# THE BODY IN

## THE MIRROR

# THE BODY IN THE MIRROR

## SHAPES OF HISTORY
## IN ITALIAN CINEMA

Angela Dalle Vacche

PRINCETON UNIVERSITY PRESS

PRINCETON, NEW JERSEY

*Library of Congress Cataloging-in-Publication Data*

Dalle Vacche, Angela, 1954–

The body in the mirror: shapes of history in Italian cinema /
Angela Dalle Vacche.

p.   cm.

Includes bibliographical references and index.

ISBN 0-691-05566-1 (alk. paper)—ISBN 0-691-00872-8
(pbk.: alk. paper)

1. Motion pictures—Italy—History. 2. Italy in motion pictures.
3. Italians—Ethnic identity. I. Title.

PN1993.5.I88D35    1991    791.43'658—dc20    91-19142

This book has been composed in Trump Medieval

Princeton University Press books are printed on acid-free
paper and meet the guidelines for permanence and
durability of the Committee on Production Guidelines for
Book Longevity of the Council on Library Resources

Printed in the United States of America by
Princeton University Press, Princeton, New Jersey

10  9  8  7  6  5  4  3  2  1

10  9  8  7  6  5  4  3  2  1
(Pbk.)

*To*

Michael Greve Petroff,

Guido and Giuliana Dalle Vacche,

Marjorie Kaufman and Jean Sudrann

# Contents

# F i g u r e s

# Acknowledgments

So MANY COLLEAGUES have helped me that I wish I could do more than just mention their names. Each one has offered unique insights, careful advice, and an interest that has sustained me. Without the cooperation of others, it is impossible to write. I am deeply indebted to J. Dudley Andrew, Francesco Casetti, Jennifer Church, Robert Kolker, Marylin Mell, Alan Nagel, P. Adams Sitney, Pierre Sorlin, Giorgio Tagliacozzo, Steve Ungar. To Marcia Landy I am grateful for having suggested that I submit my work to Princeton University Press.

At Yale University, in the Department of the History of Art, my colleagues Judith Colton, Ann Gibson, Anne Hanson, and Robert Herbert have been supportive and inspiring. Mary Miller assisted me with suggestions for the title during the final phase when I most needed fresh ideas.

The last stage of research and one semester of feverish writing and editing was made possible through funding from the Whitney Humanities Center at Yale. In the summer of 1988 I received an A. Whitney Griswold Faculty Grant, and in the fall of 1989 a Mellon Fellowship. At the Center, I had the opportunity to share my work with others. I am especially grateful to Thomas Greene, Jann Matlock, and Linda Nochlin for their questions and responses. During the writing of this book I also received crucial encouragement and practical help from Marjorie Kaufman and Jean Sudrann, my mentors at Mount Holyoke College. An Enders Faculty Grant assisted with the expense of illustrating this book.

I have conducted research at the Cineteca Nazionale of the Centro Sperimentale di Cinematografia in Rome, at the Archivio Storico delle Arti Contemporanee della Biennale in Venice, at the Film Library of the Lincoln Center, and at the Library of the Museum of Modern Art in New York. I am especially indebted to Dottor Guido Cincotti and to Signora Paola Castagna of the Cineteca Nazionale in Rome, and to Dottor Gioacchino Bonardo of the Archivio Storico delle Arti Contemporanee in Venice. I also worked at the Motion Picture Division of the Library of Congress in Washington, D.C., and at the Centre Georges Pompidou in Paris. I am most grateful to the Interlibrary Loan Office of Yale University, where the staff has coped most graciously with my endless requests.

Audrey Kupferberg of the Film Study Center, and Helen Chillman and Diane S. Torre of the Slides and Photographs Collection of the Art and Architecture Library at Yale University, and Mary Corliss of the Film Stills Archive at The Museum of Modern Art have assisted me in securing indispensable videotapes for close analysis, as well as slides and photographs for comparisons between film and other arts. I also thank Acquavella Galleries, Inc., of New York for granting me the right to reproduce Giorgio De Chirico's *The Mystery and Melancholy of a Street* on the cover. To Franco and Nora Raccuja, and to Giuliano Matteucci of the Studio d'Arte Matteucci in Viareggio, Italy, I wish to express my appreciation.

A few sections of this book have already appeared in print. An earlier version of chapter 2 is forthcoming in a collection of essays edited by Carole Zucker, entitled *Making Visible the Invisible: An Anthology of Original Essays on Film Acting* (Scarecrow Press); a previous version of chapter 3 may be found in *Film Criticism* 9, no. 1 (Fall 1984); a prior version of the Conclusion appeared in *Annali D'Italianistica* 6 (1988).

The students in my seminar at Yale, "The Past on the Screen," gave me faith that this, after all, was a project worth pursuing. In particular I wish to mention Fatimah Rony, Beverly Ballaro, Didier Maleuvre, Harsha Ram, and Wendy Wipprecht, who proved their talents with English grammar, French accents, translations from Italian, and proofreading.

From my husband Michael I still have much, much more to learn. Without his intelligence and patience, I would have never been able to write. I am also very grateful to my parents who have always done so much for me.

Needless to say, the professionalism of Joanna Hitchcock; Timothy Wardell, my copyeditor; and the staff at Princeton University Press guided me through the delicate preparation of the manuscript.

Finally, a subtext of *The Body in the Mirror* is the dialogue between my education in the Italian state school system and my training in American academia. While I still carry in the back of my mind the distant echo of an Italian historicist tradition and of *educazione umanistica*, it is at Mount Holyoke College and in the Film Program of the University of Iowa that I encountered, for the first time, an exhilarating sense of intellectual possibilities and the openness of the future.

*New Haven, January 1990*

# THE BODY IN

# THE MIRROR

# INTRODUCTION

The aim of the historian . . . is to portray time. The historian is committed to the detection and description of the shape of time.
—GEORGE KUBLER, *The Shape of Time*

We journey to abstract ourselves by fabrication. But where the fabric already has been woven, we journey to unravel. Identity recedes from us in our lives the more we pursue it, yet we are right not to be persuaded that it is unattainable.
—HAROLD BLOOM, *The Anxiety of Influence*

## THE BODY IN THE MIRROR

ALTHOUGH Italian films are intelligible to international audiences, my purpose in *The Body in the Mirror* is to explore what is unique in Italian culture and how it is translated to the screen. This study, then, will focus on origins and influences. Neither a general history, nor an intense examination of a single period, it will explore what one may learn about Italian cinema if one brings to it a consciousness both of the strength of the historicist orientation in twentieth-century Italian intellectual life and of the importance this orientation grants to an understanding of origins and cultural sources. For instance, an awareness of the historicist cast of contemporary Italian thought can help explain the continuous preoccupation of Italian cinema with the historical past. Further, this preoccupation creates an unresolved tension as filmmakers reluctantly acknowledge the power of the past by their persistent dependence on it. One of my aims is to describe the shapes this anxiety assumes when it is translated to the screen. Once projected there, corporeal entities become metaphors for the Italian body politic. They are not images of social reality, but rather reflections of an imaginary, national self. This study will show, then, that the bodies in the mirror of Italian cinema disclose ways in which Italian society perceives itself and, because such popular perceptions are never static, it will also examine the shapes that society is willing to see itself assume at specific moments.

An awareness of the connection between Italian Renaissance painting and the cinema can help explain why Italian filmmakers emphasize the modeling of the human figure, the theatricality of space, and the allegorical dimension of the visual narrative. From painting to the cinema, body, spectacle, and allegory are the three parameters that control how Italian filmmakers depict the national identity and adjust their vision of contemporary life within the restrictions of these parametric forms. Allegory, spectacle, and body not only characterize Italian Renaissance painting, but influence two art forms that in themselves are important to Italian cinema: opera and the commedia dell'arte.[1]

Enjoying a privileged status in Italian culture, opera and the commedia dell'arte occupy antipodes of size and focus. Opera, taking a monumental view, specializes in the spectacle of public history, or macrohistory. The commedia dell'arte, keeping its attention to the human scale, focuses on the spectacle of daily life, or microhistory. In opera, the written words of the libretto melt in music and in voice. On the edge of the inexpressible, the word is weak and would be hardly intelligible were it not for the support of the singers' statuesque and emblematic gestures. In the commedia, the literary script of the classical theatre is no more than a quick *canovaccio* (sketchy plot), because the bodies of the actors, their movements and behaviors, tell most of the story, along with verbal jokes note-

---

[1] The commedia dell'arte was already a well-known form of popular entertainment during the Renaissance when travelling companies of mountebanks would perform in city squares, fairs, and markets. These companies often consisted of actual families that passed on their trade to following generations. Unable to read or write and often very poor, the performers put all their attention into pantomime and acrobatics. Their illiterate audiences would identify the theatrical characters they created primarily by a series of expressions codified into a set of *maschere* (facial masks). Physiognomies were linked to a regional type, to the reputation of a city, or to a well-known social role. From the Renaissance to the eighteenth century, the commedia dell'arte became a more complex and aristocratic form of art with an international resonance. On opera and the commedia dell'arte, see Cesare Molinari, *Storia universale del teatro* (Milan: Mondadori, 1983); William Weaver, *The Golden Century of Italian Opera from Rossini to Puccini* (London: Thames and Hudson, 1980); Achille Mango, *Cultura e storia nella formazione della commedia dell'arte* (Bari: Adriatica Editrice, 1972). In *Semiotics of Cinema*, trans. from Russian and introd. Mark E. Suino, Michigan Slavic Contributions no. 5 (Ann Arbor: University of Michigan, 1981), Jurij Lotman argues that these two art forms are so familiar to Italian audiences that the artificiality of their languages cannot be perceived as such (p. 22).

worthy more for their color and rhythm than for their subtleties.[2] The victory of soma over logos travels from painting, opera, and the commedia to literature. The subordination of word to music in opera, and to gesture in the commedia, is a phenomenon literary historians explain by referring to the *questione della lingua* (chronic absence of a national literary language).[3] Unlike literature, by relying on the body rather than on the word, opera and the commedia dell'arte succeeded across different regions and social classes throughout a still-divided Italy.

The style of silent and fascist cinema is operatic; neorealist cinema, instead, relies on the tradition of the commedia dell'arte. The three elements of the commedia that are most important for neorealism are improvisation, the use of *maschere*, and pantomime. These elements are expressed in the neorealist rejection of a binding script, casting based on physical appearance, and acting emphasizing gesture.[4] Italian film style oscillates between opera and the

[2] On the status of the script in Italian neorealist cinema, André Bazin comments: "Nearly all the credits of an Italian film list under the heading 'scenario' a good dozen names. . . . Rather than the assembly line of American screenwriters, this interdependence of improvisation is like that of the commedia dell'arte or jazz." *What Is Cinema? II*, trans. Hugh Gray (Berkeley: University of California Press, 1971), 31. Pierre Sorlin reminds me that in Italian films the names of individuals who have not even read the script, let alone written it, may appear in the credits. Indeed this habit of gratuitous crediting contradicts Bazin's analogy with jazz, and I am not even sure a further analogy is quite possible between improvisation in the commedia dell'arte and in jazz. In any case, gratuitous crediting suggests that in Italian cinema, unlike in French or American film industries, the scriptwriter either enjoys a very fluid professional role or suffers from vague definition and lack of authority. On the other hand, the splendid career of Suso Cecchi D'Amico or the valid contributions of Tonino Guerra stand out as exceptions to this state of affairs.

[3] On the *questione della lingua*, see Fausta Drago Rivera, *De Vulgari Eloquentia: La questione della lingua da Dante a domani* (Milan: Centro Nazionale di Studi Manzoniani, 1980). Since the days of Dante, Petrarch, and Boccaccio, who did not write in Latin but in *volgare*, experts have been discussing the cult, but also the problem, of regional, Tuscan elements in the national literature. The *questione della lingua* is especially strong in the sixteenth century. This is the age of city-states, of great renaissance in the non-verbal arts, but also an age of extreme political division and foreign domination. In the twentieth century, the *questione della lingua* involves the place of spoken regional dialects in national life and the problem of extensive illiteracy. In *Storia d'Italia dal 1871 al 1915* (Bari: Laterza, 1967), 214, Benedetto Croce says that between 1901 and 1910, as a result of an economic renaissance, the illiteracy rate was down to 38 percent.

[4] The neorealist use of non-actors is not a radical innovation; non-actors have worked in films since the beginning of cinema. Perhaps the most notable use of non-actors occurred in another genre, one which impressed André Bazin, the scripted "ethnographic" or documentary film, from the late teens to the 1930s. Some exam-

commedia dell'arte. Silent and fascist cinema represent the fast-changing surface layers of national life punctuated by heroic leaders and famous battles. By contrast, thanks to "comedic" microhistory, neorealist cinema depicts the slow-changing patterns of daily life. Operatic macrohistory and comedic microhistory meet in recent Italian cinema, because its project is to combine the legacies of fascism and neorealism.

The body in opera is different than the body in the commedia. On stage, the body in opera is bound to statuesque poses and gestures that can be seen at a distance. The size of the body has to be commensurable with the monumental sets that surround it. Sculpture, then, is the art form that best describes the treatment of the body in opera. Paradoxically, this statue in opera embodies great movements of history, and yet hardly moves. By modeling itself on a motionless sculpture, the body in opera points to a single component of the cinema—the still frame of photography—and to the feeling of death that hangs over the arrested image.

In contrast, the body in the commedia seems more in tune with a bustling street life caught unawares, even when performed indoors. The body in the commedia also expresses a paradox. While it refers to the slow-moving, deep structures of daily life, it is in constant motion. The body in the commedia, with its agility of a dancer and its careful choreography, nonetheless produces an effect of spontaneity. By virtue of movement, the body in the commedia resembles more a living document than a still monument.

By itself, however, the image of the dancer can do justice only to some of the many patterns of movement performed by the Italian body politic. From the films of Vittorio De Sica, Luchino Visconti, and Roberto Rossellini in the immediate postwar years, to recent Italian cinema, with Bernardo Bertolucci, Lina Wertmuller, Federico Fellini, Liliana Cavani, Pier Paolo Pasolini, Ettore Scola, and the

---

ples are: Edward Curtis' *In the Land of the Headhunters* (1914), Robert Flaherty's *Nanook of the North* (1922), and *Moana* (1926), Karl Brown's *Stark Love* (1927), Flaherty and Murnau's *Tabù* (1931), and André Roosvelt and Armand Denis' *Goona-Goona* (1932). The question of authenticity that underlies the use of the non-professional actor is as important for the construction of the primitive "other" in the ethnographic film as for the representation of the average Italian in neorealist cinema. On acting, see Umberto Barbaro and Luigi Chiarini, *L'arte dell'attore* (Rome: Bianco e Nero Editore, 1949); Carlo Ludovico Ragghianti, "L'attore nel film," in *Cinema arte figurativa* (Turin: Einaudi, 1952), 203–10; Alberto Abruzzese, *L'immagine filmica* (Rome: Bulzoni, 1974).

Taviani brothers, the language of the body acquires more range, its nuances increase, its possibilities expand. The Italian body moves from dance to mime, from mimicry to pose, from the leaps and somersaults of a clown to the jumps and swirls of his ancestor: Maciste in Giovanni Pastrone's silent opera for the screen, *Cabiria* (1914).

In antithesis to the power of the studios in classic Hollywood cinema, neorealism, as a directors' cinema, set the stage for the masters of the art film. The art film learned from Rossellini, De Sica, and Visconti to slow down or flatten the Aristotelian plot based on climax and denouement, and to use instead *temps morts*, real locations, narrative ambiguity. Through these techniques, the art film avoids too artificial a closure, and, at times, even achieves an open ending. Even though neorealism was a cinema of directors and not of actors, its construction of character had great impact on the art film. The *maschere* belonged to actors of the commedia dell'arte who performed the same role, performance after performance. Because these actors relied so much on physical mimicry, when a performer died, so might that performer's particular *maschera*. This dynamic of actor and *maschera* voices a modern desire to be oneself in the role one plays. Through neorealism, the *maschera* of the commedia anticipates the search for an authentic self which is an objective of the art film.

In the art film, behavior and movement tell stories. De Sica in *Umberto D* (1951), Antonioni in *The Eclipse* (1962), and Fellini in *La Strada* (1954) all utilize fluid movements, expressive gestures, and mimicry. It is as if their actors and actresses had received a training in the tradition of the commedia dell'arte. These directors use behavior, instead of psychology, to make visible a private space (Umberto D's routine upon going to bed); to explore a certain restlessness (Monica Vitti's African dance in a modern apartment) (fig. 1); to suggest the earth-bound spirituality of half-wits and tramps (Gelsomina's dance in the tomato field) (fig. 2).

Finally, an awareness of the connections between Catholic thought and the cinema can explain why the national body politic on the screen is a modern version of the medieval *corpus mysticum*. In the Middle Ages, the community of believers organized itself around a figure of authority, the Christ-King, whose body integrated religious and secular dimensions. In modern times, the lay, Hegelian nation-state became the term of reference that regulated the

**1.** Dance in Michelangelo Antonioni's *The Eclipse* (1962). Courtesy of The Museum of Modern Art, Film Stills Archive.

**2.** Giulietta Masina as Gelsomina in Federico Fellini's *La Strada* (1954). Courtesy of The Museum of Modern Art, Film Stills Archive.

interface of public and private identity. The modern body politic has an ancient history, the complex stages of which are the subject of Ernst H. Kantorowicz's *The King's Two Bodies: A Study in Political Medieval Theology*.[5] As the title of Kantorowicz's book indicates, the medieval king needed two bodies. One was personal, physical, and subject to death; the other was institutional, ideal, and eternal. The king's second body was the unifying term of identification for the community over which it ruled. It also guaranteed the continuity of the dynasty wearing the crown, hence the saying: "The king is dead, Long live the king!" The doubling of the king's body articulates the gap between the abstract and the concrete, the individual and the social, the personal and the political, which two Italian art forms, opera and the commedia dell'arte, represent through spectacle and allegory.

## SHAPES OF HISTORY

As we have seen, allegory, spectacle, and body in Italian cinema grew out of Renaissance painting, opera, and the commedia. These parameters are reinforced by the long-standing authority of Giambattista Vico's (1668–1744) views on language.[6] Vico believed that human beings acquire knowledge only by representing themselves, and by translating mental processes into visible, anthropomorphic forms. For Vico, self-knowledge was possible only through the agency of the body. Furthermore, for Vico, the earliest form of language was closer to painting than to writing, and was based on gestures and behaviors, images and objects. Most important, this early language was without sound. The visual dimension played a crucial role in this mute language because primitive people had no speculative skills, only imaginative ones. They thought not through ab-

[5] On the history of this concept, see Ernst H. Kantorowicz, *The King's Two Bodies: A Study in Political Medieval Theology* (Princeton, N.J.: Princeton University Press, 1981), 193–272; Cecil Grayson, "Rev. of Ernst H. Kantorowicz' *The King's Two Bodies: A Study in Political Medieval Theology*," *Romance Philology* 15, no. 2 (November 1961): 179–84; Geoffrey Barraclough, "The Sovereign State," *The Spectator* (August 1, 1958): 171; Leonard Barkan, *Nature's Work of Art: The Human Body as Image of the World* (New Haven, Conn.: Yale University Press, 1975); and Marc Ferro, "From Christ the King to the Nation State: History in European Eyes," in *The Use and Abuse of History or How the Past Is Taught* (London: Routledge and Kegan Paul, 1984), 94–113.

[6] Gianfranco Cantelli, *Mente, corpo, linguaggio: Saggio sull'interpretazione vichiana del mito* (Florence: Sansoni, 1986).

stractions, but through metaphors. Thus they depended on the body to articulate their thoughts and relied on visual shapes and corporeal images to grasp what was abstract, absent, or intangible. Vico's sense that the first language of humankind was *mute, visual,* and *corporeal* may very well have been preserved in the cinema.

In addition to his views on language, Vico is of importance to Italian cinema for his philosophy of history.[7] As we shall see in greater detail later on, Vico believed that history was cyclical. Each cycle included three stages: the first stage, the age of gods (the father of the family being the highest authority); the second, the age of heroes (the fathers form an aristocracy as the families unite into a community); and the third, the human age, in which the community passes under the rule of a single monarch. Once these stages have been completed, a *corso,* or a cycle, has taken place. Changes in the social organization, for Vico, were analogous to the stages of intellectual development in the individual: from the imagination of children and of primitive cultures, to the mature, rational thought of philosophers in the age of humans. Furthermore, changes in the body of the individual parallel changes in the national identity. From childhood to adulthood, from poetry to philosophy, from imagination to reflection, the body of the individual is an historical variable and, as such, whether as a still monument or a moving document,[8] it tells the history of the national body politic to which it belongs. In short, for Vico, history was made of patterned repetitions, *corsi* and *ricorsi,* occurring in different contexts, yet in comparable situations. Italian cinema seems to have appropriated Vico's thought and, in representing the national identity with films systematically built like palimpsests, continues to call attention to the

[7] On Vico's historicism, especially useful is Emanuele Riverso, ed. and intro., *Leggere Vico: Scritti di Giorgio Tagliacozzo ed altri* (Milan: Spirali, 1982). Although Riverso uses the term "historicism" in relation to Vico, this term may be too modern a description of Vico's genetic view of causality. The philosopher took issue with Descartes who privileged logic and non-temporal explanations, synchrony over diachrony. In *Recoding Metaphysics: The New Italian Philosophy* (Evanston, Ill.: Northwestern University Press, 1988), Giovanna Borradori individuates a tradition from Vico to Croce to Gianni Vattimo, the proponent of "weak thought" in the recent debate on postmodern culture.

[8] The terms "document" and "monument" come from Michel Foucault, *The Archaeology of Knowledge and the Discourse on Language,* trans. A. M. Sheridan Smith (New York: Pantheon Books, 1972). There Foucault writes, "History is that which transforms documents into monuments" (p. 7).

*corsi* and *ricorsi* of isomorphic, yet changing stylistic choices and historiographical dilemmas.

Vico not only developed a cyclical philosophy of history that was influential, but, in a very real sense, he invented in *The New Science* (1744)[9] a modern definition of human history for Italians. He argued that history was the science of sciences, the founding discipline of all other disciplines. For Vico, to know a thing was to know its origin, to understand a word was to master its etymology, to read a text was to recognize its sources. The remnant of this view is reflected in Italian cinema by its constant preoccupation with history. The kind of history relevant to the cinema, the "Book of History," is not an academic product. Rather, that "History" is a pool of stories referring either to political or daily life. When these stories refer to fast-moving political events, they are represented in the cinema by the macroscopic scale of opera; when these stories deal with the long duration[10] of deep structures of behavior, they are represented in the cinema by the microscopic scale of the commedia. Where Vico saw history as the fundamental discipline, Italian cinema, either through opera or the commedia, seems to see it as the inescapable subject.

Vico's modern definition of human history became influential in Italian culture thanks to three early twentieth-century Italian intellectuals, Giovanni Gentile (1875–1944), Benedetto Croce (1866–1952), and Antonio Gramsci (1891–1937). Flourishing in the period immediately following the Risorgimento (the creation of modern unified Italy), they not only spread Vico's historicism, but refashioned it in an Hegelian direction. Not surprisingly, in the context of Italy's newly born political identity, Hegel's theory of the state as an organic entity and as the supreme stage of a linear historical process, became quite popular. Gentile, Croce, and Gramsci, however, were Hegelians in different degrees and for different reasons. Croce's and Gramsci's sense of historical identity is by far more dynamic and nuanced than Gentile's view of the national self. By pushing the Hegelian legacy to its limits, Gentile abstracts identity

---

[9] Giambattista Vico, *The New Science* (1725), trans. of 3d ed. (1744) Thomas Goddard Bergin and Max Harold Fisch (Ithaca, N.Y.: Cornell University Press, 1968). With this work, Vico replaced the *Prisca Theologia* of the Renaissance by arguing that the development of humanity was not based on God's will, but on internal mechanisms and social processes for which humans alone are responsible.

[10] On the concept of long duration, see Fernand Braudel, *On History*, trans. Sarah Matthews (Chicago: The University of Chicago Press, 1980).

into pure logos and reduces history to a phantasmic teleology. For Croce and Gramsci, the self is a unified body, but resonating from and fully inserted into a multifaceted and thickly layered historical process. It is true, however, that Croce rejected Vico's cyclical view of the *corsi* and *ricorsi* in favor of Hegelian linear historicism. Croce was the passage-way to Hegelian Marxism for Gramsci,[11] because, in Gramsci's Italy, Croce had the intellectual authority of a "lay Pope." While Croce, along with Gramsci, accepted Hegel's historicism, with *What Is Alive and What Is Dead in Hegel's Philosophy* (1907), Croce expressed an antipathy for the anti-humanist abstractions of Hegel's philosophy of history. For Gentile, instead, the fascist ethical state was the perfect application of Hegel's view that logos is outside the self and in the "World Spirit."

Again, although both men nourished themselves on Vico's cyclical philosophy of history, Croce and Gramsci produced competing interpretations of the Risorgimento by handling differently the themes of unity and continuity. Gentile's historiography was quickly dismissed after World War II due to the philosopher's long involvement with the regime. By contrast, Croce's and Gramsci's views on the nineteenth century persisted in the "Book of History" until May 1968. Both thinkers held on to a belief in the unitary nature of consciousness.

With his interpretation of the Risorgimento, Croce posited a relation of historical continuity between the patriotic values of the political brain of the Risorgimento, Camillo Benso, count of Cavour (1810–1861), and the liberal oligarchy led by Giovanni Giolitti (1842–1928) in early twentieth-century Italy. By contrast, Gramsci wanted to see historical continuity between the popular democratic forces in the Risorgimento and the class struggle in a country lagging behind its European neighbors in industrialization. By unity, Croce meant national unity, beyond class and regional differences. On the other hand, by unity Gramsci meant the alliance of the working class in the north with the rural masses of the south, for the sake of a shared identity rooted in the experience of economic exploitation and social oppression.

[11] Edmund E. Jacobitti writes, "To Gramsci Croceanism was the Hegelianism of the twentieth century, and any advancement of Marxism would therefore have to be within the Crocean framework just as Marx had advanced within the Hegelian framework." "From Vico's Common Sense to Gramsci's Hegemony," in Giorgio Tagliacozzo, ed., *Vico and Marx: Affinities and Contrasts* (Atlantic Highlands, N.J.: Humanities Press, 1983), 379.

Croce wanted to salvage both the organic self of the nineteenth century and Giolitti's unified liberal state.[12] Gramsci felt that class identity could be the founding premise of a new "national-popular" culture in modern Italy.[13] This belief in the unitary nature of consciousness is reflected in Croce's and Gramsci's common hostility toward the Futurist avant-garde and Gabriele D'Annunzio.[14] Through fragmentation and excess, respectively, rather than through continuity and unity, the Futurists and D'Annunzio were beginning to describe a new subjectivity and use of the past. By contrast, Croce, somewhat cautiously, and Gramsci, more fervently, were trying to hold on to or update nineteenth-century notions of the self in order to respond to the advent of modernity.

These conflicting views of Croce and Gramsci on the Risorgimento are reflected in cinema's presentation of Fascism and the Resistance. In dealing with the "Book of History," Italian filmmakers have woven into their narrative not only the theme of historical continuity, as both Croce and Gramsci defined it, but also the

[12] On Croce's "organic holism" in art, see Hayden White, *Metahistory: The Historical Imagination in Nineteenth-Century Europe* (Baltimore, Md.: The Johns Hopkins University Press, 1987), 385–86. The revival of the Renaissance in Fascist Italy is also at the heart of the *Novecento* movement in painting. See Rossana Bossaglia, "L'iconografia del novecento italiano nel contesto europeo," *The Journal of Decorative and Propaganda Arts 1875–1945* 3 (Winter 1987): 53–65. More specifically, Croce's preferences in art tended to the decorum of classical antiquity and to the emphasis on the body in Renaissance Italian painting. Croce viewed Futurism as the negative expression of the irrational forces of modernity.

[13] The ideology of the medieval *corpus mysticum* is apparent in Gramsci's definition of culture: "But what does 'culture' mean in this case? undoubtedly it means a *coherent, unitary, nationally* diffused 'conception of life and man,' a 'lay religion,' a philosophy that has become precisely a 'culture,' that is, it has generated an ethic, a way of life, a *civil* and *individual* conduct." Antonio Gramsci, *Letteratura e vita nazionale* (Rome: Editori Riuniti, 1971), 20, as cited in Jacobitti, 370, n. 6 (emphasis is mine). Also notice the use of the body as a metaphor for a unifying political identity in Gramsci's conception of party-structure: "The party therefore became a kind of school (*un partito come scuola*) for Gramsci, and as such it was divided into the 'conscious' instructors ('captains,' 'directors') and the 'unconscious' pupils (the 'soldiers,' the 'ordinary people') and, for want of a better term, the teaching assistants, or 'cadres,' (the link between the 'head' and the 'body' of the movement)." Jacobitti, 383.

[14] On Gramsci and Futurism, see *Antonio Gramsci: Selections from Cultural Writings*, trans. William Boelhower and ed. David Forgacs and Geoffrey Nowell-Smith (Cambridge, Mass.: Harvard University Press, 1985), 46–54. Gramsci looked favorably upon pre-World War I Futurism, as long as he could assimilate the Futurists' desire for radical change to the Marxist cause. Gramsci decried Filippo Tommaso Marinetti's involvement with Fascism after the Great War.

theme of unity, which to Croce meant national unity and to Gramsci class unity. Thus unity and continuity in films exploring the "Book of History" have functioned as two additional parametric forms, regulating the representation of the Italian identity, from the silent film period to the students' revolts of May 1968.

In films made during and after May 1968, unity turned to disunity among regions and classes, and continuity to discontinuity with one generation questioning the legacy of the previous one. Because, in the wake of Vico's historicism and under the influence of Catholic thought, they assume that the past is the father and that the Italian body politic is male, filmmakers translate this interrogation of the past into the plot of the Oedipal myth.

According to the myth, Oedipus makes love to his mother, Jocasta, and longs for the father, Laius, he has unknowingly killed. Thus Oedipus and Laius share the same woman, while both love and hate characterize the son's predicament with the father. With regard to the mother, their rivalry is all the more problematic because it is the mother who makes possible a continuity between father and son, but who also separates them. The latent homoeroticism of the Oedipal myth seems to apply to Italian cinema, which employs "homosocial"[15] narratives to represent fathers and sons in history and public life, while pushing mothers toward biology and the private sphere. By "homosocial" I mean a patriarchal culture that represses a homoerotic core behind a strong, heterosexual façade. Like Kantorowicz's king, in Italian cinema the allegorical embodiment of national self is not only male but also has two bodies, a masculine and a feminine self. This heterosexual, homosocial order needs a woman to insert a discontinuity, so to speak, between two men, often a father and son, thus keeping the threat of homosexuality at bay. In this scheme, the woman is also an agent of biological continuity enabling genealogies between fathers and sons, thus reinforcing the heterosexual façade of male bonding and historical legacies.

Nine films support the argument of this book: Giovanni Pastrone's *Cabiria* (1914), Carmine Gallone's *Scipio Africanus* (1937), Bernardo Bertolucci's *The Conformist* (1970), Alessandro Blasetti's

[15] I have borrowed the concept "heterosexual, homosocial culture with an unconscious homoerotic component" from Eve Kosofsky Sedgwick, *Between Men: English Literature and Male Homosocial Desire* (New York: Columbia University Press, 1985).

*1860* (1933), Luchino Visconti's *Senso* (1954), Paolo and Vittorio Taviani's *Allonsanfan* (1973–1974), Roberto Rossellini's *Paisà* (1946), Paolo and Vittorio Taviani's *Night of the Shooting Stars* (1982), and Bernardo Bertolucci's *Spider's Stratagem* (1970). *Cabiria* represents pre-Fascist Italy and the new art of cinema looking at antiquity; *Scipio Africanus* represents Fascist Italy looking at antiquity and at silent cinema; *The Conformist* represents Italy after May 1968 reinterpreting Fascism and looking at fascist cinema; *1860* represents Fascist Italy interpreting the Risorgimento according to Giovanni Gentile; *Senso* represents postwar Italy reinterpreting the Risorgimento according to Antonio Gramsci, reevaluating the Resistance through Gramsci's Risorgimento, and weaving together the styles of fascist and neorealist cinema; *Allonsanfan* represents Italy, after May 1968, looking at Visconti's Risorgimento in *Senso* and evaluating May 1968; *Paisà* represents Italy in the present tense at the very end of World War II; *Night of the Shooting Stars* represents Italy after May 1968, reinterpreting the Resistance and moving beyond neorealism; *Spider's Stratagem* represents Italy, after May 1968, exploring the dark side of antifascism and taming the movement of neorealism through the fixity of opera.

The reader may wonder why I discuss the representation of the Risorgimento in *Senso* and not in Visconti's *The Leopard* (1963), or why I analyze *The Conformist* and *Spider's Stratagèm* in much greater detail than Bertolucci's *1900* (1975–1976). The controversies surrounding *Senso*, a much bigger cinematic and political scandal than *The Leopard*, allow me to examine the film culture and the historical context of 1954. The year 1954 is an indispensable term of reference for an understanding of how the popular knowledge of history (doxa) changed from 1945 to 1968. *The Conformist* and *Spider's Stratagem* interest me because these films are so much in tune with the climate of 1968. Furthermore, in comparison to *1900*, where Bertolucci slips into myth-making about the early days of the Resistance, *Night of the Shooting Stars* seems to offer a more subtle critique of the status of 1945 in the postwar perception of Croce's and Gramsci's historiographies. In *Night of the Shooting Stars*, the Tavianis look at the end of World War II from a viewpoint well beyond 1968 and well after the season of the "historical compromise," when a coalition between Catholics and Marxists seemed to be possible. Finally, the Tavianis themselves have spoken of Visconti and Rossellini as seminal influences on their work, so that intertextual connections between *Senso* and *Allonsanfan*, *Paisà* and *Night of the Shooting Stars* are not at all gratuitous. This does not mean that the parameters of Italian cinema do not apply to *The Leopard* or to *1900*, because they certainly do, but simply that my intertextual intarsia is meant to highlight how important 1945, 1954, and 1968 are to an understanding changes in the popular perception of historical interpretations originally developed in the 1920s and in the 1930s.

# ONE

Fascism
before World
War I, after
World War I,
and after
World War II

## UNITY, CONTINUITY, AND KITSCH

IN 1928, under Fascist rule, Benedetto Croce (1866–1952) published his *History of Italy from 1871 to 1915*.[1] In this book, the Neapolitan philosopher describes the newly born Italian nation in a positive light. Croce also establishes a relation of continuity between the yearning for "liberty" expressed by the Risorgimento and Giovanni Giolitti's (1842–1928) modern state. In those days, Italy was under the control of a liberal, upper-bourgeois-aristocratic oligarchy. For Croce the Risorgimento was a successful phase of civic awakening, paying little attention to the fact that the northern Italian upper bourgeoisie benefited from the "national" movement for unification much more than the rural masses in the south. For Croce "liberty" is a moral imperative. "Liberty" is the driving force of human history even when the light of liberty barely flickers in the surrounding darkness. This Crocean hope that fundamental human values will transcend the horrors of history reappears in the dialogue of Francesco and Pina (Anna Magnani) in Roberto Rossellini's *Open City* (1945). Pina tells Francesco she is pregnant

---

[1] Benedetto Croce, *History of Italy from 1871 to 1915* (1928), trans. Cecilia M. Ady (Oxford: Clarendon Press, 1929). In Italian: *Storia d'Italia dal 1871 al 1915* (Bari: Laterza, 1967). To better understand how Croce's view of the Risorgimento sustains an antifascist stance, compare the preface written in 1927 with the one written in 1947. Both prefaces appear in the Laterza 1967 edition, the one from which I cite throughout the book.

and expresses hope for a better life, once the struggle against the Nazis is over.

Croce's light of "liberty" recalls Giambattista Vico's (1668–1744) humanist credo that because history is created by humans, its processes can be understood by them: "But in the night of thick darkness enveloping the earliest antiquity so remote from ourselves, there shines the eternal and never-failing light of a truth beyond all question: that *the world of civil society has certainly been made by men*, and that its principles are therefore to be found within the modifications of our own human mind."[2] For Croce, history is neither a philosophy nor a science searching for general laws, but an art form which, through narrative, reaches out for the concreteness and individuality of human experience. For Croce, human responsibility for the historical process is a source of hope rather than a reason for despair. Croce's preference for the concrete over the abstract, his faith in human nature, and his emphasis on the subjective experience of history are at the heart of Roberto Rossellini's neorealism—a cinema in the present tense, where spiritual quests acquire a sensual edge,[3] and where a documentary approach prevails over abstract speculation.[4]

Yet, for Croce, only the past can be an object of knowledge; history can tell us nothing about the immediate future. Moreover, Croce's historian can hardly philosophize about the present since he is standing in the middle of an unfinished sentence. While Croce's antipathy for the Hegelian philosophy of history is a powerful revisitation of Vico's awareness of the subjective dimension of history, this very same attitude of neutrality about the future leads to a stance of impotence in the face of the degeneration of created history. Consequently, Croce's light does not shine but only flickers during the dark years of the Fascist regime.

By the time Croce's *History of Italy* appeared, the Black Shirts had already marched on Rome (1922) and Fascism was a dictatorship. Fearing that the circulation of his book might encounter obstacles, Croce sent a few copies abroad. As early as 1921 Croce was

---

[2] Vico, as cited in Edmund E. Jacobitti, "From Vico's Common Sense to Gramsci's Hegemony," in *Vico and Marx: Affinities and Contrasts*, ed. Giorgio Tagliacozzo (Atlantic Highlands, N.J.: Humanities Press, 1983), 367. Emphasis is mine.

[3] Tag Gallagher, "NR = MC²: Rossellini, Neo-Realism, and Croce," *Film History, An International Journal* 2, n. 1 (1988): 94.

[4] Ibid., 90.

still supportive of Benito Mussolini, because he felt that the country needed a revitalizing force after the pain of World War I, and a return to order in response to violent strikes and social unrest. In 1925, however, Mussolini threw off his mask of constitutional scruples. That year, Giovanni Gentile composed a "Manifesto of Fascist Intellectuals" (April 21, 1925), while Croce replied with a "Manifesto of Antifascist Intellectuals" (May 1, 1925), expressing adamant opposition to Fascism and stating his belief in culture's autonomy from politics.

Croce's "Manifesto" became a rallying point for hundreds of prominent intellectuals to oppose the regime and its message stayed alive for those who went into exile. The "Manifesto of Antifascist Intellectuals" turned Croce into the living symbol of cultural resistance in Italy. From 1926 to 1943, Croce's name was banned from public mention. The philosopher, however, never went to jail as did Antonio Gramsci (1891–1937) in 1926. In isolation and protected by a wealthy family background, Croce was able to continue to write and publish. In Fascist Italy, Croce's work circulated discreetly. The adjective "crocean," with the small "c," appeared frequently in literary and film publications. Luigi Chiarini, the editor of the film journal *Bianco e Nero* (1933), for example, held on to a "crocean" orientation to aesthetics. Chiarini agreed with Croce that, while art has an ethical dimension, aesthetics should be kept separate from politics. Although it was academic suicide to visit Croce at his home in Naples, he did meet with young scholars during his vacation excursions.

In his *History of Italy from 1871 to 1915* Croce did not launch into an apology for Giolitti's administrations (1892–1893; 1906–1909; 1911–1914; 1920–1921), but did dwell on the economic renaissance of Italy between 1901 and 1910. By contrast, he analyzed much less the violent resurgence and repression of the class struggle. The serene voice in Croce's pages stemmed from his belief that the values of the fathers of the Risorgimento would eventually provide a sense of direction for twentieth-century Italy.

Croce feared that his *History of Italy* would antagonize Mussolini's censors. In fact, the regime disliked the elitist attitudes of Giolitti's liberal oligarchy and favored a populist retelling of recent history. Today, it is not surprising that Croce's *History of Italy* avoided obstacles, for his book hesitated in pushing to center-stage the structural weaknesses of Giolitti's Italy. While Croce shunned a critique of Giolitti's government, the newly born Fascist movement was interested in co-opting as many members of Giolitti's administration as possible. In contrast to Croce, historians Giustino Fortunato, Luigi Salvatorelli, and Piero Gobetti, also writing in the 1920s, argued that the contradictions of early twentieth-century Italy prepared for the advent of the Fascist regime. For Fortunato, Salvatorelli, and Gobetti, Fascism is a revelation that developed out of Giolitti's failures, rather than an inexplicable aberration as Croce would have it.[5]

Croce's hopeful outlook and his view that Italian history is a linear continuum tending toward "liberty" explain why his *History of Italy*, despite its overestimation of Giolitti's Italy, became a point of reference for antifascist circles. Faith in the values of Giolitti's Italy led Croce to underestimate early manifestations of Fascism. The regime, for Croce, was not the product of structural evils in Italian society, but an evil parenthesis. Croce's interpretation of Fascism makes possible a comparison between antifascists in the 1930s and the patriots of the Risorgimento, since both groups, according to the philosopher, are seeking "liberty."

In contrast to Croce's positive account, great difficulties in the transition from the Risorgimento to modernity characterized the administration of Giovanni Giolitti. A shrewd, well-trained Piedmontese politician, a man of sobriety and self-discipline, Giolitti preferred to avoid head-on conflicts. The color of Giolitti's working style as a statesman was grey with shifting nuances. Giovanni Giolitti became famous for his timely juggling of political allies, and for his ability to turn an enemy into a friend, and to distance himself from a former ally. Giolitti, in a word, perfected the ancient Italian art of political *trasformismo*.

Giolitti's Italy experienced the arrival of twentieth-century technology later than other European nations, mostly taking root in the north at the expense of the south. The south, a poor area of Italy, has always been exploited as a pool of cheap labor and has been weakened by heavy emigration. The major protagonists of this transition into the twentieth century were the industrial groups of the

[5] On the reception of Croce's *History of Italy*, in the 1920s and in the 1970s, see Gennaro Sasso, *La "Storia d'Italia" di Benedetto Croce: Cinquant'anni dopo* (Naples: Bibliopolis, 1979). Sasso's style is quite involuted, but his footnotes are most useful to trace the phases of an historiographical debate that brings together interpretations of Fascism, the Risorgimento, and the Resistance.

Turin-Genoa-Milan triangle. Meanwhile, the working class became more and more aggressive. Giolitti's paternalistic administration, his badly implemented reforms in the north, and his abuses in the south did not meet the needs of rural and urban proletariats. In the climate of disorientation following World War I, seeds of discontent easily germinated.

In contrast to Benedetto Croce, and in agreement with Giustino Fortunato and Piero Gobetti, the historian Luigi Salvatorelli already understood in 1923 the weaknesses inherited from Giolitti's Italy and wrote in *Nazionalfascismo*: "With a smattering of classical rhetoric, the humanist petty-bourgeoisie is inclined toward dogmatic statements, beliefs in the *ipse dixit*, in the celebration of gesture and word taking over the place of facts and ideas, in a fanaticism for undiscussed and indisputable formulae."[6] Salvatorelli clearly sees how the culture of melodrama degenerates into the cult of authority, with a taste for gratuitous spectacle prevailing. In Salvatorelli's "humanist petit-bourgeoisie," with "a smattering of classical rhetoric," it is possible to recognize the attitudes of stagnating aristocrats, displaced bureaucrats, and disillusioned war veterans. These groups' frustrations enabled the Duce to seize power.

From its early days to its zenith, Fascism was a mosaic of contradictory impulses and preoccupations, an eclectic montage of conflicting interests and alliances, with both rural and urban forces, lay and religious groups. After sedimenting for centuries, an antidemocratic mentality flourished through layers of regional traditions, economic practices, and stereotypical behaviors.

Despite the archaic and ubiquitous nature of these latent, protofascistic tendencies, neither the institutional apparatus of the regime nor the personal charisma of Mussolini succeeded in unifying Italy into the Hegelian ideal of a modern nation. Mussolini's agrarian campaigns in the Roman countryside, xenophobic policies in the South Tyrol, and anti-Mafia purges in Sicily did not defeat strong regionalism and social disequilibrium.

The most popular interpretation of the Risorgimento is the one that celebrates a unified nation, an imaginary celebration since the real Italy remains, instead, deeply divided. Likewise, the body poli-

---

[6] From Luigi Salvatorelli's *Nazionalfascismo* (1923) as cited in Umberto Silva, *Ideologia ed arte del fascismo* (Milan: Mazzotta, 1973), 92. On Giolitti's age and, especially, on the industrial triangle, Milan-Turin-Genoa, see Giampiero Carocci, *Giolitti e l'età giolittiana* (Turin: Einaudi, 1961).

tic of Fascism amounted to an artificial cohesion, rather than any common awareness of civic responsibilities. The Duce was the head of a corporate state the function of which was to homogenize from above a proteiform, ever-shifting maze of competing interests, alliances, and partisanships. Popular consent was the effect of an apparatus whose practices ranged from the brutally coercive to the subtly persuasive, with the educational documentaries of L.U.C.E. (November 1925) and the commercial films of Cinecittà (April 1937) forming the backbone of the Fascist culture industry.

Fascism did not resolve well-known tensions operative in Giolitti's Italy: an oppositional view of social change and political stability; a fascination with modernity and a nostalgia for antiquity; the temptation of a populist mentality and the lingering of aristocratic aspirations; an oppressive rural past and an all too recent urban lifestyle. According to the historian Renzo De Felice, Fascism responded to these tensions by glorifying the role of brutal action in the 1920s, and by putting up a respectable façade in the 1930s after having seized power. In *Interpretations of Fascism* (1969),[7] Renzo De Felice distinguishes between fascism as a revolutionary movement, after World War I, and Fascism as a regime, in the 1930s.

The two outfits worn by the regime, the black shirt of the *manganellatore* and the *doppiopetto* of the government official, use the body as if it were a stage for the spectacle of the national self.[8] In order to homogenize composite audiences, Fascism staged great spectacles of national unity and impressive displays of popular consent.

[7] Renzo De Felice is the first to conduct research on Fascism in private archives. His books: *Mussolini Il rivoluzionario (1883–1920)* (Turin: Einaudi, 1965) and *Interpretations of Fascism*, trans. Brenda Huff Everett (Cambridge, Mass.: Harvard University Press, 1977) have stirred great controversies in Italy. In 1969, when the Italian edition, *Interpretazioni del Fascismo*, came out, the Left accused De Felice of an apology of Fascism and was uneasy about his contentions on the revolutionary nature of early fascism as a political movement. For comprehensive overviews of daily life in corporate Italy see Edward Tannenbaum, *The Fascist Experience: Italian Society and Culture 1922–1945* (New York: Basic Books, 1972); Victoria De Grazia, *The Culture of Consent: Mass Organization of Leisure in Fascist Italy* (Cambridge: Cambridge University Press, 1981).

[8] On Fascism defining itself through the staging of a unified, imaginary, but also diversified national self, see Claudio Pavone, "Italy: Trends and Problems," in *The New History: Trends in Historiographical Research and Writing since World War II*, ed. Walter Laqueur and George L. Mosse (New York: Harper and Torch Books, 1967): "Fascism should be regarded as an anomalous interlude or disease, as Croce would have it, or rather as a 'revelation' and a 'national self-description,' according to the well-known interpretation of Giustino Fortunato and Piero Gobetti" (p. 63).

While Mussolini relied on the power of spectacle to unify, he was also aware of the necessity to personify a multiplicity of roles. The Duce's body became the mirror of the fantasy-selves of Italians. The fascist man supposedly has the efficacy of an athlete and of an intellectual, of a warrior and of a father. In the popular culture of the times, the public personae of the Duce (and of his best "public relations" man, Achille Starace) loom over an art-deco landscape cluttered with Roman ruins, beneath billboards advertising American products, for a culture industry catering serialized icons of high art to the masses.

The Fascist culture industry confronted a situation in a manner comparable to the cinema. Since its invention, cinema has tried to reconcile its identity as a mass medium with its status as one of the new art forms of the twentieth century. The newly born regime elicited support from well-established, high art forms, but also experimented with representational solutions appealing to the masses. Kitsch was Fascism's pseudo-democratic answer, an anti-democratic ideology using a popular form of address while simulating the authority of high art.

Classical art made for consumption and ancient history at the service of spectacle were the components of Fascist "Roman" kitsch. Kitsch refers to menial objects raised to the realm of the aesthetic, while high art is lowered through serial reproduction. Kitsch describes a thriving on status symbols, or on effects of artistic vitality and presence that hide, instead, a death-like stasis, and an absence.[9] Through kitsch, Fascism projected an image of cultural prestige on a national level that bridged the gap between high and popular arts. By concealing an inadequacy, kitsch repeated the logic of the spectacles staged by the regime to cover up poverty and abuse, repression and violence. With its aura of prestige, kitsch worked like a therapeutic device for a country in the aftermath of World War I haunted by a demoralized self-image.

Through a kitsch cinema, Fascism reconciled the populist basis of the 1920s with the elitist aspirations of the 1930s and, in so do-

[9] On kitsch, see Clement Greenberg, "The Avant-garde and Kitsch," (1939) in Gillo Dorfles, Kitsch: The World of Bad Taste (New York: Universe Books, 1969), 116–26; Saul Friedlander, Reflections on Nazism: An Essay on Kitsch and Death (New York: Harper and Row, 1982); Thomas Elsaesser, "Myth as the Phantasmagoria of History: H.-J. Syberberg, Cinema and Representation," New German Critique 24–25 (Fall–Winter 1981–82): 115.

ing, glossed over differences due to class, region, and gender. This unifying function of kitsch implemented the construction of a corporate state and the production of an ideal mirror-image of the national self. The visual spectacle and allegorical characters of Carmine Gallone's *Scipio Africanus* (1937), in which kitsch refers to the exploitation of high-culture clichés, correspond to this ideological agenda. Images traditionally associated with great men, crucial battles, and famous events of antiquity grant a narrative authority to the cinema as a mass medium.

Kitsch is the style of cinema where fiction comes closest to propaganda. In Gallone's film, Scipio is a God-like, disembodied protagonist. He is the embodiment of an heterogeneous, but also unified nation: Rome in antiquity, Italy in Mussolini's times. The construction of Scipio's character rehearses the model of the perfect Fascist citizen; Scipio's Rome provides audiences with a mirror image of what the perfect Italian society ought to be.

With the natural forcefulness of an athlete and with the instinctive authority of a statesman, Scipio shapes the course of history as if he were an abstract principle,[10] rising above history itself. Scipio's history-making power recalls Giovanni Gentile's view that ideal forces are the motor of mankind and that the corporate state embodies the spirit of the nation. The Fascist corporate state was the political fulfillment of an "ethical," but also inhuman ideal. Gentile was the official philosopher of the regime and the cinema contributes to the popularization of his Hegelian philosophy of history and view of the state.

From Gentile to Croce, during and after Fascism, a view of the historical process based on continuity and a belief in the unitary nature of consciousness remained pervasive in Italian historiography. In this regard it is important to notice that a linear historicism of Hegelian descent precedes and follows Fascism. Gentile died in 1944. To some extent Gentile's assassination all too quickly put to rest further inquiries into the political uses and abuses of idealist philosophy and of Hegelian historicism. It is also important to remember that these philosophical orientations, either through Gentile or through Croce, were operative in both the fascist and the

---

[10] On *Scipio Africanus*, see James Hay, *Popular Film Culture in Fascist Italy* (Bloomington: Indiana University Press, 1987), 155–61; and Francesco Bolzoni, ed., *Il progetto imperiale: Cinema e cultura nell'Italia del 1936* (Venice: Edizioni de la Biennale, 1976).

antifascist camp. In the immediate postwar period, Croce's intellectual authority, his reputation as an antifascist, and his interpretation of fascism as a disease interrupting Italian history as the "Story of Liberty" caused a delay in the popular diffusion and further development of alternative interpretations of fascism. Put another way, Croce's argument prevents a full appreciation of the early theses by Gobetti, Fortunato, and Salvatorelli about the genesis of fascism in Giolitti's Italy.

This is not to say that, among historiographers, the Crocean interpretation of the Risorgimento prevailed unchallenged until May 1968. In 1952, Federico Chabod, for example, rehashes the objections to Croce put forth by Fortunato and Gobetti in the 1920s, while pointing once again to the limitations of *History of Italy from 1871 to 1915*. Furthermore, in 1965, by maintaining that, early on Mussolini presented himself as a revolutionary, De Felice locates the origins of the regime in the frustrations of Giolitti's Italy. It is only with May 1968, however, that all these arguments massively invade popular culture and the cinema. All these discourses congeal into a new doxa of history that calls for a rethinking of Crocean "liberty."

Not being a political historian, I am unable to provide a detailed account or full explanation of the impact that postwar historiographical research on Fascism and the Resistance might have exercised on the student movement. However, I would underline that Italian students, such as myself, developed ideas about subjectivity and history in a national school system that was originally designed by Benedetto Croce and later by Giovanni Gentile. With Croce and Gentile as the founding fathers of the national school system, it is not surprising that the themes of national unity and historical continuity lived on in students born in the 1950s.

The social unrest surrounding May 1968 and thereafter the resurgence of research on the 1930s and 1940s, culminating in Renzo De Felice's *Interpretations of Fascism* (first published in Italy in 1969), turned the 1970s into a decade of interrogation. The Oedipal conflict of May 1968 was between fathers, who had lived under the regime, and sons, who saw the historical Left mythologize the Resistance. The glorification of the Resistance was most effectively carried out by the Italian Communist and Socialist parties. These groups were eager to appeal to voters on a national level, rather than on a class scale. Hence they quickly ignored the historiographical limitations of an antifascism based on the theme of unity, and of a linear historicism based on continuity with the democratic forces of the Risorgimento.

The generation of May 1968 challenged the popular knowledge of an antifascism of Crocean descent which the Christian-Democrat Alcide De Gasperi (1881–1954), in the postwar period, exploited to the advantage of Catholic forces against the Communist threat. As we shall see later, the generation of May 1968 also became aware of the limits of the communist Palmiro Togliatti's (1893–1964) Gramscian interpretation of the Resistance. Togliatti held on to Antonio Gramsci's belief in the unitary nature of consciousness for the sake of class identity. Furthermore, Togliatti depicted the Resistance with the formula of "unity within diversity."

## CONTINUITY: FROM A SILENT TO A FASCIST SCREEN

The stylistic similarities, as well as the differences, between Giovanni Pastrone's *Cabiria* (1914) and Carmine Gallone's *Scipio Africanus* (1937) challenge Croce's view that in pre-World War I Italy the positive values of the Risorgimento flourished undisturbed. By contrast, a comparative analysis of these two films supports Luigi Salvatorelli's claim that there is a continuity of mentalities[11] between Giolitti's and Mussolini's Italy. More specifically, in the wake of De Felice's distinction between fascism as a movement and Fascism as a regime, a fictional, national self, stereotypical enough for *all* spectators to recognize, moves from a phase of full embodiment, with Pastrone's Maciste, to one of gradual disembodiment, with Gallone's Scipio.

Bartolomeo Pagano, a non-professional actor, played the role of Maciste.[12] Scipio, instead, was impersonated by a trained performer,

[11] For a definition of "mentality," see Pierre Sorlin, *Sociologia del cinema* (Milan: Garzanti, 1979): "Mentalities include thus the intellectual apparatus relevant to the different subdivisions of society, that is to say not only words, specific ways of saying, idioms, but also attitudes, fashions, rituals and symbols" (p. 24).

[12] On the use of non-actors in silent cinema, see Claudio Camerini, "La formazione artistica degli attori del cinema muto italiano," *Bianco e Nero* 44, no. 1 (January–March 1983): 7–43. According to Camerini, Bartolomeo Pagano and Emilio Ghione are the only non-actors who became stars. However, it was not uncommon for aristocrats to play themselves in melodramas and epics. When aristocrats acted, their compensation was sometimes given to charity and their presence on screen enhanced the marketing of the film. In the silent film period, aristocrats were also heavily involved in production. The cinema was often a hobby for the jet set.

Annibale Ninchi. At the level of casting in these films, we immediately encounter an opposition that would later be exploited by neorealism. The character of Maciste is "in-the-body" of Pagano, a non-actor. By contrast, Ninchi's Scipio belongs to a professional actor who is "acting-in-character." The second approach is in line with the classic Hollywood style. Hollywood is a cinema of scriptwriters, and depends on the power of words to explore psychological nuances. In Italian neorealism, in contrast, the physiognomy and behavior of non-professionals, rather than the script, make visible the characters' interiority.

Pastrone's Maciste was cast on the basis of type or physical appearance, according to a theatrical tradition that, in Italian culture, dates back to the commedia dell'arte. His muscles tell the story. Despite Pagano's lack of experience on the set, the non-actor performs in an historical film. Ranking at the top of all the other genres, the historical film demands an operatic scale. The comedic body of Maciste, however, is not inappropriate for an heroic construction of character. In the commedia dell'arte, just as in opera, soma wins over logos, and Maciste's lack of training does not prevent the insertion of his body in an operatic mise-en-scène where emphatic gestures and postures are much clearer and one-dimensional than are the literary and overwrought intertitles attributed to Gabriele D'Annunzio.

The comedic elements of *Cabiria* point to an early phase of kitsch. In Pastrone's film the serialization of icons of high culture does not completely drain the comedic into the operatic, the athletic into the statuesque. *Cabiria*'s kitsch is comparable to a shifting kaleidoscope of different art forms. On the contrary, kitsch in *Scipio Africanus* operates as extreme reification, redundancy, and stillness.

De Felice's distinctions between movement and regime, popular revolution and bureaucratic establishment, historicize Fascism and describe the two stages of kitsch at work in Pastrone's and Gallone's films. The images of *Cabiria* vibrate with the self-awareness of a newly invented art. In 1914, the ambition of cinema was to challenge the relations in place among older art forms. In *Cabiria*, the uses of camera movement, the hypertrophy of the settings, and the emphasis on decorative patterns are constant reminders of the potential of the cinema as an art form.

More than twenty years later, in 1937, Italian cinema no longer had the élan of a newly born art form. Carmine Gallone and Luigi Freddi, the head administrator of Cinecittà, ignored innovative American and Soviet contributions to editing and camera movement. In a stagnant environment of cultural autarchy, Gallone and Freddi imitated the style of Italian silent cinema. In *Scipio Africanus*, the weight of Hannibal's elephants, the width of the Roman columns, and the clichés of famous speeches fail to revitalize an exhausted narrative universe, despite a spectacle of quantity, size, and scale.

The styles of *Cabiria* and *Scipio Africanus*, respectively, exemplify an "early" kitsch that disregards canonical distinctions and a "later" kitsch that reasserts the authority of high culture. In superimposing the unique on the common, and the low on the high, kitsch marks the transition from the physical to the heavenly, from pulsing flesh to lingering aura. It is this transition from Maciste's to Scipio's body, from the dancer to the statue, that brings Salvatorelli's claim of continuity to bear on De Felice's interpretation of fascism as a movement and as a regime.

## KITSCH AND THE ARTS

Both *Cabiria* and *Scipio Africanus* express the rampant nationalism of their times. Both convey the delirious atmosphere of a prewar climate. In 1914 *Cabiria* became an international success. Pastrone's film articulated a correspondence between the ambitious producers of the newly born industry and the hopeful supporters of Giolitti's colonialism in Libya (1911–1912). New audiences saluted a young art form, as the Libyan territory fell prey to a young nation.

In the footsteps of *Cabiria*, Gallone's *Scipio Africanus* reverberated with the excitement of the daily war bulletins from the Ethiopian campaign (1935–1937). Luigi Freddi wanted *Scipio Africanus* to display the popular basis of Mussolini's colonialism. Gallone's film is an operatic spectacle. It allegorizes contemporary history through the culture of classical antiquity, for a mass audience. Unlike *Cabiria*, *Scipio Africanus* was not successful at the box office, suggesting that Fascist spectacles did not always effectively foster a consensus.

From the nineteenth to the twentieth century, operas and historical films fulfilled comparable ideological functions in Italian culture. Both of these mass media bring together different audiences.

As in the opening sequence of Luchino Visconti's *Senso* (1954), opera is the only high-art form that can appeal at the same time to an aristocratic and to a popular audience. Nineteenth-century operas and silent, or fascist historical films tend to set private narratives against public backgrounds. The injection of an historical dimension into a private realm requires the space of a spectacle where individual characters may allegorize the national body.

Both *Cabiria* and *Scipio Africanus* follow the classical dictum that only grandiose images can adequately represent famous historical events, namely the Roman and the Fascist colonial successes in Africa. By relying on the art historical and literary patrimony, in 1914 and in 1937, Pastrone's and Gallone's films tell us about two different ways of envisioning the relation between cinema and the other arts. In *Cabiria*, Pastrone integrates Gabriele D'Annunzio's literary intertitles with art nouveau designs à la Aubrey Beardsley. Pastrone plays the fin-de-siècle fascination for the savage Orient off a morbid, European sensibility. In sequences set in the Temple of Moloch, the director implements Hieronymus Bosch's sensuous detailing of horrific situations with Gustave Moreau's precious textures.

*Cabiria* is a survey of conflicting traditions. This hybrid constellation of cultural sources documents a changing taste. Pastrone's eclectic use of cultural sources reveals how the advent of cinema reconfigured the landscape of the arts. Cinema broke the division between elitist and popular arts. The international success of *Cabiria* proved the existence of new kinds of audiences with a composite, social physiognomy.

In contrast to *Cabiria*'s polymorphous textuality, the rhythm and the make-up of Gallone's film remain monotonous and monolithic. By relying on redundancy, Gallone's film does not boost the artistic traditions it exploits. *Scipio Africanus* reduces art forms to the same level, under the auspices of fascist populism. Literature, painting, theatre, and music become interchangeable trademarks of high culture, available for mass consumption.

As a kitsch opera for the screen, *Scipio Africanus* is an example of how the Fascist culture industry supervised the production and circulation of art in order to construct one, socially homogeneous, national audience. This populist turn offered no constructive alternative to the division between high and popular arts. It merely drew a mystifying equivalence among different artistic traditions, historical periods, and social contexts.

Despite their different ways of appropriating the high culture patrimony, both Pastrone and Gallone allow episodic, spectacular tableaux to slow down causal narrative development. The domination of spectacle over narrative is typical of opera. In this art form, gestures are fixed to a transcendent meaning as ineffable as music. In Pastrone's and Gallone's films, the opposition of stillness and movement matches the operatic placement of one element against the other. With little room for psychological nuances, spectacle, in opera and in cinema, deflects attention away from the void lurking between extreme polarities.

Opera's tendency to polarize reappears in kitsch. Kitsch works on the cinematic mise-en-scène in two opposite, but complementary, directions. It either magnifies objects into monuments or it reduces them to gratuitous details. In kitsch, the too large or the too small are meant to fill in the void, the deficiency that is behind the spectacle. The logic of kitsch, then, matches that of spectacle, for both simulate presence to hide absence, while they strive toward superlative effects to make up for a sense of inadequacy.

In *Cabiria*, sequences are linked by the use of decorative motifs frequently placed in the corner of the intertitle. The draping of a stage curtain, or the silhouette of a palm tree, or the curvilinear volume of a cornucopia, become figurative allusions to either theatrical, exotic, or fantastic traditions. In moving from the close-up of a round Carthaginian vase to the concentric pattern of a Roman shield, Gallone's camera provides an ornamental punctuation mark between sequences. As in kitsch interior decorating, there is in *Scipio Africanus* an excessive attention to functionless detail. The material culture of antiquity assumes the subordinate position of a glorified accessory.

The use of choreographic and acting conventions drawn from opera is apparent in both films. In *Cabiria*, the volcano Aetna erupts when the Carthaginians attack Cabiria's villa (fig. 3). The frantic movement of the extras follows precise screen directions. In the first scene, a line of extras enters the center of a stagy frame. Within a pattern of alternation, this line bifurcates into two opposite wings of figures, respectively exiting on the left and on the right side of the frame. This splitting into two opposite screen directions produces an orderly configuration of disorder. Likewise, in the sec-

**3.** Interior decorating in Giovanni Pastrone's *Cabiria* (1914). Courtesy of The Museum of Modern Art, Film Stills Archive.

ond scene, one line of running extras, with their arms raised toward the sky in desperation, crosses the frame from left to right. The reverse movement from right to left of a second line of extras, with the same posture, intercepts the first group. The expression of strong emotions follows a careful choreography, even though emphatic gestures signal uncontainable feelings.

Sofonisba, the queen of Carthage, and Massinissa, an ally of Scipio, embody love and war. The anguish of Sofonisba emerges from Gallone's choir-like groupings. In opera, the group amplifies the dramatic intensity of the single voice. When Sofonisba throws herself at Massinissa's feet, the curvilinear silhouette of her body reappears in the slaves' postures as they lie on the floor. The repetition of this visual pattern discloses a studied arrangement of bodies and objects. From an operatic viewpoint, the postures of the slaves enlarge the scale of Sofonisba's feelings, as she pleads at her lover's feet. From an historical viewpoint, Sofonisba and the slaves allegorize the helplessness of Carthage.

Highly stylized gestures of happiness, fear, and despair punctuate Gallone's static choreography of still postures. These gestures belong to acting codes that have migrated into silent cinema from opera. In moving from opera to cinema, and, eventually, to comic strips, gestural codes with low information value, but high expressivity, persist. Across different media, the use of stylized gestures resolves specific problems of space. On an operatic stage, the singers' movements must be seen in the distance by the audience. The operatic gesture does not just echo the dramatic sound of the voice. Its emphatic quality provides a visual solution to a problem of scale. Through the magnification of its properties, the scale of an operatic gesture also conveys the heroism of individual struggles against overwhelming forces.

The scale of an operatic gesture is proportional to the monumentality of the settings. In silent cinema, emphatic gestures solve not just problems of scale, but also make up for the absence of recorded sound. Just as in opera, bigger-than-life gestures in silent cinema outdo the word and melt in the music that accompanies the projection. In comic strips, characters perform one gesture at a time. The narrative develops through a fragmented succession of simplified gestures. Each gesture speaks for itself. Through successions of decreasingly smaller or increasingly larger gestures effects of movement and impressions of spatial depth are produced.

In *Scipio Africanus*, when her companion Arunte leaves for the war against Carthage, a Roman woman, Velia, puts her hand on her heart, as if illustrating the intertitle "Farewell." Velia's movement of the hand, accompanied by the appearance of a chanting procession of volunteers, takes place in an operatic setting, without dialogue and during a static medium shot. Gallone integrates such gestures with spatial codes from opera and silent cinema, codes that are adaptable to comic strips.

In *Scipio Africanus*, the camera never intrudes during the dialogues of Roman citizens in the forum. It remains on the outside of their small groups, on the border of the dramatic space, ready to pan as soon as the group moves. In surveying arguments about Scipio's politics, Gallone does not employ the shot/reverse shot. While talking, the bodies of three or four characters address the camera. The characters' glances converge toward one single point, at the center of the frame. The pan does not interrupt, but further underlines the constant frontality of the characters' postures and the circularity of their glances. These elements presuppose the hidden presence of blocking marks, such as those strategically set on the floor of an operatic stage. In opera, spotlighting, in contrast to panning in cinema, carves a dramatic space for each group or singer.

Gallone's references to classical sculpture and architecture tell us little about antiquity. The statues, temples, and columns do tell us, however, much about ancient Rome in the fascist imagination. The fountain statue in Velia's garden belongs to a junk shop rather than to an archeological museum (fig. 4). In the eyes of a popular audience, statues are ancient if they exhibit some mutilation. The pan from an armless statue to Velia's hands sets death against life, and reasserts the logic of polarization typical of the operatic mise-en-scène. Like the columns and the togas, Gallone's fountain statue is a decorative reminder that these characters live in ancient Rome. By depriving art of its hermeneutic function in relation to history, kitsch reinforces a visual tautology.

Gallone's choice of Ildebrando Pizzetti as the composer for *Scipio Africanus* was consistent with the filmmaker's allegiance to the

**4.** Statue, woman, and child in Carmine Gallone's *Scipio Africanus* (1937). Courtesy of The Museum of Modern Art, Film Stills Archive.

aesthetics of opera and silent cinema. Pizzetti was the author of *The Symphony of Fire* in *Cabiria*. In both films, music and gesture charge static scenes with an artificial energy. Pizzetti's contribution to Gallone's film is inflected by the mentality of a silent film composer, that the ineffable music of opera and the ordinary speech of sound cinema are incompatible. For Pizzetti, the film script of *Scipio Africanus*, a sound film shot as if it were a silent film, is subordinate to the music just as the writer of a libretto enjoys a lower rank than the composer of an opera.

Pizzetti's score does not reinforce the impression of real life inherent in the movement of the cinematic image. In contrast, his music turns the characters into lifeless creatures and exposes the very stuff of which films are made: celluloid, shadows, and light. Instead of breathing life into Gallone's characters, Pizzetti's music points out their ghostly presence. Pizzetti's score invokes the phantoms of silent cinema.

The psychological personae of the major characters is not fleshed out by Pizzetti through the use of identifying themes. Antithetical to the Wagnerian solution of the leitmotif, in *Scipio Africanus* Pizzetti's score de-emphasizes the characters' psychology. It stresses, instead, the theatrical similarities among the settings, the lighting, and the compositions of tableaux. Pizzetti explains his method:

> Themes, leading themes? No: but musical nuclei from which, the characteristic features of the generating nucleus remaining recognizable, other themes, other motifs, rhythmic and melodic patterns are generated, according to the requirements of impressions and feelings which are different from that impression and feeling the original nucleus developed from, but which are related to that primitive feeling or impression.[13]

Pizzetti's musical nuclei fit Gallone's subordination of characters' psychology to gestures and a monumental mise-en-scène. When Hannibal and Scipio confront each other, the music does not convey these two leaders' personalities. In a Roman as well as a Carthaginian setting, very different themes concerned with violence, fear, and anxiety develop from the same musical nucleus.

Gallone's characters remain puppets. Pizzetti's music does not bring them to life. Music only sets the pace for their dramatic action and the rhythm of their gestures. The music accomplishes the

---

[13] Ildebrando Pizzetti, "Significato della musica in *Scipione l'Africano*," *Bianco e Nero* 1, nos. 7–8 (July 1937): 13.

dehumanization of Scipio and Hannibal, Massinissa and Sofonisba. These shallow figures undermine the ambition of Pizzetti's score. The result is a dissonance between an operatic film and a comic strip of togas and elephants. Pizzetti's expertise does not rescue *Scipio Africanus* from its failure to simulate the effects of great spectacle and high culture.

From the overlapping story-lines of *Cabiria* and *Scipio Africanus*, a tale of heroism emerges. Individuals, either the obedient Maciste or the noble Scipio Africanus, significantly affect the course of history, giving voice to the aspirations of the nation as a whole.

Both films celebrate a unified consciousness which defies historical change and lasts *corso* after *corso*. Pastrone and Gallone represent Maciste and Scipio as makers of history. The two directors ignore the remapping of subjectivity brought about by the advent of mechanical reproduction in the twentieth century. In antithesis to the Futurists' interest in disjunction and simultaneity of perception, Pastrone's and Gallone's characters stand for two unified selves. This belief in the unitary nature of consciousness is at the basis of Gentile's theory of the corporate state and of Croce's organismic holism. In fact, both philosophers would have liked to see separate members of the national body cooperate with each other.

Maciste's humble origins do not prevent his cooperation with the noble Fulvio. They discover that a young Roman girl, Cabiria, has been kidnapped by the Carthaginians. They succeed in rescuing the child from a horrible death in the flaming mouth of an evil god, Moloch. The dictum of interclassist cooperation against a foreign enemy can be seen in Pastrone's and Gallone's films. Patrician origins do not separate Scipio from the masses. The Romans follow his lead enthusiastically in the struggle against Carthage, in order to avenge their fellow countrymen who, earlier on, perished in the battle of Cannes.

The behaviors of Maciste and Scipio stress cooperation in the name of a national self, encompassing class, regional, and sexual differences. This ideal Italian identity transcends time and space. It rings as true in 1914 as in 1937. It speaks to the continuity of a colonial role in North Africa, from ancient to Fascist Rome. This ideal is, of course, a mass fiction and an ideological construct. Its function is to unify and control, while claiming to be universal and natural.

A similar strategy of effacing differences and naturalizing history is at work in the characterization of Maciste and Scipio. The depiction of Maciste tends toward the athletic, emphasizes movement, and suggests spontaneity. The depiction of Scipio leans toward the statuesque, privileges stillness, and underlines self-control. As allegorical embodiments of the national self, Maciste and Scipio are terms of identification.

Silent-fascist cinema capitalizes on Vico's argument that the body tells history; it updates the humble Maciste into a Roman senator of Scipio's stature, thus refining a previously popular character in order to unify composite audiences through the image of a male hero. According to Vico, the changing image of the body politic mirrors the stages nations, like individuals, experience. On a reduced scale, one example of these Viconian stages could be the shift from revolutionary movement to bureaucratic regime De Felice ascribes to Fascism. This shift becomes tangible through the disembodiment of the athletic Maciste into the phantasmic Scipio. This is not to say, however, that Pastrone and Gallone see their characters as historical variables. On the contrary, the two directors see Maciste and Scipio as mythical heroes who exist beyond history, even though they belong to an historical mise-en-scène. In a similar fashion, as an idealist Hegelian philosopher, Gentile thought of the national self as a spiritual entity that makes history, but whose essential traits remain unchanged.

Maciste and Scipio are mythical and epic characters rather than historical and novelistic.[14] They are endowed with immutable traits and pursue an irreversible destiny. These two characters fit a popular imagination that believed history to be a repetition of Manicheistic confrontations between antithetical forces. In this vulgarized and Hegel-influenced Viconian scenario, good prevails over evil; the domestic triumphs over the foreign; noble idealism defeats petty materialism; historical processes are reduced to biological cycles; the call for unity wins over the expression of differences.

On the basis of Honoré de Balzac's historical novels, Georg Lukács argued that the realist character embodies the constitutive dilemmas of an epoch. For Pastrone and Gallone, Maciste and Scipio are neither the products of their age, nor the representatives of a social class. Rather, as mythical heroes they embody a natural law,

---

[14] On the difference between a mythic and a novelistic character, see Umberto Eco, "The Myth of Superman," *The Role of the Reader* (Bloomington: Indiana University Press, 1979), 109.

and their actions are in response to a universal demand. Maciste's humble origins and Scipio's patrician lineage widen and elevate a populist mode of spectatorial address. With the plebeian Maciste, the lower classes appear to cooperate with the aristocracy. With Scipio, instead, the aristocracy appears popular with the masses. The national ideal warrants that all classes happily cooperate in the corporate, Fascist state.

The representation of crowds in *Cabiria* and in *Scipio Africanus* throws light on the status of the hero's body in the fascist imagination. In *Cabiria* and in *Scipio Africanus*, crowds at the Temple of Moloch and at the Roman forum are as compact and self-contained as the muscles of Maciste and the posturing of Scipio. In these scenes, architecture keeps an enthusiastic mob in check. The huge columns and thick walls of the temples in the forum contain the unpredictable movement of the masses. There is no open public space for wandering off. The architecture blocks the crowd's inclination for sudden disorder (fig. 5).

Gian Piero Brunetta's remarks on the choreography of crowds suggest that Pastrone's and Gallone's scenes do not correspond to the real psychology of Italian audiences. For Brunetta, these crowds on the screen spell out an ideal image of an orderly body politic that does not really exist.

Brunetta acknowledges the power of Fascist spectacles to mobilize the masses and build popular consent. Yet, he also argues that these events are only circumscribed, exhilarating moments of unification within an overall pattern of quasi-anarchic behavior. This defiance of authority is, perhaps, a reaction to centuries spent under foreign rule. Brunetta writes, "There are no reliable and consistent traces that all the followers rigidly conform to the rules of the ritual. The ceremonial, at least during the first decade, draws its inspiration from scholastic and theatrical models more often than from religious ones."[15] By juxtaposing a classroom and a theatre with a church, Brunetta implicitly sets the response of a Fascist crowd against a Nazi one. The critic does not spell out his second term of comparison, but this term nevertheless emerges from Brunetta's reference to a religious model.

Here Brunetta suggests that a Nazi audience, in contrast to a Fascist one, is more sensitive to the mystical overtones surrounding

[15] Gian Piero Brunetta, *Storia del cinema italiano 1895–1945* (Rome: Editori Riuniti, 1979), 373.

**5.** Architecture in Carmine Gallone's *Scipio Africanus* (1937). Courtesy of The Museum of Modern Art, Film Stills Archive.

the Führer. Mussolini's crowds, instead, are more irreverent and child-like than their stern, German counterparts. Italians appear to unify in the image of the leader only for the span of a spectacle. By contrast, German crowds seem more appreciative of social regimentation and conformist behavior.

After setting up a distinction between a Nazi and a Fascist crowd, Brunetta concludes that the marketing of Mussolini's image is characterized by a tendency to favor the physical over the spiritual, the concrete over the abstract, the body over the voice of the leader, the visual over the acoustic. Brunetta borrows this insight from Edward Tannenbaum, who explains, "Unlike Hitler . . . who achieved with radio remarkable results not so much because of what he was saying, but most of all because the medium was perfectly suited to his project of bringing back the German people to a tribal state, Mussolini *had to be seen* in order to make an effect."[16] Since the begin-

---

[16] Gian Piero Brunetta cites Tannenbaum in ibid., 374. Emphasis is mine.

ning of his rise to power, Hitler remained a disembodied presence, a mystical leader, a voice emitted by a bodiless uniform. The Führer's moustache is, perhaps, the only noticeable sign of an uncomfortable physicality in a face of phantasmic pallor.

Brunetta's and Tannenbaum's speculations on the differences between Italian Fascism and German Nazism are stimulating and should be further pursued by cultural and film historians. Let us now move from Brunetta and Tannenbaum to De Felice. It would seem, by emphasizing the concrete over the abstract, action over thought, that the Fascism of the 1920s gained ground as a revolutionary movement. In the 1930s, instead, the regime veered toward non-figurative, non-anthropomorphic political icons. Once its power was consolidated, according to Brunetta and Tannenbaum, Fascism could afford to imitate Nazi Germany with its use of radio.

Italian cinema of the 1970s was keen on the exploration of the changing image of Fascism in the 1930s. In Bernardo Bertolucci's *The Conformist* (1970), Italo Montanari, a blind radio commentator and spokesman for Fascist propaganda, embodies the acoustic stage of Mussolini's regime. During a broadcast, Italo celebrates Italy's allegiance to Hitler's disembodied and abstract ideals.

In Liliana Cavani's *The Night Porter* (1974), Bert dances for an audience of SS officers in a concentration camp (fig. 6). He embodies the soul of the German *Volk*. By contrast, in Pastrone's *Cabiria* Maciste is the Mediterranean body of the commedia dell'arte. Cavani explains:

> If Mussolini was to make use of a Mediterranean machismo, the cocksure swagger of the Italian male, then Hitler relied on quite the reverse: a profoundly military ethos, an esprit de corps that was far more congenial to Germanic culture. Hitler inspired a devotion deeper, more aestheticizing and less rustic than that which the Duce enjoyed. . . . The SS was a body endowed with a great capacity for narcissism. Hitler's charisma, moreover, was based on an ambiguity: he was the "virgin" while Mussolini was the "male." Fascist Italy spoke of "male beauty" while Germany instituted a cult of physical beauty and purity of race.[17]

Cavani's remarks indicate that the Italian and the German popular perception of the leader's body differed greatly. Cavani suggests that the Fascist and the Nazi imagination express themselves through two different approaches to national identity. The Italian self ap-

---

[17] Liliana Cavani, *Il Portiere di notte* (Turin: Einaudi, 1974), xiii.

**6.** Dance in Liliana Cavani's *The Night Porter* (1974). Courtesy of The Museum of Modern Art, Film Stills Archive.

pears to be earth-bound and eclectic; the German seems introspective and ethereal.

It would be interesting to assess whether Nazi Germany identified earlier than Fascist Italy with an abstract representation of the national self, as a result of an older political identity. Italy's limited national history and inferiority complex toward more industrial neighbors might explain why fascism, in the 1920s, relied on an athletic mirror image of the national self. Only once it congealed into a regime was Fascism able to sublimate the earthly features of its revolutionary identity into the abstract aura of a unified body politic. This fictional image of cohesion operated to defy the threat of dismemberment put forth by real differences due to class, region, and gender.

### FROM THE ATHLETE TO THE STATUE TO THE PHANTOM

In *Cabiria* and in *Scipio Africanus*, the representation of the hero's body is inflected by the changing traits of Mussolini's public persona. From the 1920s to the 1930s, the Duce was one of the most powerful images in Italian culture. Maciste's brute physical force and the god-like attributes of Scipio correspond to two phases in the history of the social circulation of Mussolini's image.[18]

The shift from the arrogant days of the March on Rome to the daily administration of power in the 1930s emerges from a comparison of Pastrone's and Gallone's characters, in terms of fashion. Maciste's attire recalls the outfit of a Roman gladiator and stands for the aggressive appearance of the Black Shirts. Scipio's toga, instead, stands for the *doppioppetto* worn by Fascist bureaucrats. With Maciste and Scipio, the image of Mussolini moves from the infinite reproducibility of a comic-strip superman to the charisma of a divine appearance.

This process of disembodiment becomes apparent through references to Mussolini's body, voice, posture, gestures, and clothing in Pastrone's and Gallone's films. *Cabiria* was closer in time than *Sipio Africanus* to the athletic milieu of the circus, an art form that, like opera, shares the mass appeal of the cinema. Physical valor redeems the humble origins of Pastrone's athlete. If Maciste had not become the male star of silent cinema, he might have had a successful career in the circus. He is an acrobat of the arena more than a divo of the operatic stage (fig. 7).

The operatic label "divo" refers to a male star of private melodramas and to a public hero of historical films. The male stars of melodrama, however, are weak artists and effete aristocrats, and not strong athletes. Consequently, their status on the screen is weaker than that of their female counterparts, who, as goddesses of the opera, divas, eclipse them in the public eye. As stars subordinate to the divas, male actors in melodrama are not quite worthy of this title reserved for operatic singers and for military leaders in the historical film. Outside the cinema, in Italian popular culture, Benito Mussolini and Gabriele D'Annunzio were divi. As objects of collective desire, Mussolini and D'Annunzio shared stardom with three great divas of the silent film period: Francesca Bertini, Lyda Borelli, Pina Menichelli.

Scipio is an aristocratic, corpse-like character. Gallone moves

---

[18] An excellent visual account of the history and the circulation of Mussolini's image is Renzo De Felice and Luigi Goglia, *Storia fotografica del fascismo* (Rome: Laterza, 1982). On fashion in Fascist culture, see Natalia Aspesi, *Il lusso e l'autarchia: Storia dell'eleganza italiana 1930–44* (Milan: Rizzoli, 1982).

7. Bartolomeo Pagano as Maciste and the diva in Giovanni Pastrone's *Cabiria* (1914). Courtesy of The Museum of Modern Art, Film Stills Archive.

away from Maciste's proletarian muscles to narrate the transformation of the leader's body into a cult object. This shift from the physical to the heavenly, from the ordinary to the unattainable, is the constitutive contradiction of kitsch.

Once reified, the kitsch object does not become obsolete. On the contrary, it ascends to the status of an irreplaceable fetish. A similar process goes on in the transition from the spectacle of Maciste's physical force to the spectacle of Scipio's institutional power. In contrast to Maciste's, the nobler origins of Scipio signal a refinement of character. They express a will to distance this heroic figure from the masses. In the turn from a populist to an aristocratic persona, Scipio's white toga replaces the nakedness of Maciste's muscles.

Scipio's generosity and wisdom recall standard allegories about the moral and intellectual virtues of the Roman people. Scipio's traditonal traits are firmness and courage, rationality and clemency. Gallone depicts these virtues through statuesque postures, all-embracing gestures, and sober costuming.

A comparable allegorical impulse hovers over Giambattista Tiepolo's paintings of episodes in Scipio's life.[19] Clothed in a red cloak, Tiepolo's Scipio takes on a chivalric twist. The muscles of his body still shape the outline of his costume, yet the foldings in the cloak and the graceful hanging of the sword turn the Roman Scipio into an effete Venetian admiral fit for a fresco in a Palladian villa.

The opposition between an aristocratic leader and a Tarzanesque hero emerges from Scipio's cameo appearance in *Cabiria*. In Pastrone's narrative, Scipio is not a major character as is Maciste. Nevertheless, historical fame alone makes Scipio quickly recognizable. Maciste, instead, needs a story of rescue to attain the status of a mythical character.

In the eyes of an audience in 1937, Scipio's "Roman" profile was the blueprint of Mussolini's official portrait. According to Luigi Malerba, these two faces come together as in a filmic superimposition: "Well, yes, the Duce's image had become fixed in my memory against my will, precise and cinematographic, sepia-toned like a figure of *Scipio Africanus*. A mute image, as if cut out of a silent movie."[20] Malerba's words stress that the iconicity of Scipio's image in relation to the Duce's is so strong that it achieves a dehumanizing effect. Malerba is more interested in the impression of reality produced by the cinema, rather than in the historical referent. Malerba's pairing of the adjectives "precise" and "cinematographic" underlines how Scipio's cinematographic image is more "real" the more precisely it fits the heroic mold stored in the popular imagination.

Scipio's traits, such as his stern profile, his authoritative posture, and his immaculate toga, stand in for separate parts of Mussolini's body. The jutting chin of the Duce conveys an attitude of boldness. The bald area of his skull makes the forehead look more spacious and the expression more thoughtful. The protruding lips, the squared jaw, are also typical aspects of Mussolini's public image.

In the popular visual culture of the 1930s, all these features came together in a montage which fit the stereotype of the leader, piece

[19] On Tiepolo's Scipio, see Valentino Crivellato, *Tiepolo* (New York: W. W. Norton & Co., Inc., 1962), plate 6.

[20] Luigi Malerba, "Quella voce che mi segue" in "Mille facce per un duce," *La Repubblica*, July 10–11, 1983, n.p.

by piece. Each separate trait was stylized to such a degree that alone it signified Mussolini's whole body. The chin, the forehead, the lips became the trademarks of an age.

Extreme stylization also applies to the body of Sofonisba. Standing in profile against a wall, she looks like an Egyptian hieroglyph. This stylization is kitsch, because it combines what is inaccessible and unique with what is common and consumable. Sofonisba is both a distant, undecipherable letter and an exotic cliché, a trite character.

The fact that both Scipio and Sofonisba undergo a comparable kitsch stylization suggests that one is the alter ego of the other. This symmetry between male and female is typical of the scenario of the battle of the sexes and depends on an effacement of the sexual difference that implements the theme of national unity.

The cinema of the 1970s explored the components of the Duce's popular image, piece by piece. Lina Wertmuller's *Love and Anarchy* (1973) begins with a montage sequence, in black and white, of separate parts of Mussolini's body. The flashing of each detail on the screen is accompanied by a booming sound that evokes the customary explosions following the operation of an old-fashioned photographic apparatus. It is as if Mussolini's body were exploding into a thousand pieces, while imprinting itself in the spectator's minds. Frank Burke's commentary on this sequence illustrates the reifying effects of kitsch:

> Inherent in all that goes on in the opening sequence is the denial of the cinematic. The limitations of black and white, the stasis of photographs, the disconnection and death of the eye, the dominance of abstraction—all are mortal enemies of cinema, which lives through the multiplicity of color, the vitality of the moving image, the marriage of seer and seen, and above all, the "enlighted" activity of the unique, concrete, individual. Wertmuller, sensing that the values of movies are the values of life itself, sets *Love and Anarchy* up as an exercise in anti-cinema—note even the abstractness of the title—providing yet one more negative dimension to the life-denying conditions that pervade the film's action.[21]

I agree with Burke that *Love and Anarchy* calls attention to the abstract idealism underpinning unattainable political goals and to the myth of eternal love. Yet, I would also add that, despite this

[21] Frank Burke, "Death-By-Abstraction, A Discussion of the Opening Sequence and Tunin's Demise in Wertmuller's *Love and Anarchy*," *Film Studies Annual: Theory-French-German-Italian* (Lafayette, Ind.: Purdue University Press, 1976), 227.

undeniable level of critique, Wertmuller cannot help but look back, with a certain indulgence, at the strong images of Maciste and Scipio.

Instead of *Love and Anarchy*, Wertmuller's film could be retitled *Life and Death*, as it explores the work of kitsch. In cinema, kitsch drains the life of the moving image into the death-like stasis of sculpture. Sculpture, the art of stillness, is closer to photography than to the cinema. Like dance, the cinema is an art of movement. While *Love and Anarchy* rejects the inhuman side of idealist philosophy, Wertmuller's handling of the male body as an historical variable suggests that the legacy of Vico's thought has survived intact the generational tensions of May 1968.

Brunetta's remarks on the achievement of respectability for Fascism in the 1930s echo De Felice's thesis that Mussolini's image shifts from an athletic-revolutionary phase à la Maciste to an institutional-statuesque phase à la Scipio: "with the increasing tendency of Fascist Italy to become more and more bourgeois . . . the balancing of the body on two legs spread apart, the tossing about of the bust disappear. . . . In comparison to the paroxysm of the 1920s, gestures appear to undergo a *ralenti* process, words are enunciated and isolated in a more clear-cut way."[22] During his first appearance in *Cabiria*, at the center of the frame, Maciste's weight is distributed on both legs, which are set apart from each other. This posture evokes one of Mussolini's favorite photographic poses. Viewers do not see the object of Maciste's glance to the left of the frame. They can only look at Maciste looking. Maciste's muscles, then, are the spectacle that engages the viewers' attention.

Prior to any interest in Maciste's psychology, the body alone signifies the heroic status of this character in the narrative. Gallone's Scipio never assumes this athletic posture. When he first appears under an arch, like a sun rising in the distance, he dominates the acclaiming crowd below. From Maciste's stance to Scipio's ascension to power, the change of posture is accompanied by slower gestures and words. Movements do not convey a sense of physical energy. The lifted arm of the Fascist salute has the rigidity of Gallone's wooden standard rising over the battlefield of Cannes, as a sign of revenge across a blank sky.

The visual parallel between the Fascist arm and the Roman stan-

[22] Brunetta, *Storia del cinema italiano 1895–1945*, 377.

dard announces the transformation of human movement into mechanical performance. The Fascist body of the 1930s belongs to an automaton. Gallone's kitsch drains all that is bodily out of the hero's body, which becomes a lifeless envelope. In Vittorio Emanuele Bravetta's poem *Hail the Duce*, a succession of images produces a comparable effect of artificiality. With Bravetta, the iconographic commonplaces of *Scipio Africanus* unfold as if they belonged to a comic strip. In kitsch, low becomes high, and even a comic strip can take on the structure of a prayer:

Blessed by the sun.
By the Earth.
By Bread.
By mothers' hands.
By children's smiles.
By shining hoes.
By far-away ships.
Blessed by Rome, on the 21st of April.
God sends you to Italy as he sends light:
Duce.
Duce.
Duce.
Take the twenty-year-old blood
that burns in our veins.
Turn the blood into the flame
that defends the empire.
Dictate laws of glory.
Break shackles and chains.
Worker.
Shepherd.
Constructor.
Warrior.
God sends you to Italy
as he sends light:
Duce.
Duce.
Duce.[23]

[23] Vittorio Emanuele Bravetta, "Saluto al Duce," in Bolzoni, ed., *Il progetto imperiale*, 44.

Mussolini's presence is invoked line after line, with the fragmentation of the comic strip and the repetitiveness of religious chanting.

The kitsch mode, here, requires the absence of the body, while it uses redundancy to mask a void. Mussolini, who is "blessed by the sun," becomes pure light at the end. The dematerialization of Mussolini's body, in Bravetta's verses, parallels the disembodiment of Scipio in Gallone's film. Images of hands without arms, of smiles without faces, of farming tools and military weapons without a user, reinforce the theme of the absence of the body.

Like Bravetta's Mussolini, Gallone's Scipio is a farmer and a warrior. He is a *pater* and a *dux*. In bringing these rural, familial, and military roles together, Gallone refers to the versatility of Mussolini's public persona. The Duce is the term of identification of the "new Italian man," of the "Fascist *vir.*" *Scipio Africanus* fits in Luigi Freddi's manifesto for a "virile cinema." "It is absolutely right that, in the Italy of today, one demands, also from cinema, visions that are inspired by the energetic and active way of life of the new Italian man. Also, it is reasonable that films of the revival genre draw their inspiration from those aspects of our past that are pleasant and acceptable to our present form of mind."[24] This "virile cinema" celebrates the strength of the body, the physical courage of leaders, and the congruence of individual with national interests within the corporate framework of the Fascist state.

This emphasis in the cinema on the virile body came from the spectacles of physical fitness, coordination, and endurance staged in German and Italian stadiums. Instead of the Renaissance stage built for an aristocratic audience, Fascism preferred the open space of the gymnasium, of the military courtyard, and of the Roman circus for the masses. The cult of the body was at the center of this public space. The spectacle of sports became a mass religion in Fascist Italy in which both men and women participated. In this religion, the material world was sublimated to the spiritual, according to the logic of kitsch disembodiment that links *Cabiria* to *Scipio Africanus*. Anton Giulio Bragaglia speaks of "an intense spiritualization through sport of the education of the human body. . . . The soul defeats brutal animality, which is feared in the cult of physical power and dexterity."[25] Despite Freddi's call for a "virile cinema," the re-

[24] Bolzoni, ed., *Il progetto imperiale*, 69.
[25] Anton Giulio Bragaglia, "Sport e Teatro di Massa," in Bolzoni, ed., *Il progetto imperiale*, 84.

dundant images of *Scipio Africanus* look crowded by shallow figures.

The flesh of Pastrone's Maciste turns into the marble of Gallone's Scipio. The leader assumes the posture of a neoclassical statue. In the Senate, Scipio's body acquires the inhuman stillness of a bust. The close-ups of Scipio's stern, "Roman" profile, his hair style, and hawkish gaze turn the cinematic frame into a commemorative medallion.

In discussing Mussolini's changing image, the writer Italo Calvino argues that the medallion version of the Duce's profile sanctions his elevation to the all-powerful, medieval Christ-King. This aristocratic look of Fascism was replaced by a modernist Mussolini, in profile, wearing a helmet. Italo Calvino recalls:

> For Mussolini's iconography, this is a major turning point: the classical image of the Duce is now the one with the helmet, like a metallic amplification of the smooth surface of his head. His jaw is emphasized beneath the helmet and acquires a decisive importance because the top part of his head (including his eyes) has disappeared. . . . The Duce's head, . . . then, appears to be essentially composed of helmet and jaw, whose volumes counterbalance each other and counterbalance the curve of his stomach, which is now beginning to stand out.[26]

This iconographic metamorphosis marked a change in mood. The enthusiasm surrounding Mussolini's colonial conquests was replaced by the dark journey toward World War II, after the Italian alliance with Germany.

This change of look constitutes a good example of "styling." By this term, the art critic Gillo Dorfles does not mean kitsch stylization. Rather, Dorfles describes a kitsch upgrading performed on objects: "The object is submitted to a particular *cosmetic* treatment which accentuates the line, and the so-called aerodynamic quality, but has no basic and genuine functional purpose."[27] As a result of this cosmetic styling, the Duce's "Roman" profile turns into a cubist arrangement of volumes. In kitsch styling, just as in kitsch generally speaking, there is again something gratuitous. It is a useless embellishment. Kitsch styling updates the markers of antiquity and makes them appealing to the aggressive taste of modern audiences.

[26] Italo Calvino, "Cominciò con un cilindro" in "Mille facce per un duce," *La Repubblica*, July 10–11, 1983, n.p.
[27] Dorfles, *Kitsch: The World of Bad Taste*, 254.

The styling is also a symptom of Mussolini's military commitment to Hitler's Germany.

In the cinema of the 1970s, Mussolini's image oscillated from the haunting to the ridiculous. Federico Fellini latched on to this second extreme. In *Amarcord* (1974), the Duce's body is a huge float of pink petals (fig. 8). With Fellini's carnivalesque approach, signs are turned upside down or against themselves. Through a mise-en-scène of flowers and uniforms, Fellini dramatizes the processes of kitsch. The circular shape of the float with eyes, nose, and mouth makes Mussolini's face resemble an anthropomorphic sun, drawn by a child. Indeed, with their cult of strong men, the onlookers of Fascist spectacles come to occupy a child-like position. Furthermore, children are the most avid readers of comic strips where the hero always wins.

The Duce's face is made of flowers and, like other kitsch objects, is an artificial emblem of natural life. This aura of naturalness

**8.** Fascist kitsch in Federico Fellini's *Amarcord* (1974). Courtesy of The Museum of Modern Art, Film Stills Archive.

builds upon the sexualized scenarios couched in Fascist rhetoric. The Duce is either the beloved father or the spouse of Italy, which is both woman and land. In *Scipio Africanus*, the battle of the sexes allegorizes a military confrontation. Hannibal makes advances to Velia in anticipation of his conquest of Rome.

The symmetry of the battle of the sexes implies the effacement of sexual difference for the sake of national unity. This scenario defines women as alter egos of men and, reversely, men as potential objects of feminization. Undoubtedly, femininity is not just a prerogative of women in a cinema where the male body continues to be an object of spectacle from the 1930s to the 1970s.

In Fascist culture, the athletic muscles of Maciste and the composed gestures of Scipio become objects of desire and, as such, slip into a feminized realm. Femininity, in turn, is a threatening reminder of castration and becomes the subtext for the depiction of Carthage in *Cabiria*. This foreign city is overly decorated and sensous, leading one to believe that its inhabitants, too, are deceiving and decadent. It is important to remember that Moloch, who lives off human sacrifices, is not a god, but a goddess. This evil creature embodies an horrific male fantasy of castration, recalling the destructiveness of the divas of melodramas.

Lounging on a sofa, Gallone's Sofonisba behaves like a diva, the beautiful, but dangerous, goddess of opera and silent cinema. As threatening as the foreign queen Sofonisba may be, the Roman heroes need her Medusa-like, intense gaze to become statues. Even the static camera of Gallone cannot resist the pull of Sofonisba's eyes, which it seeks during a lengthy tracking shot.

Fellini's flowers signal the potential slippage from masculinity to femininity latent in the cult of the male body. The float is an emblem of domestic embellishment, rather than of military imperialism. In Bravetta's poem and in *Amarcord*, the Duce is the sun. Like Gallone's Scipio, Fellini's flowery face exhibits a stern, severe expression worthy of a Roman leader. In *Amarcord*, the Duce leads a corporate state of faceless, obedient bodies in uniform.

Fellini carnivalizes, but does not deconstruct, the Fascist body. The float sequence is the fantasy of a fat boy who dreams of marrying the girl of his dreams during a military parade in honor of the Duce. The marriage ceremony takes place under the eye of the father, as if only his gaze could guarantee the naturalization of the historical process into a sequence of generations.

*Amarcord* unfolds along the cycle of the seasons. This kind of narrative structure neutralizes the carnivalesque potential of the images, for Fellini's choice of a seasonal frame suggests the alignment of historical with biological continuity and the reduction of the processes of culture to the *ricorsi* of an Hegelianized Vico.[28]

In a similar fashion to Fellini, Wertmuller's explosion of the Duce's body in *Love and Anarchy* is not a gesture of deconstruction, but a piece-by-piece dismantling that further eroticizes. In the 1970s, *Amarcord, Love and Anarchy*, and Bertolucci's *The Conformist* exorcise Fascism into a desirable object of guilt, without giving up the unconscious homoeroticism of the heterosexual, homosocial culture *Cabiria* and *Scipio Africanus* exemplify.

After all, *Amarcord* is about the sexual frustrations of a group of boys growing up in the isolation of a small town. The exorcism of Fellini's provincial past took place in the aftermath of May 1968. This was a time when the sons interrogated the fathers and when Fellini, Wertmuller, and Bertolucci were able to deal with an era Togliatti's historical Left and De Gasperi's Catholic establishment, in the 1950s, could not fully come to terms with. This is why the carnivalesque styles of Fellini and Wertmuller have an Oedipal rather than a deconstructive coloring. Fellini and Wertmuller stop at the investigation of origins only recently rediscovered, whose pull their films hardly overcome.

### BODY BUILDERS AND BEAUTY QUEENS

The involution of neorealism into pink neorealism, in the 1950s, and into Comedy Italian Style in the 1970s, indicates the strength of the parameters of Italian cinema. Allegory, spectacle, history, unity, continuity, and body are valid categories for the silent film period as well as for pink neorealism and Comedy Italian style. From the mid-1950s to the mid-1960s, in the "peplum" film, the body-documents of neorealist comedic microhistory revert to the body-monuments of operatic macrohistory. The precursors of the postwar peplum are the "strong man" adventure and comedy films of the 1920s, with Maciste and his imitators, Ajax (Carlo Aldini)

[28] On the representation of history and nature in Fellini's *Amarcord*, see Pier Paolo Pasolini, "The Catholic Irrationalism of Fellini," trans., introd., and notes Frank and Pina Demers, *Film Criticism* 9, no. 1 (Fall 1984): 63–73.

and Saetta (Domenico Gambino), as star-athletes.[29] In the context of pink neorealism, the peplum revamps the spectacle of the male body and the passion for antiquity promoted by Fascist historical films like Gallone's *Scipio Africanus*. In postwar Italy, the role of the athlete à la Maciste passed to Steve Reeves, an American body builder, who became a star of Italian cinema and of the Via Veneto overnight.

The Marshall Plan, the Cold War, De Gasperi's anti-Communist stance, and Giulio Andreotti's Studio Law (1949)[30] against the neorealist denounciation of social evils all contributed to the transformation of black-and-white newsreel neorealism into pink neorealism. Emerging like a phoenix from the ashes of Gallone's fascist kitsch, the life-span of the neorealist body-document was quite brief, as Rossellini sadly pointed out in a letter from Rome to Brunello Rondi, dated December 19, 1955: "But at the end of the war the production of kitsch in Italy came to a sudden halt. . . . This despite the fact that, with the reorganization of kitsch production, neorealism felt besieged, and isolated."[31] In his analysis of the role the Marshall Plan played in the containment of neorealism, Michael Silverman isolates a telling image of the return of the kitsch body in 1948 in a film by the neorealist Giuseppe De Santis:

[29] On the "strong man" film and the peplum, see Alberto Farassino and Tatti Sanguineti, eds., *Gli uomini forti* (Milan: Mazzotta, 1983); Giovanni Calendoli, "*Cabiria* e il film della romanità," *Materiali per una storia del cinema italiano* (Parma: Maccari, 1967), 63–111; M. Domenico Cammarota, *Il Cinema Peplum* (Rome: Fanucci, 1987); Claude-Michel Cluny, "Le Péplum," *Cinéastes* 2 (Paris-Tournai: Casterman, 1971), 245–46; Olivier Curchod, "Cinéma et représentation du passé l'antiquité dans le *Fellini-Satyricon*," *Film et histoire*, ed. Marc Ferro (Paris: Éditions de l'École des Hautes Études en Sciences Sociales, 1984), 53–63; Raymond Durgnat, "Homage to Hercules," *Motion* 6 (1963): 48–50; Derek Elley, *The Epic Film: Myth and History* (London: Routledge and Kegan Paul, 1984); Goffredo Fofi, "Maciste sugli schermi," *Catalogo Bolaffi del cinema italiano 1945–65* (Turin: Bolaffi, 1967), 254–60; Jacques Siclier, "L'Age du Péplum," *Cahiers du Cinéma* 22, no. 131 (May 1962): 26–38; Vittorio Spinazzola, "Ercole alla conquista degli schermi," *Film 1963* (Milan: Feltrinelli, 1963), 75–111; Mario Verdone, "Il film atletico e acrobatico," *Centrofilm* 3, no. 17 (1961): 3–36; Roland Barthes, "Les Romains au cinéma," *Mythologies* (Paris: Éditions du Seuil, 1957), 27–30.

[30] A member of De Gasperi's Christian-Democratic Party, Giulio Andreotti favored shooting in studios with trained actors and skilled labor because, he argued, this kind of more traditional cinema would raise the employment rate at Cinecittà. On Andreotti's Studio Law, see Liehm, *Passion and Defiance*, 90–93.

[31] Roberto Rossellini, *Il mio metodo: Scritti e interviste*, ed. Adriano Aprà (Venice: Marsilio, 1987), 126.

Mangano in *Riso Amaro* walks left of the frame through a rice paddy perpendicular to an undifferentiated mass of less strikingly attractive women, all of whom are bent over their work. As she moves to the middle distance she raises her skirt out of the water to just below her buttocks. Our eyes no longer watch the right side of the frame, the mass of working women, but take in the movement of the skirt, the revelation once again of the body. Not only voyeurism and the gaze, not only the Bazinian middle distance, but the documentable trace of American capital investment is marked by the movement of that skirt.[32]

De Santis' kitsch body is male, just as Pastrone's Maciste and Gallone's Scipio, to the extent that Silvana Mangano is the projection of a male sexual fantasy. Silvana Mangano is a character with a neorealist profession: a day-worker in a northern Italian rice paddy. This class feature, however, is eclipsed by her looks, since she has the sex-appeal of an American pin-up (fig. 9).

Mangano started out as Miss Italia, like many other beauty queens who in the 1950s quickly ascended to stardom in the cinema, in the footsteps of Maciste. He was the first non-actor to become a star. Gina Lollobrigida, Marisa Allasio (the Italian Jayne Mansfield), Renato Salvatori, and Maurizio Arena also started as non-actors starring in the escapist comedies of pink neorealism, embodying different manifestations of the fictional, national self. The fact that comedy, with light-hearted social commentary, flourished in conjunction with the involution of neorealism, confirms that, along with opera, the commedia dell'arte endures in the 1950s to become a term of reference of Comedy Italian Style in the 1970s.

On the screen of pink neorealism, men and women loose the vibrant physicality of Luchino Visconti's non-professional actors in *La Terra Trema* (1948), the spontaneous movements of Vittorio De Sica's children in *Shoeshine* (1946), and the erratic fluidity of Roberto Rossellini's crowd scenes in *Open City* (1945) and *Paisà* (1946). In comparison with the characters of fascist cinema, these *bulli e pupe*[33] lack the contrived purity of neoclassical sculpture. With their sexy rags and sweaty biceps, they seem closer to life, but really are not. Their higher degree of humanization is a kitsch up-

[32] Michael Silverman, "Italian Film and American Capital, 1947–1951," in *Cinema Histories/Cinema Practices*, ed. Patricia Mellencamp and Philip Rosen (Frederick, Md.: University Publications of America and the American Film Institute, 1984), 43.

[33] In English, "guys and dolls."

**9.** Dance in Giuseppe De Santis' *Bitter Rice* (1948). Courtesy of The Museum of Modern Art, Film Stills Archive.

dating called for by the documentary aesthetics of early neorealism. This styling is a picturesque disguise intended to recycle the ideological continuity of the same imaginary, national self that informed the construction of character in silent and fascist cinema.

Pink neorealist comedies and the peplum films are *filoni*, rather than "genres" in the Hollywood sense, that is, well-planned investments of the industry into a regulated, but also stimulating, oscillation between repetition and difference, convention and invention. Unlike the Hollywood genre, the Italian *filone* has a brief life-span and an hypertrophic size. It would seem that the *filone* is a genre that degrades itself into empty redundancy; it does not achieve that meaningful layering which, from Vico's theory of history, lives on across Italian culture in the spectacular-allegorical styles of opera and the commedia dell'arte.

In the 1960s the fixed scripts of the peplum and the spectacle of the male body lose their energy. The industry, then, recycles the well-known parameters—body, history, spectacle, allegory—into the Spaghetti Western. While thriving on the politicized climate of May 1968, this new *filone* challenges Hollywood's view of the American frontier and restages American history as if it were a popular, Marxist allegory. The superficial politicization of the Spaghetti Western, its rereading of the Hollywood western without overturning its epistemology, its ability to produce simultaneously pleasure and distance, work both as a strength and a weakness.[34]

Sergio Leone, the most famous director of Spaghetti Westerns, started out with a peplum, *The Colossus of Rhodes* (1960). In the Spaghetti Western, Leone's style integrates operatic with comedic elements. The neorealist interest in the long duration of structures of behavior and the comedic impulse to magnify details of physiognomy and daily life, explain why Leone combines hyperbole with duration, extreme close-ups with an unmotivated stretching of suspense.

An Italian horse-opera, Leone's *Once Upon a Time in the West* (1968), is a film about the American past. Such a middleground distance—undoing Hollywood without moving beyond it, Italian pop-Marxism, and American mythology—indicates that Leone's film belongs to the intersection of operatic macrohistory in silent-fascist cinema and the comedic microhistory of neorealism and the art film. Leone amplifies the spectacle of the male body along minimalist rhythms which, in length, are comparable to the *temps morts* of Michelangelo Antonioni's *L'Avventura* (1960).

[34] On the Spaghetti Western, see Mary Ann Doane, "*Once Upon a Time in the West*: The Politics of Genre," in "The Dialogical Text: Filmic Irony and the Spectator" (Ph.D. diss., University of Iowa, 1979), 259–90.

# TWO

## Fascism after May 1968

### OPERATIC MACROHISTORY IN CRISIS

THE RESTRAINED acting style of Jean-Louis Trintignant in Bernardo Bertolucci's *The Conformist* (1970)[1] recalls the stiffness of Carmine Gallone's kitsch statue in *Scipio Africanus* (fig. 10). Trintignant's Marcello Clerici models his public self in the image of the perfect Fascist citizen. Clerici supports the regime to hide a homosexual encounter during his childhood. This experience haunts the adult Marcello as a sin that cannot be erased. This sexual initiation stands as an indelible origin, a fathering principle of his male identity. The inescapable circularity of the past with the present leads Marcello to hide his homosexuality until the fall of Fascism.

Marcello Clerici is split between a heterosexual, public identity and a homosexual, private one. In contrast to Bertolucci's character, the private self of Gallone's Scipio is hardly an issue, since it is an unproblematic flip side of his public behavior. This comparison between Marcello and Scipio is drawn in order to propose that, in the cinema of the 1930s and of the 1970s, the body of the male

[1] The bibliography on Bertolucci, in general, and *The Conformist*, in particular, is quite rich, for example: "Bernardo Bertolucci Seminar," *American Film Institute Dialogue on Film* 3, no. 5 (April 1974): 14–28; Andrew Britton, "Bertolucci: Thinking about Father," *Movie* 23 (Winter 1976–77): 9–22; Francesco Casetti, *Bernardo Bertolucci* (Florence: La Nuova Italia, 1978); Joan Mellen, "A Conversation with Bernardo Bertolucci," *Cineaste* 5, no. 4 (1973): 21–24; Millicent Marcus, "*The Conformist*: A Morals Charge," *Italian Film in the Light of Neorealism* (Princeton, N.J.: Princeton University Press, 1986), 285–312; Robert Philip Kolker, *Bernardo Bertolucci* (New York: Oxford University Press, 1985), 87–104.

**10.** The statue and the text of history in Bernardo Bertolucci's *The Conformist* (1970). Courtesy of The Museum of Modern Art, Film Stills Archive.

protagonist is a site for the negotiation of the private with the public, of the personal with the political. This negotiation is by far more peaceful with Gallone than with Bertolucci.

In *The Conformist*, Bertolucci turns to the operatic macrohistory of silent-fascist cinema. From the 1930s to the 1970s, the endurance of the statue summons the specter of Ernst H. Kantorowicz's medieval Christ-King with two bodies: one public and eternal, the other private and contingent. These two bodies easily coexist in Gallone's Scipio, but are in painful conflict in Bertolucci's Marcello.

Gallone's monuments of Fascism reappear in Bertolucci's film, but their status is under scrutiny as if one of Giambattista Vico's cycles in the history of the nation had reached its end and its emblems were about to collapse. If Vico's law of the *ricorso* is still operative in Bertolucci's revisitation of the 1930s in the 1970s, Benedetto Croce's historiography does not survive the blunder of May 1968. For Croce, Fascism was an interruption of the history of Italy, unfolding from the Risorgimento to the Resistance as the "Story of Liberty." Croce's Fascism was containable within a parenthesis. According to a postwar popular historical knowledge of Crocean descent, 1945 marked a clean break with the regime. In *The Conformist*, Bertolucci challenges Croce's comparison of the fall of the regime to a sort of ground-zero.[2]

After May 1968, Fascism can no longer fit inside a parenthesis. In *The Conformist*, Bertolucci may reject Croce's historiography, but the sins of the fathers remain indelible and the operatic macrohistory of the 1930s continues to exercise its appeal. Marcello can neither forget his encounter with Lino, a homosexual chauffeur, nor restrain himself from accusing his father, a former Black Shirt and a madman. Likewise, the mise-en-scène of *The Conformist* is as monumental as Gallone's in *Scipio*, even though Bertolucci's statue is only the compact façade of a split self.

Marcello's father participated in the rise of Fascism. Tormented by his violent past, he ends his life as a recluse inside a black-and-white asylum, with long, rigid lines receding into the horizon. The absence of color and the layering of contained volumes into a haunting perspective underline the pull of origins. Likewise, the sins of the fathers weighed over the revolt of the sons during May 1968.

Bertolucci's stance toward Italian historical thought is characterized by ambivalence, fitting the climate of generational tensions typical of the late 1960s. While the enfant terrible of Italian cinema rejects Croce's historiography, Bertolucci's conceptualization of history is based on Vico's view that the body is an historical variable, the features of which change on the basis of two scenarios: the Oedipal conflict or the battle of the sexes. Sons confront fathers, in the first case; men and women challenge each other, in the second.

[2] On Croce's interpretation of Fascism, see Claudio Pavone, "Italy: Trends and Problems," *The New History: Trends in Historical Research and Writing since World War II*, ed. Walter Laqueur and George L. Mosse (New York: Harper and Torch Books, 1967): "Croce's optimism about the Giolittian age in his *History of Italy* has been amply contested in many quarters; and indeed his undeservedly successful medico-bacterio-logical metaphor (a healthy body but with a predisposition to harbour the germs of future disease), which was later used by Chabod, no longer seems adequate to explain the relation between the 1900–1915 period and fascism" (pp. 53–54).

These two scenarios interlock under the sign of a heterosexual male identity in a homosocial context. The more the sons of May 1968 questioned the generation of the 1930s, the more the power exercised by the fathers and their haunting historical past became apparent. History is, thus, reduced to a father-son, man-to-man social pact.

History as a series of legacies between males presupposes a marginalization of women. The effacement of sexual difference in the historical process fits the symmetry of the battle of the sexes. In this scenario women are either reassuring male alter egos or threatening reminders of castration. The dominant term of reference in the battle of the sexes is heterosexual masculinity, a homosocial orientation of male desire that keeps in check the unconscious, homoerotic subtext of the Oedipal conflict.

Marcello's identity is artificial. Hence, the battle of the sexes becomes a metaphor for a personality split between a heterosexual and a homosexual side. The outcome of Bertolucci's inquiry into Marcello's past is that history layers itself within the individual, generation after generation, just as, according to Vico, entire nations go through a series of fixed stages. But the Oedipal scenario in *The Conformist*, and the inscription of Bertolucci's film in the context of 1968, are so strong that Vico's emphasis on history as meaningful changes within a pattern of reoccurrences does not lead to Croce's Hegelian linear, forward-moving historicism. Rather, with Bertolucci, a director especially sensitive to the power of origins, Vico's *ricorso* is made to feed a pattern of regressive circularity.

From the days of *Scipio Africanus* to the making of *The Conformist*, Croce's belief in the unitary nature of consciousness, and its translation into a unified, national self, breaks down. The connection between Bertolucci's film and the atmosphere of May 1968 becomes clear through an opening reference to Jean Renoir's *La Vie est à Nous* (1936). In the guise of a throbbing neon light, the title, *La Vie est à Nous*, occupies one side of the frame. Born out of the Popular Front and financed by the French Communist Party,[3] Renoir's film received its first public release in 1969, at the peak of the student movement in the streets of Paris.

---

[3] Jonathan Buchsbaum, "Vote for the Front Populaire! Vote Communiste! *La Vie est à Nous*," *Quarterly Review of Film Studies* 10, no. 3 (Summer 1985): 183–212.

From the barricades of Paris to the huge strikes of the Italian "Autunno Caldo," the operatic macrohistory of the 1930s underwent a crisis. If confidence in this style of filmmaking collapsed, its rhetorical power did not vanish. Although recast in a critical light, the visuals of operatic macrohistory continued to appeal to Bertolucci and to a whole generation of filmmakers formed during the postwar period: Lina Wertmuller, Paolo and Vittorio Taviani, Sergio Leone, and Ettore Scola. All these directors engage in an Oedipal interrogation of fascist and neorealist cinema.

The intertextuality of *Cabiria* with *Scipio Africanus* is based on the transformation of the athlete into the statue. Scipio's body stands for the Fascist body politic as a corporate state. In *The Conformist*, Bertolucci depicts the breakdown of the statue into a dance of fleeting and contradictory movements. Bertolucci's allegorical use of sculpture, the art of stillness, and dance, the art of motion, suggests that Renzo De Felice's theory of Fascism as a movement in the 1920s and a regime in the 1930s has come full circle, after the events of May 1968.

The impact of May 1968 explains Bertolucci's ambivalence toward the role of spectacle in building consent. Operatic macrohistory has the authority of a father figure. In the position of a rebellious son, Bertolucci loves and hates this style of the past. May 1968 marked a crisis of bourgeois, heterosexual male identity and a phase of generational tensions. May 1968, however, did not lead to a viable long-term alternative. This is why, in *The Conformist*, dance does not allegorize a new Italian body politic, but only its loss of unity in the late 1960s, after the failure of the Center-Left parliamentary coalition between Catholics and Socialists (1963–1968), and the resurfacing of the class struggle which had been put on hold during the economic "boom" of the early 1960s.

In *The Conformist*, the relation of sculpture to dance takes the form of a battle of the sexes between Marcello Clerici, the Fascist, repressed, homosexual, and Anna Quadri, an antifascist whose sexuality is as polymorphous as her dancing routines and multiple roles. According to the symmetrical scenario of the battle of the sexes, Anna Quadri is not an embodiment of feminine desire, but a reflection of Marcello's fear of losing control over his hidden, homosexual self.

In the climate of revolt against tradition during May of 1968, Bertolucci acknowledged the stylistic legacy of fascist cinema and, through a series of modernist techniques, turned it against itself. Bertolucci's modernism, however, does not alienate the viewer. The director's self-reflexive style does not follow the Brechtian dictum of alienation between performance and spectators that Jean-Marie Straub and Danielle Huillet apply in their monotone, disjunctive avant-garde films.[4]

Because Bertolucci is both attracted to and rejects the style of the 1930s, modernism in *The Conformist* is a style of ambivalence. On one hand, Bertolucci's modernism calls attention to the deceptions of the apparatus and to the illusion of a unified, heterosexual subjectivity. On the other hand, Bertolucci's modernism lures the spectators into a representation of the past as mesmerizing as the transformation of the father into an ambivalent object of love and hate.

Through a series of symmetrical oppositions, such as consent and interpellation, spectacle and performance, stillness and mobility, tracking shots and fluid pans, sculpture and dance, Bertolucci explores in *The Conformist* how fascist ideology constructs identity. Under Mussolini's regime, subjectivity found, in the idealized image of the body politic, a ground for the self-realization of the individual in a public forum.

National unity, in the Fascist corporate state, expressed an ideal congruence of individual and collective interests, and obscured the persistence of very real class, regional, and sexual differences. The obscuring of social divisions based on class, regional, and sexual identity is not new to Italian historical thought. As an idealist philosopher tied to a nineteenth-century notion of selfhood, Croce, for example, felt that an individual's desire for "liberty" could play a role in the historical process. In contrast to Croce's emphasis on individual will, in *The Conformist*, Bertolucci proposes an interpretation of Fascism explicitly based on class identity and grounds the genesis of the regime in the vices of the bourgeoisie. Bertolucci's emphasis on class stems from the radicalization of the class struggle following May 1968.

For Bertolucci, fascist ideology exploited the image of a unified body politic to validate itself through the same effects of coherence and intelligibility sought by narrative, commercial cinema. *The Conformist* is a spectacle film, a Paramount production, where Ber-

---

[4] Dana B. Polan, "Brecht and the Politics of Self-Reflexive Cinema," *Jump-Cut* 17 (1978): 29–32.

tolucci plays the game of enticing the viewer with exactly the same representational strategies used by Fascism to gain the consent of a nation.

## REPRESENTATION, SPECTACLE, PERFORMANCE

Bertolucci's *The Conformist,* based on the novel by Alberto Moravia,[5] is a self-reflexive text; it meditates on how representation, spectacle, and performance function when cinema looks at the Fascist past. The culture of the regime becomes a testing ground for the theses Louis Althusser borrowed and developed from Antonio Gramsci's *Prison Notebooks* (1929–1935). In particular, Gramsci's concept of hegemony acquired a seminal value in Althusser's work. By hegemony, Gramsci meant "The 'spontaneous' consent given by the great masses of the population to the general direction imposed on social life by the dominant fundamental group; this consent is 'historically' caused by the prestige and (consequent confidence) which the dominant group enjoys because of its position and function in the world of production."[6] Bertolucci's handling of representation, spectacle, and performance in *The Conformist* can be better understood in the light of poststructuralist and neomarxist categories, such as the positing of imaginary relations, the construction of consent, and the interpellation of the subject.

Rosalind Coward and John Ellis explain that, in borrowing from Jacques Lacan the concepts of the imaginary and interpellation, "Althusser only acknowledges the inadequacy of the terms available in Marxism, rather than uses the full implications of the psychoanalytic canian terminology [La]."[7]

For Coward and Ellis, Althusser's imaginary means "that which is not real"[8] and interpellation indicates "the calling on the individual as an homogeneous, non-contradictory whole—or subject—

[5] Bertolucci's film is based on Alberto Moravia, *The Conformist,* trans. Angus Davidson (New York: Playboy Paperbacks, 1982). In Italian: *Il Conformista,* 2d ed., (Milan: Bompiani, 1951). Moravia's *The Conformist* is the literary source of the film, but the visuals and decor of the 1930s also come from Moravia's first novel and lucid analysis of the times he was living in, *The Time of Indifference (Gli Indifferenti),* (1929).

[6] Quintin Hoare and Geoffrey Nowell-Smith, eds., *Antonio Gramsci: Selections from the Prison Notebooks* (New York: International Publishers, 1971), 12.

[7] Rosalind Coward and John Ellis, *Language and Materialism* (London: Routledge and Kegan Paul, 1977), 75.

[8] Ibid.

which is then the coherent support for ideological representations."[9] *The Conformist* lends itself to a reading based on a parallel
between Althusser's and Bertolucci's views, as both the philosopher
and the filmmaker raise questions about subjectivity in culture and
history.

Bertolucci's critique of historical continuity and national unity in
Croce's historiography echoes Althusser's anti-humanist conten-
tion that idealism postulates a transcendental subject. As Andrew
Britton explains, Althusser denies "the primacy of the self-conscious subject as a theoretical category and suggests that the subject
is an ideological construct whose conviction of self-determination
is illusory."[10]

In maintaining that self-determination is only an illusion, Althusser and Bertolucci disagree with Croce's belief in the unitary
nature of consciousness. It is this unified self that, according to a
popular historical knowledge of Crocean descent, has found expression in the national movements of the Risorgimento and the Resistance. For Croce, there was historical continuity in the striving for
political unity from the nineteenth to the twentieth centuries.
Thus Italian history became the "Story of Liberty," an ongoing national effort stretching from the Risorgimento to the Resistance.

Representation is a broader term than spectacle and performance,
because it includes all sorts of mise-en-scènes, behaviors, images,
and artifacts—in short, a whole range of signs engaged in the production of a vision of the past. George G. Iggers observes that for
Hayden White history is representation and, therefore, no vision of
the past is ever definitive. White's awareness of the narrative dimension of historical writing seems to be an important issue for
Bertolucci as well, who uses the cinema to expose the Fascist past
with a tale full of ambivalences. Iggers explains that for White,
"History is in no sense a science and its generalizations are products
of a historical or poetical imagination in no way capable of being
'refuted' or 'disconfirmed' by evidence."[11] Although history is not a
science, its generalizations are powerful narrative constructs, capable of making a claim of truth about the past.

[9] Ibid.

[10] Andrew Britton, "The Ideology of *Screen*: Althusser, Lacan, Barthes," *Movie* 26
(Winter 1978–79): 2–3.

[11] George G. Iggers, *New Directions in European Historiography* (Middletown,
Conn.: Wesleyan University Press, 1975), 175.

The representation of the past in cinema draws its power from a comparable paradox. On the one hand, history in film is enticing to the point that the viewers believe in what they see, even if only for a moment. The images on the screen are, at the same time, lies and lures. To this tension between enticement and simulation corresponds a game of disclosure and concealment, light and darkness. Cinematic representation produces the appearance of a life-like reality. Its movement is at once *illusion* and *elusion*,[12] from the Latin *ludere*, to play. The etymology of these words confirms the metaphor.

Like Marcello Clerici in Fascist Italy, cinema, too, plays a game of conformity. Through the representation of different, unrelated, or conflicting elements, cinema constructs a surrogate world the cohesiveness of which satisfies our desire for truth. According to a similar logic, the unified body politic of fascist ideology hides disunity and tensions. Behind Marcello's conformist identity exists a difficult secret. In a sequence set in a radio station, Bertolucci divides the screen between an area of darkness and one in full light. The director draws an analogy between the split configuration of Marcello's self and the deceptive way in which cinema and radio link sound with image, voice with body.

On the screen, incongruous elements appear congruous with each other, as if they neatly fit in a bigger-than-life and seamless narrative. This narrative with its seamless pattern, in turn, interpellates the spectators, as if they were unified selves. Marcello is torn between a public, heterosexual façade and a private, homosexual secret. His dilemma calls attention to the illusion of Croce's unitary nature of consciousness.

In narrative, commercial cinema, representation is conformist. It relies on the stitching together of sounds and images, looks and movements, to construct coherent, but misleading, pictures. Spectacle is the most conformist form of representation, because it gains the consent of the viewers by giving them images that are pleasurable to look at. Spectacle is a particular type of representation which conceals an absence or inadequacy behind a pleasurable façade.

Spectacle comes from the Latin verb *spectare*, to look at. Specta-

[12] For this etymological remark, see Ulrich Wicks, "Borges, Bertolucci and Metafiction," in *Narrative Strategies*, ed. Syndy M. Conger and Janice R. Welsch, with introductory essay by Dudley Andrew (Macomb: Western Illinois University Press, 1980), 22.

cle describes a region accessible to the public gaze, or the display of animate and inanimate elements. A spectacle is a mise-en-scène with superlative features that declare their endurance regardless of transient audiences or of historical changes.[13] A performance is a particular type of spectacle in that it assumes the work of performers whose voices, gestures, and actions are consumable by either a potential or an actual audience. Performance brings to life a mise-en-scène which, until that moment, is frozen into a spectacle. The discourse of spectacle is based on passivity and is comparable to a monologue. Performance, instead, is dialogical. A tacit recognition of boundaries, or a mutual acknowledgment of roles, must take place between actors and spectators.

Since its invention, cinema has fulfilled the dream of representing life in motion. In the passage from the stage to the screen, performance does not *give life*, but *is* life. In the theatre, the contrast between the inertia of spectacle and the dynamism of performance anticipates the technology of cinema, which is based on a comparable tension between stillness and movement. The mechanical projection of images on the screen is possible as long as the actual stillness of each individual frame allows for the illusion, through the projector, of movement.

Performance in film means that the actors' words, gestures, and expressions are executed by bodies capable of speaking, moving, and signifying. As Jean-François Lyotard explains, the performance of these moving bodies "is intended for other living bodies—the spectators—who are capable of being moved"[14] by these words, gestures, and expressions. Lyotard's definition of performance as that which gives life leads him to the formulation of an anthropomorphic model, whose "elementary unit is polyesthetic like the human body: capacity to see, to hear, to touch, to move, . . . the idea of performance seems linked to the idea of the inscription of the body."[15] For Lyotard, the body is the main site through which this exchange between the cold celluloid and the warm theatre, the moving performers and the still spectators, shadows of bodies and

---

[13] For a most interesting and esoteric collection of quotes, images, and ideas on spectacle, see Carlo Romano, *Lo spettacolo e i suoi prodigi* (Rome: Arcana Editrice, 1975).

[14] Jean-François Lyotard, "The Unconscious as Mise-en-scène," *Performance in Post-Modern Culture*, ed. Michel Benamou and Charles Caramello (Madison, Wis.: Coda Press, 1977), 88.

[15] Ibid.

bodies in darkness, takes place. Lyotard's emphasis on the body as a site of exchange between performers and spectators is relevant to Bertolucci's use of the actors' performances to depict the constitution of subjectivity in fascist ideology.

In *The Conformist*, spectacle and performance refer, respectively, to the passivity fostered by consent and to the desire of seeing one's own identity represented as an acting subject. It is this desire for motion in stillness, difference in sameness, which Althusser describes as "interpellation." Sculpture and dance[16] are the two art forms Bertolucci uses to make explicit the association of spectacle with stillness and consent, of performance with movement and interpellation.

Through the family of Marcello Clerici, Bertolucci describes the upper bourgeoisie hiding its decadent way of life behind a façade of respectability. With Marcello, performance is an act of simulation whose reward is the pleasure of conforming to a system of authority. Regardless of their political beliefs and sexual inclinations, all the characters of *The Conformist* practice the art of deception. Lino (Pierre Clementi), the chauffeur of Marcello's family, thinks of himself as Giacomo Puccini's Madame Butterfly. Under Lino's uniform, a beautiful woman with long hair lives. Marcello's fiancée, Giulia (Stefania Sandrelli), feigns virginity until her honeymoon. In Paris, Clerici approaches his former mentor at the University of Rome, the antifascist Professor Luca Quadri (Enzo Tarascio), with the secret intention of murdering him. Anna Quadri (Dominique Sanda), the professor's wife, flirts with both Marcello and Giulia. Even Professor Quadri, whose name evokes a clear, geometric figure, has a shady side. Although he is an antifascist, he tolerates his wife's flirtation with his most dangerous enemy, the Fascist Marcello. This aura of ambiguity hovering over Professor Quadri is not surprising. Indeed, it may be a symptom of Bertolucci's dissatisfaction with Croce's argument that the antifascist movement is a stage in the "Story of Liberty."

Manganiello (Gastone Moschin), Marcello's brutal assistant, is

[16] On a visual tradition sensitive to the erotics of the dance-studio, see Angela McRobbie and Mia Nova, eds., *Gender and Generation* (London: Macmillan, 1984): "In most of Bertolucci's films dance plays this highly sexual role, and it was his portrayal of Dominique Sanda as the ballet mistress in *The Conformist*, surrounded in her studio with all the paraphernalia of dance: the ballet shoes, the mirrors, the bar and the leotard, which first alerted me to the mysterious eroticism of the rehearsal room (so obsessionally pursued in the visual arts by Degas)" (pp. 133–34).

the only character who does not simulate. Renzo De Felice would say that Manganiello, a former participant in the March on Rome (1922), embodies the most aggressive version of Fascism as a regime. With Manganiello, Fascism lifts the mask of respectability it adopted in the 1930s and shows its violent origins in the 1920s. The surname, Manganiello, brings to mind the *manganello*, the baton used by the Black Shirts during their raids, before and after the March on Rome. The *manganello* is the Fascist version of the baton held by Pulcinella, a mask of the commedia dell'arte whose irreverent *lazzi* are associated with the city of Naples.[17]

All these characters inhabit a Freudian scenario whose directors are the unconscious and Bertolucci. The director empowers his actors with disguises, so that they can perform on the stage of Fascist public life. In assuming the position of the unconscious, Bertolucci's direction of actors follows a double strategy that parallels the ambiguity of the filmmaker's modernist techniques: to explore the surfacing and the repression of desire, to expose the artificiality of the images, and to lure the spectators with them. Furthermore, the ambivalence of Bertolucci's modernism corresponds to the tensions between generations during May 1968. Bertolucci's interest in sexual politics emerges from his vision of the past, from his direction of actors, and from his use of camera movement and editing. In *The Conformist*, the sexual and the political aspects of Marcello Clerici's identity interface and suggest an interpretation of Fascism based on a model that would like to integrate psychoanalysis with Marxism.

## IDEOLOGY, CONSENT, SUBJECTIVITY

With a profusion of details from the period, Bertolucci's Fascism is seductive in its fashion, architecture, industrial design, and painting.[18] Like Bertolucci, the regime understood the power of persua-

---

[17] Millicent Marcus makes this point in "Wertmuller's *Love and Anarchy*: The High Price of Commitment," *Italian Film in the Light of Neorealism*, 329.

[18] In "Fascinating Fascism," *Under the Sign of Saturn* (New York: Farrar, Straus & Giroux, 1980), Susan Sontag remarks: "Art Nouveau could never be a fascist style; it is, rather, the prototype of that art which fascism defines as decadent; the fascist style at its best is Art Deco, with its sharp lines and blunt massing of material, its petrified eroticism" (p. 94); also on the visuals of fascist material and popular culture, see Sergio Coradeschi, "Lo stile novecento italiano: Grafica di massa e design esclusivo," *The Journal of Decorative and Propaganda Arts 1875–1945* 3 (Winter 1987): 67–82.

sion and propagated images of modernity for a country still tied to a rural past.

The Fascist production of illusions for the masses corresponds to Althusser's definition of ideology: "Ideology represents the imaginary relationship of individuals to their real conditions of existence."[19] When a culture internalizes this imaginary relationship, the imaginary becomes the "real."

Althusser's definition of ideology can be seen in Bertolucci's critique of the bourgeois life style. The director suggests that the value system of this class is based on religious practices, moral obligations, social codes, and hence does not correspond to a set of universal and natural rules. For Bertolucci the values of the bourgeoisie are strategies of control, and it is through these strategies that the regime maintains hegemony.

For Gramsci, a ruling class maintains its hegemony by fostering consent to legitimize the use of coercive powers: "The 'normal' exercise of hegemony on the now classical terrain of the parliamentary regime is characterised by the combination of force and consent, which balance each other reciprocally, without force predominating excessively over consent. Indeed, the attempt is always made to ensure that force will appear to be based on the consent of the majority."[20] Gramsci's definition of hegemony as a mixture of force and consent leads to Althusser's argument that it is not a reality of coercion that men represent to themselves in ideology, but a relationship based on a consent which is wholly imaginary.

The staging of spectacles, such as athletic events and military parades, fostered consent for the regime.[21] The relationship of consent between the governed and the governing was perceived as real, rather than imaginary, because the spectators were under the illusion of performing spontaneous roles in Fascist spectacles. According to Gramsci, an artificial preparation is behind the "spontaneous" consent of the masses who must "live" those directives, modifying their own habits, their own will, their own convictions to conform.[22] The exploitation of consent as a disguise of coercion

---

[19] Louis Althusser, "Ideology and Ideological State Apparatuses," *Lenin and Philosophy and Other Essays* (New York: Monthly Review Press, 1971), 162.

[20] Hoare and Nowell-Smith, *Gramsci*, 80, n. 49.

[21] Ibid., 266.

[22] Ibid.

occurs in daily Italian life and in cinematic spectacles meant to foster a condition of passivity in the viewers.

In *The Conformist*, Bertolucci evokes the artificial climate of the 1930s by imposing a polished mise-en-scène over situations of disruptive violence. Bertolucci's sleek images for this horrifying tale correspond to Fascist spectacles which hid signs of disturbance beneath a surface of regimentation. Series of arched, identical windows reminiscent of Marcello Piacentini's architecture, the art-deco lintels framing Clerici's figure, the muted colors of Giulia's clothing, and Marcello's military gait are icons of regimentation. They express the individual's desire to project one's own self in the "imaginary relationships" of fascist ideology.

The tension between regimentation and loss of control becomes explicit in the sequence where Giulia dances in front of Marcello. To a syncopated tune from America, she tries to seduce her composed fiancé. Her provocative, fluid movements contrast with the black-and-white striped pattern of her dress. Stripes, bars, shadowy lines block all threats to the established order.

With dance, Bertolucci stages Giulia's attempt to seduce Marcello. When associated with spontaneity, tribal rituals, or entertainment, dance evokes emotions and calls attention to energies stored in the body, in opposition to control and ratiocination. While dancing, Giulia embodies a femininity associated with the pleasure of the senses and mindless behavior. Without upsetting her apartment's orderly decor, Giulia's performance increases the sensuousness of the mise-en-scène. Her dance is more a tease for Marcello and the male spectator, than an expression of female desire.

Instead of teasing Marcello, dance threatens him in a Parisian ballroom. There he finds himself trapped in the coils of a snake-like *farandole* (fig. 11). The dancers' spiralling movement immobilizes Marcello. Giulia's jazz dance may satisfy a private, heterosexual male fantasy, but, significantly, it does not move Clerici. A heterosexual masculinity, however, is the term of reference for Marcello's forced involvement in a communal dance. Marcello's entrapment in the *farandole* spins out of his obsession to be "the same as everybody else." Recreational, public dance becomes an emblem of consent whose price is the loss of a private, homosexual individuality.

Consent rests on the illusion of individuality, an imaginary relationship posited by ideology. Through performance, the individual subject plays out the role of his or her own self in the spectacle

TC-3758-42

**11.** Dance in Bernardo Bertolucci's *The Conformist* (1970). Courtesy of The Museum of Modern Art, Film Stills Archive.

staged by the regime. Since consent, rather than coercion, enables this playing out of the self, the individual "is interpellated as a (free) subject in order that he shall submit freely to the commandments of the Subject; i.e., in order that he shall (freely) accept his subjection, i.e., in order that he shall make the gestures and the actions of his subjection all by himself."[23] Conformity between ideas and actions is comparable to congruity between private values and public behavior in daily life, sound and image in cinema, voice and body in radio. Individual subjects think that they are "free" to the extent that their actions fit the national body politic to which they belong.

In *The Conformist*, the actors' performances cover a range of styles, conveying the ways in which individuals construct themselves in the system of fascist ideology. Bertolucci surveys interpel-

[23] Althusser, "Ideology," 182.

lation through the performance styles of his actors, assuming that "the ideas of a human subject exist in his or in her actions."[24] Put another way, conformism is functional to a subjectivity that believes itself to be free when its public actions conform to its private ideas. Conformism, then, is not an evil prerogative of Fascism, but rather the product of an "idealist scheme"[25] which, from the days of Giolitti's Italy to the economic "boom" of the 1950s, perpetuates a belief in a "free," unified consciousness.

Fascism makes interpellation explicit through "hailing."[26] For Althusser, ideology hails "subjects among individuals," singling individuals out and conferring on them the status of "subjects." Hailing marks a closed circuit where the subjection of individuals is the *conditio sine qua non* for the acquisition of one's own subjectivity. The circularity of hailing echoes the belief that the present cannot shake the past off its shoulders. Likewise, the son who rejected his father after May 1968, was, inevitably, acknowledging the authority of that figure.

Hailing is a gesture of subjection to a leader. Hailing is also the gesture of a policeman identifying suspects. Hailing means both *subjection to* and *subjection of*. Hailing indicates how interpellation functions in Fascist daily life. Interpellation enables the individual to hail his fellow citizens as subjects, because he has received authority from the leader he has previously hailed. In *The Conformist*, Bertolucci defines interpellation in terms of the allegory of the cave, which Marcello recounts during his first encounter with Professor Quadri (fig. 12). Interpellation affects individuals who, like Plato's slaves, do not realize that their subjectivity is not real, but only a fiction of an ideology.

By volunteering his services to the O.V.R.A., Mussolini's secret police, the homosexual Marcello Clerici gains access to a heterosexual self. This new identity gives Marcello the right to hail other homosexuals, Jews, and antifascists. After the fall of the regime, Marcello hails his friend Italo Montanari as a Fascist. Due to this gesture of accusation, Marcello remains a "subject" whose newly found identity as a heterosexual antifascist conforms to the new political climate of the Resistance and of the postwar period.

In the cave-like study of Professor Quadri, Marcello's hailing does

[24] Ibid., 168.
[25] Ibid.
[26] Ibid., 174.

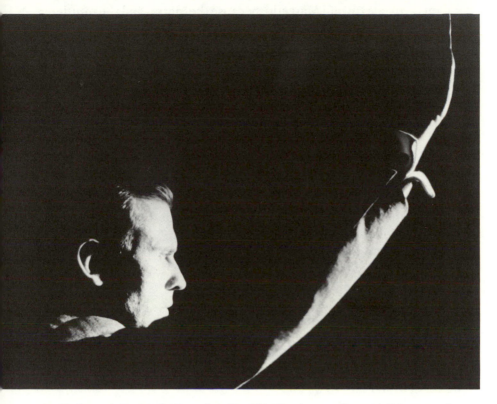

**12.** Hailing in Bernardo Bertolucci's *The Conformist* (1970). Courtesy of The Museum of Modern Art, Film Stills Archive.

not betray him in front of his victim. Rather, it is a gesture of acknowledgment, from the disciple to his former mentor. Marcello hails Professor Quadri as the ultimate father figure, whose idealist Crocean culture allows the former student, in the role of son, to consider himself a free subject in exchange for his subjection to fascist ideology.

Albeit an antifascist, Professor Quadri's physical deformity suggests that the germ of Fascism grows within the body politic of Giovanni Giolitti's liberal state and is not, as Croce would have it, an evil from outside.[27] Quadri wavers between a paternal and a suspi-

[27] Critics (Bondanella, Liehm, Kolker, and Casetti) have proposed different interpretations of the character of Professor Quadri. In English, the professor's last name means "squares," an image of clarity and precision. Despite the connotations attached to the last name, critics agree that the professor's politics are ambiguous.

cious attitude toward Marcello, because the victim and the murderer, father and son, share a common ground based on class identity and a humanist education reserved for members of the bourgeoisie. The bond between the professor and the student blurs the distinction between Fascism and antifascism. Bertolucci turns to the 1930s to tell the story of his generation's struggle in 1968 against the legacy of Croce's historiography.

Bertolucci's alternation of light and darkness, violence and seduction, corresponds to the generational and erotic tensions of the Oedipal conflict and the battle of the sexes. Chiaroscuro envelops walls, furniture, and blurred patches of color. The heavy curtains in the dressing room of Anna Quadri, and the hanging bed sheets in the deserted corridors of Lino's house, hide the secret of erotic encounters followed by dramatic confrontations. These regions of cool darkness, muffled whispers, and echoing footsteps, clash with the blinding sunlight on the dock at Ventimiglia, or with the dazzling snow of the murder scene.

In this final sequence, the battle of the sexes between Marcello and Anna reaches a climax (fig. 13). Confronted with the choice of saving Anna, his homosexual alter ego, Marcello finds himself on the edge of a dangerous slippage from a masculine to a feminine realm. Marcello chooses to stifle his homosexual side, or feminine alter ego, and lets Anna die.

Dressed in white, Anna runs through a forest of thin, tall, black trees chased by Fascists as ferocious as hunting dogs. Her red blood stains the white snow. The use of black and white and the iconography of a runner chased by dogs in a forest recalls the story of Actaeon. This mythological character is well-known as a *figura Christi*. Diana, the goddess of the hunt, turns the white-clothed Actaeon into a deer and punishes him in the forest. Marcello, like Diana, subjects the white-clothed Anna to punishment when he lets the dogs chase her. Kantorowicz's medieval king receives from the Church the duality of Christ's nature, for Christ is both human and immortal. This doubling reappears in Actaeon, who is half-human,

---

Some argue that the antifascist politics and the physical deformity of this character are an allusion to Antonio Gramsci; some associate Quadri with the antifascist brothers, Carlo and Nello Rosselli, assassinated in France (1937); some feel that Quadri's ambiguous position is comparable to Bertolucci's predicament as a bourgeois intellectual with a membership in the Italian Communist Party; Quadri is a hunch-back, a "gobbetto," in Italian, which may recall the name of Piero Gobetti, an antifascist historian.

**13.** The Medusa in Bernardo Bertolucci's *The Conformist* (1970). Courtesy of The Museum of Modern Art, Film Stills Archive.

half-animal, a lover for Diana at one time, and now a helpless deer for the dogs. Anna, too, has two bodies: one lesbian, the other heterosexual. Anna's two sides enable her to mirror Marcello's conflict between a public and a private side.

The "fascinating Fascism"[28] of Bertolucci's many "fathers"—Benedetto Croce, Attilio Bertolucci,[29] Alberto Moravia—casts a romantic light on the son who rejects authority, tradition, and the past that obsesses him all the same. In *The Conformist*, Bertolucci

[28] Sontag, "Fascinating Fascism," 73–105.

[29] Nearly every critic discusses the Oedipal theme in Bertolucci's work, but especially see T. Jefferson Kline, "The Unconformist Bertolucci's *The Conformist* (197[1]) from the novel of Alberto Moravia," in *Modern European Filmmakers and the Art of Adaptation*, ed. Andrew Horton and Joan Magretta (New York: Ungar, 1981), 222–37; T. Jefferson Kline, "Orpheus Transcending: Bertolucci's *Last Tango in Paris*," *International Review of Psychoanalysis* 3 (1976): 85–95. Attilio Bertolucci, prominent literary critic and poet, is Bernardo's real father.

is unable to free himself totally from the binding power of his fathers' cultural tradition. As if performing a gesture of mea culpa, the director admits he cannot reconstitute his identity outside his bourgeois origins. Yet, like the sons of May 1968, Bertolucci rejects the historiography of the fathers and sets Croce's interpretation of Italian history as the "Story of Liberty," against his own story of bourgeois desire for order.

In the end, Bertolucci comes to the standstill of an indelible class identity. This paralyzing awareness explains the director's involvement with Paramount Studios. The alliance with American capital is congruous with the interests of the social class he represents and rejects at the same time. Bertolucci's modernism is characterized by a stifling circularity: the past is not easy to forget, origins are haunting, and class identity cannot be discarded. In a narrative where dance is the flip side of sculpture, motion must end in stillness, while the social upheaval of 1968 leads mostly to a sense of paralysis.

Bertolucci points to the incongruities beneath pictures that seem to fit with each other. When Marcello steps into a car in the garden of his mother's villa on his way with her to visit the deranged father, movement comes to resemble stillness, in a narrative where comparable historical circumstances reoccur in different contexts, generation after generation, or, as Vico would say, cycle after cycle. The car remains fixed to the ground, while yellowish brown leaves of autumn fly up toward the viewers on the wave of nostalgic music. As disjunctive as Bertolucci's modernism may be, his cinema runs against the wall of Plato's cave. The movement of the leaves lures the viewer's eye away from the absent motion of the car, while providing a smooth transition from the fixed tableau in the garden to the one in the asylum, where the father is raving about his past political sins while the homosexual Marcello wears a black shirt just as his father did.

From the standpoint of the 1970s, Bertolucci conducts a critical interrogation of the 1930s. Although he is seduced by the Fascist style, the director denounces the complicities of the bourgeoisie with the regime. In a sense, Bertolucci is trying to incriminate the past with a mixture of resentment and attachment comparable to the one Oedipus must have half-understood when he unknowingly killed his own father. According to the myth, Oedipus blinds himself with Jocasta's brooch after discovering that he has killed his father and made love to his mother. The motif of blindness, then, fits the tensions between fathers and sons, the seductive visual style, and a haunting class identity.

Blindness is associated with Marcello's best friend, Italo Montanari, a voice at the E.R.I., the Fascist radio network. For Bertolucci, as for Hayden White, history is made of narratives. And, despite their claims of truthfulness, narratives are misleading. In this manner, Bertolucci establishes a parallel between the blind, Fascist radio speaker and all of Italy under Mussolini.

Like the slaves in Plato's cave, Italians had confused shadows moving on the walls with the real objects used to produce those shadows. Blindness in relation to Fascism refers to the manner in which the regime duped the masses for decades. Furthermore, for Bertolucci, as for Althusser, all ideologies are deceiving narratives and we, as spectators, are blind to these forms of deception. As such, ideologies interpellate through mass media like radio and the cinema. In so doing, ideologies enable subjects to identify with imaginary public selves, while keeping them entrapped inside the Plato's cave of their private illusions. In a sense, Bertolucci tends to collapse history into narrative and ideology into history.

Two themes become apparent at the end of *The Conformist*: the entrapment of identity in ideology and the inescapable circularity of history. Without doubt, these two themes contribute to an overall sense of paralysis. With Bertolucci, the linear historicism of the Hegelianized Vico degenerates into a closed circle, while the spiralling of *corsi* and *ricorsi* takes on a haunting quality. In the end, it becomes apparent that the individual cannot break through the wall of class identity handed down from one generation to the next. Marcello, however, pretends that it is indeed possible to switch political affiliation on the wave of powerful historical change. Right after the collapse of Fascism, he points an accusing finger against Italo. After hailing his friend as a Fascist, Marcello feigns a break with the past. He allows a crowd singing the national anthem, "Fratelli d'Italia," and the Communist party song, "Bandiera Rossa," to surround and nearly trample him. By blending the national anthem with a song of the working class, Bertolucci suggests that the Resistance was both a national effort and a class experience. In this manner, the director reminds us that postwar historiography is characterized by a confusion between nation and class.

## THE STATUE AND THE DANCER

Through his actors' performances, Bertolucci depicts the constitution of subjectivity in fascist ideology. The performance styles of Bertolucci's actors disclose that the effects of interpellation subtend the identities of all the characters. Professor Quadri's tolerance of his wife's lesbian inclination, Anna's contradictory behavior, Marcello's need for approval, and Giulia's brainless drive for pleasure stand for different positions in the construction of the same idealist subject. Whether this subjectivity perceives itself as "free" in the realm of normality or of perversion, it assumes, all the same, the conformity of its public actions as well as the private ideas it "freely" recognizes as its own.

All the characters of *The Conformist*, from the Fascist Marcello to the antifascist Professor Quadri, have been hailed by ideology. In exchange for subjecting themselves to this hailing, they gain the illusion of a coherent and independent self, regardless of the political camp to which they belong. Both the antifascist Croce and the fascist Gentile share a belief in the unitary nature of consciousness and in history as the expression of the continuity of national traditions. Antonio Gramsci, too, subscribes to a belief in a unified subjectivity, one, however, linked to class identity and not to the national self of Gentile and Croce.

It is just this commonly held view of individuality as an organic category, either for the sake of nation or class, that enables Marcello, at the end of *The Conformist*, to step out of a Fascist role and assume an antifascist stance. These two roles, undeniably, belong to opposite political camps, but can also be interchangeable by virtue of a shared theatrical and allegorical dimension. The two roles, Fascist and antifascist, are isomorphic. They both depend on a conceptualization of subjectivity dating back to nineteenth-century liberalism. It is this bourgeois notion of individuality that Althusser criticizes when he says that an individual is free as long as public gestures match private ideas.

The multiple roles performed by Dominique Sanda do not situate the character of Anna Quadri outside the interpellation of ideology. Anna's shifting personae are not about her, but make up Marcello's repressed alter ego. Anna's multiple roles voice Marcello's impossible desire to be himself and others, to be an individual and many at the same time. In the case of Fascism, ideology circumvents this

desire for both an individual and a communal identity, by sublimat-
ing the clash of interests of the single citizen and the state into an
abstract, corporate ideal.

Bertolt Brecht, in the 1930s, argued that the negotiation of the personal with the social performed by Fascism represented a mystifying strategy of consent. Brecht maintained that "The continuity of
the ego is a myth. Man is an atom that perpetually breaks up and
forms anew."[30] Brecht's attention to the contradictions of subjectivity, however, can be considered a corrective to Althusser's stifling
view that we are all entrapped in ideology. Althusser persuasively
points out that the continuity between public role and private behavior is a bourgeois illusion, one aimed at feeding a myth of individual freedom. Yet the French philosopher is not quite interested
in taking full advantage of the discrepancies between public and private.

In contrast to Althusser, Brecht seems more attentive to the pro-
ductivity of all these discrepancies or contradictions. For Brecht,
one's own identity is not so much an ideological product, but rather
an ideological process, one constantly shaped and reshaped by history itself. Bertolucci's view of subjectivity seems closer to Althusser's pessimistic and stagnating sense of entrapment in history
rather than to Brecht's dialectic, dynamic interface of public and
private realms. Along with his characters, Bertolucci defines himself as a "conformist." In producing ideology through the cinema
and in hailing spectators with the high-production values of Paramount, the director must work, always and only, from inside the
cave.

Sanda's multiple roles do not refer to Brecht's discontinuity of the
ego. Rather, Sanda's polymorphous identity fits the challenging, but
not disruptive, conventions of the European art film. Her contradictory persona defies the viewers' expectations for the coherent character of classic Hollywood films, while it does not overturn Croce's
belief in the unitary nature of consciousness. Anna's fluid identity
is comparable to Giulia's sinuous movements. If Giulia's dance fulfills a heterosexual male fantasy, Anna's character is elusive enough
to lure in a pleasurable way the most demanding spectators. Sanda's
character acquires coherence through Marcello, for Anna's poly-

---

[30] Coward and Ellis, *Language and Materialism*, 75.

morphous personality is there to amplify the facets of Trintignant's split character.

Conformity of ideas with actions is comparable to congruity of private values with public behavior. By turning actors' bodies into embodiments of the national body politic, Bertolucci updates Giambattista Vico's view of the body as an historical variable, while adding a Freudian twist to it.

Bertolucci's use of the body brings to mind more Norman O. Brown's popularization of Freudian thought[31] than Jacques Lacan's theory of the subject. Vico argued that the unfolding of the historical process undergoes different stages. Within these stages, intellectual transformations at the level of the individual are analogous to political changes in the social body. In line with Vico's argument that the private body tells public history, Bertolucci suggests that the image of the body politic is subject to historical change. Yet, the changing appearances of the Italian body politic refer to different styles of performance whose common function is to allegorize the same ideal, national subject before and after the fall of Fascism.

Bertolucci's use of the actors' bodies for the allegorization of the national subject depends on a popular reading of Freud. The performances of Trintignant and Sanda embody the struggle between sculpture and dance, the political and the personal, death (Thanatos) and pleasure (Eros) which Freud locates in the body. Trintignant's acting style recalls the granite-like look of Fascism and its unequivocal visual emblems. Sanda's acting style, instead, is a fleeting succession of ambivalent images. Marcello, as the statue, and Anna, as the dancer, stand for the two extreme poles of Bertolucci's representation of the body: from the hypnotic stillness of a crowd in front of a leader, to the shimmering fluidity of shadows on the walls of Plato's cave. Marcello's and Anna's performances are complementary, to the extent that the passage from his monolithic to her proteiform persona signals the crisis of values and beliefs triggered by the fall of the regime and by the student movement. In perfect consonance with Vico's law of the *ricorso*, the statue crumbles twice—in 1943 and in 1968.

The movements of Marcello and Anna suggest that stillness and mobility, normality and perversion, duty and pleasure are not "absolute" categories, but symmetrical and exchangeable pairs. Ac-

---

[31] Norman O. Brown, *Closing Time* (New York: Vintage Books, 1974), 21.

cording to the symmetrical scenario of the battle of the sexes, dance is *in* sculpture and sculpture is *in* dance. Sculpture locks movement within a still mass. Classical dance, in turn, consists of highly controlled steps moving toward the stillness of an ideal pose. The complementariness of sculpture and dance signals the blurring of boundaries between homosexual and heterosexual, male and female, private and public. All these distinctions, Althusser argues, remain always "internal to bourgeois law"[32]; they function to perpetuate the authority of an ideal, unified subject.

With his direction of camera movement, Bertolucci juxtaposes the rigid poses of Marcello to the flowing motions of Anna. In conforming to his actors' performances, Bertolucci acknowledges that his camera cannot signify outside interpellation. His tracking shots toward altar-like desks, across marble halls, under black lintels, trace the obsessive flow of Marcello's memory and exhibit the compulsive quality of a regression in time. Moving along the seductive shopwindows and the fashionable streets of Paris, Bertolucci's pans, instead, unfold with the soothing tempo of Georges Delerue's musical score. As if a third site of performance, Bertolucci's camera enacts the movement from hostility back to attraction, between Marcello and Anna.

Bertolucci's camera becomes an acting subject and a participant in the exploration of the past, along with the actors' performances. In commenting on his direction of camera movement, Bertolucci distances himself from the classic Hollywood style: "And I move the camera as if I was gesturing with it. I feel that the cinema is always a cinema of gestures—very direct, even if there are fifty people in the crew. But imperialism is an enemy of these 'gestures.' . . . This is why . . . one cuts out all that was direct and 'gesticular' in the rushes; . . . I employed the editing to underline the gesticulation of the film."[33] Bertolucci's contrast between "a cinema of gestures" and imperialism might be an encouragement to the critic to draw a parallel between direction of camera movement in the nouvelle vague and direction of actors in neorealist cinema. In neorealism the observation of daily behavior and a comedic construction of character mobilizes the statues of operatic macrohistory.

And yet, Bertolucci's direction of actors owes more to the classic

[32] Althusser, "Ideology," 144.
[33] Amos Vogel, "Bernardo Bertolucci: An Interview," *Film Comment* 8, no. 3 (Fall 1971): 26.

Hollywood style than to the hand-held cameras of neorealism, of the nouvelle vague and of his mentor, Jean-Luc Godard. Bertolucci's direction of camera movement is carefully keyed to the actors' performances; there is little room left for neorealist improvisation. The congruence between camera movement and actors' behavior is as pleasurable as the smooth development and clarity of meaning sought by Hollywood narrative cinema.

Bertolucci's editing does have the unpredictable quality of a sudden "gesticulation" and the erratic rhythm of Godard's character in *Breathless* (1959), Michel Poiccard, in flight. The editing of Marcello's flashbacks is a convoluted *mise-en-abîme* of memories. The non-chronological organization of the narrative proposes affinities between viewing a film and dreaming. Both these activities are based on condensation and displacement. Acting style is congruous with camera movement, while the editing of Marcello's memories discloses a loss of control. Camera movement matches the polished mise-en-scène to the actors' enticing performances. The visceral quality of the editing, by contrast, points to the darkest regions of the subconscious. The desire to recover a private, homosexual identity spills over a public, heterosexual subjectivity.

Bertolucci illustrates Freud's concepts of repression and sublimation through two acting styles, or patterns of movement: pulling in and flowing out; the self-absorbed look of a sculpture and the spinning away of a dancer. By constantly intersecting each other, these two movements shape the battle of the sexes between Marcello and Anna. Because Marcello's character is an embodiment of conformism, Trintignant's restrained acting style eschews open gestures that reveal no emotion. His public image supports Susan Sontag's insight that fascist aesthetics are based on "the containment of vital forces; movements are confined, held tight, held in."[34]

The statue-like Marcello wears an impenetrable mask on his face. Unlike Giulia and Anna, he never lies down or sprawls on a comfortable chair. Sitting on the bed, or on the back seat of the car, Marcello is straight-backed and stiff, his hat low over his eyes. Anna and Marcello speak many languages. Anna's poised Italian signals an aristocratic persona, while her exasperated French reveals an aggressive sensuality. In the car, Marcello mumbles a few lines in Latin, a sign of his humanist education and of his class identity.

---

[34] Sontag, "Fascinating Fascism," 93.

Marcello's words are incomprehensible and cast a veil on his thoughts. In her dance studio, Anna's black cane alludes to her sophisticated charm. The cane can be seen as an emblem of sexual independence and, in the hands of Marcello's alter ego, invokes the theme of masculinity as domination. Rather than with a cane, Marcello is associated with a bouquet of flowers that he stiffly carries to Giulia's house.

The battle of the sexes underpins the oscillation between Marcello's constrained conformity and Anna's decadent behavior. The symmetry of this scenario becomes explicit when Marcello's and Anna's sexual roles are reversed. The statue becomes dancer and the dancer becomes statue. After teaching a dance routine, Anna, her leg bent, leans against the wall of her studio. When Marcello appears, she maintains her lithe and provocative posture. As he bends down, Marcello mimicks the graceful bow of children after a performance. Marcello, then, violently jerks Anna into the next room. He turns the ritual greeting at the end of a dance lesson into a challenge to Anna's pedagogical role. For a moment, he hurls at her all the rebellion he would have liked to project against the ultimate teacher, Professor Quadri. At the same time, Marcello pretends to be a student of dance to force Anna into a partnership and, thus, assert his control over her.

In the ballroom, while she dances with Giulia, Anna replaces Marcello in the role of husband. The two women, one clothed in black, the other in white, form a plastic unit of balanced volumes in motion. Their arms stretch out as they execute a sensuous tango. The male's traditional stiffness in the tango is softened by Anna's careful lead—her swift, sinuous turns blending with Giulia's mindless flexibility. When Anna allows Giulia to step outward and dance around her, she takes on the statue-like immobility of Marcello with which she controls her partner from a distance.

Despite his desire for conformism, Marcello longs for Anna's unconventional sexuality. This attraction leads to Marcello's psychological dependence on Anna. By catering to both Marcello's private homosexual self and to his heterosexual public image, Anna acquires a bisexual identity, and, in the role of femme fatale, becomes Marcello's alter ego. When Anna undresses in front of Marcello, his aggressiveness gives way to insecurity. The spectacle of Anna's pale skin glaring in the darkness paralyzes him, forcing the truth of his homosexuality to surface. Anna's glistening body becomes the mirror of Marcello's repressed identity. Marcello pulls a blanket on top of Giulia's nude back while she is asleep. He is annoyed when he sees his mother's decaying body on display. Marcello instinctively perceives that the unveiling of the female body can illumine his own sexual truth, hitherto disguised under the clothing of male conformity.

Sanda's performance style refers to a traditional view of femininity as being moody and unreliable. This stereotype amounts to the famous operatic "La donna è mobile qual piuma al vento. . . ."[35] Anna's lesbianism teases out Marcello's homosexual inclination. Anna's promiscuous life style glows with the lure of that very same freedom Marcello thinks he will find in the sirenesque call of ideology: interpellation.

Anna obsesses Marcello's memory, because her changing image links together the contradictory facets of his sexual identity. As the mistress of a Fascist official, Anna becomes a mother figure to Marcello when he witnesses a reenactment of the primal scene, a scenario of voyeurism. In spying upon Anna and the official, Marcello assumes the role of a child who surprises parents in the bedroom. The zoom underlines the intensity of Marcello's gaze, and reminds us that we, as spectators, are also voyeurs hidden in the darkness. After traversing the empty space of the room, Marcello's eyes land upon Sanda's leg swinging under a huge, marble tabletop. The child, then, focuses on the mother's profile hidden behind a short, black veil.

The fragmentation of Sanda's body into a few, eroticized components measures the power of the visual associations in Marcello's memory. Anna's traits of motherhood become compatible with her role of deranged prostitute in the whorehouse of Ventimiglia. After rejecting his guilt-ridden and corrupt parents, Marcello protectively hugs Sanda. He rests his cheek against hers, as a child, but not a lover, would do. The Oedipal scenario, here, takes over the battle of the sexes, while the motif of blindness recedes in opposition to the role transgressive vision plays in the primal scene of sexual intercourse of parents viewed by a child.

Shortly before her death, Anna presses her face against the window of Marcello's car. For a moment she looks like a Medusa. The

---

[35] This line appears at the beginning of a famous aria from Giuseppe Verdi's *Rigoletto*, act 1, scene 1. In English: "Woman is as mobile as a feather in the wind."

Medusa's stare turns men into stone. It is only through the death of the dancer and the repression of the feminine in him that Marcello can become the statue he wants to be in public. But Marcello's yearning for statue-like immobility outgrows the need for a heterosexual façade, perhaps as a symptom of deep horror for the heterosexuality of parents seen in sexual intercourse.

Anna's clothing combines seduction with sobriety. By wearing pants she projects an image of self-confidence, yet, the silky textures and the drooping cut of her shirts strengthen her appeal as a well-heeled femme fatale. In her living room, Sanda's soft silhouette clashes with one of her legs arrogantly dangling from the arm of a chair, or with the palm of her hand decisively resting on her hip. In her performance, Sanda imitates the masculine postures of Marlene Dietrich's cabaret routines. Likewise, in playing Giulia, Sandrelli exploits the whining voice, the childish pouting, and gullible expression of Hollywood starlets in early sound comedies and melodramas.

Sanda's and Sandrelli's performance styles throw light on Bertolucci's method of evoking the atmosphere of the period. In keeping with Vico's view that the body is an historical variable, Bertolucci's "cinema of gestures" refers to famous stars' movements in genre films of the 1930s. A case in point is Bertolucci's casting of a popular singer in Mussolini's Italy, "Milly," to play the role of Marcello's mother. Milly still sang in the postwar years for R.A.I., the national television network (fig. 14).

Milly's enduring fame points to an unsettling continuity in taste, one that links the audiences of Mussolini with those of the postwar period. Through the casting of Milly, Bertolucci adheres to an anti-Crocean, post-1968 popular interpretation of history. By arguing for continuity between the 1930s and the 1950s, Bertolucci defies Croce's claim that Fascism is containable within a parenthesis and that 1945 was a new beginning.

Continuity between Mussolini's and De Gasperi's Italy emerges from another performance, one which echoes Milly's. Giulia's mother is played by Yvonne Sanson, the star of Raffaello Matarazzo's "black telephone" melodramas, a genre flourishing in the 1950s when the dimension of social denunciation typical of neorealist cinema was beginning to die out (fig. 15). The period casting of Milly and Yvonne Sanson repeats the symmetrical configuration of the battle of the sexes. In this scenario, the woman is an alter ego

**14.** "Milly" in Bernardo Bertolucci's *The Conformist* (1970). Courtesy of The Museum of Modern Art, Film Stills Archive.

of the man. Likewise Giulia's mother, Yvonne Sanson, is the alter ego in the 1950s of Marcello's mother Milly, in the 1930s.

Anna's sexual and political ambivalence corresponds to Marcello's wavering between fascist virility and infantile frailty. Anna's oscillation between a heterosexual and a lesbian identity is comparable to Marcello's wavering between child-like insecurity and the display of fascist authority. The perfect citizen hides a helpless *bambino*.[36] The uncontrollable bodily manifestations of the child signal a return to an originary, pre-historical state of being. A comparable folding of adulthood back into childhood occurs in Vico's last phase right before the beginning of a new cycle. This is when the most advanced stage of civilization, the age of humans, rhymes with the earliest phase, the age of gods. During the murder of the Quadris, Manganiello's urination is a degraded example of fascist sexual infantilism.

---

[36] Felix Guattari makes this remark during a conversation with Liliana Cavani published in Liliana Cavani, Franco Arcalli, and Italo Moscati, *Al di là del bene e del male* (Turin: Einaudi, 1977), 175.

**15.** Yvonne Sanson in Bernardo Bertolucci's *The Conformist* (1970). Courtesy of The Museum of Modern Art, Film Stills Archive.

Marcello's rigid postures deny sexual duplicity. In the office of a Fascist official, Marcello holds a gun with his arm rigidly stretched across a doorframe. This posture of aggression has a sculptural quality. On the steps of his mother's house, with his arms crossed on his chest, Marcello encases an attitude of inwardness, signaling his need for control.

In the radio studio, when Marcello describes his fiancée's unrestrained behavior to Italo, he performs a gesture of embrace, crossing his arms over his chest. In his mind, Marcello relates to his body as if it were Giulia's body. The embrace discloses the feminine alter ego of his undeclared homosexuality. Yet the dancer cannot quite emerge from the statue. Marcello's transformation into a feminine counterpart does not lead to a sensuous embrace, but to a gesture of containment. It resembles the straitjacket position assumed by Marcello's father in the asylum.

Trintignant's indecipherable expression masks a fragile identity. During an eerie blackout in 1943 a couple of motor vehicles drag huge Fascist sculptures of heads, busts, and eagles across a bridge over the Tiber (fig. 16). Bertolucci might have found these haunting emblems of the fall of the regime in the iconography of L.U.C.E. documentaries. Bertolucci stages the dismantling of Fascist ideology by dramatizing the collapse of the ideal statue Marcello tries to model himself on.

Susan Sontag finds significant the fact that the physical perfection of the fascist body conceals the violence of its repressed sexuality.[37] The proteiform traits of Sanda's body stand for the crum-

**16.** The statues in Bernardo Bertolucci's *The Conformist* (1970). Courtesy of The Museum of Modern Art, Film Stills Archive.

---

[37] For a more specific discussion of the representation of the body in Leni Riefenstahl's work, see Sontag, "Fascinating Fascism," 73–105.

bling of the Fascist statue. Her metamorphoses allegorize the disgregation of the national body politic in two *corsi*, one in 1943 and another in 1968.

The term "corporativism," used to describe the organization of daily life in the Fascist state, alludes to how powerful the image of a unified body politic can be. With their majestic and virile look, neoclassical, Fascist sculptures express the desire of individuals to model themselves on a transcendent subject. For Bertolucci, the regime uses the body as a site to stage consent. Through the national body politic, the individual self interiorizes an ideal image of public identity, thus effacing real contradictions.

At the end of *The Conformist*, Marcello looks into the camera. It is possible to read this gesture along the grain of Bertolucci's modernist project and endow his text with a self-reflexive edge. Marcello's gaze exposes the spectacle through which cinema hails viewers and places them in a position comparable to that of Plato's slaves in the cave, the archetypal movie theatre. By looking into the camera, Marcello breaks the spell of cinema and denounces the viewers' seduction. They have subjected themselves to Bertolucci's images of Fascism, in exchange for the plenitude of an illusory, unified self.

Marcello's gaze into the camera is also relevant to the sexual politics Bertolucci explores in *The Conformist*, through the scenarios of the Oedipal conflict and the battle of the sexes. Moreover, Marcello's oblique look at the camera pushes the enslavement of the viewers to an extreme. The viewers fall into Marcello's field of vision and, inevitably, participate in all his sexual and political secrets. This moment of complicity occurs when the viewers have just seen Marcello shift his allegiances: denouncing Italo as a Fascist and losing himself in a crowd.

Most importantly, the gaze into the camera and the direct address to the viewers follow Marcello's first, explicit manifestation of homosexual desire. In the dimly lit passageway of the Colosseum, a man with a soft voice and squatting posture offers another male a cigarette and a meal. This man is Lino, whom Marcello denounced as a homosexual after having heard his mellow voice and recognizing a scar on his face. In the role of prostitute, Anna's face also bears the trace of an old wound. Lino's homosexuality threatens Marcello, whereas Anna's lesbianism is a reminder, through the scar, that heterosexuality is predicated on a fear of castration.

Those familiar with the physiognomies of Italian cinema cannot help but notice that Lino's companion resembles a non-professional actor Pier Paolo Pasolini would have cast to play himself as a sub-proletarian youth. The homosexual encounter depicted in this scene is reminiscent of paintings by Caravaggio, an artist who, like Pasolini, found his models in the street. Caravaggio's and Pasolini's young men flaunt their seductive selves in defiance of heterosexual norms regulating male behavior. Lino's friend has dark, curly hair, like Pasolini's Ninetto Davoli in *Teorema* (1968), and speaks with a Roman accent like Pasolini's Franco Citti in *Accattone* (1961). In addition to Croce and Alberto Moravia, Godard and Attilio Berto-lucci, Pasolini was a father figure for Bertolucci, who worked as an assitant director on the set of *Accattone* (fig. 17).

The allusion to Pasolini, a public defender of homosexuality, and Marcello's unmistakable attraction for a half-naked young man fall-ing asleep nearby, charge Trintignant's gaze into the camera with

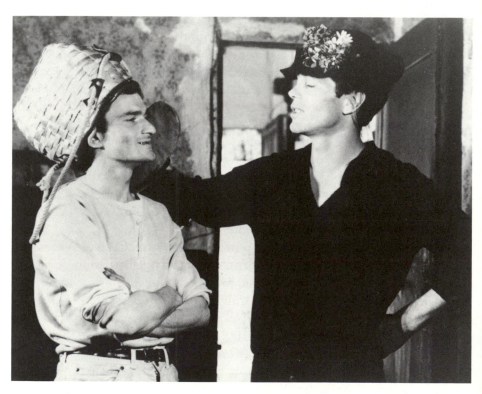

**17.** The male masquerade in Pier Paolo Pasolini's *Accattone* (1961). Courtesy of The Museum of Modern Art, Film Stills Archive.

all the intensity of an explicit, homosexual desire. Furthermore, Marcello's direct address presupposes a viewer who can acknowledge his newly assumed identity. Through Marcello's gaze, the actor, Trintignant, takes over the director Bernardo Bertolucci. The intentional homoeroticism of Trintignant's silent address to the camera exposes the unconscious homoerotic component of the appeal to the audience Bertolucci has been developing through the heterosexual scenarios of classical cinema: the Oedipal conflict and the battle of the sexes.

In analyzing conformism in Fascist culture, Bertolucci surrenders along with us to its pleasures, except for this last image where Marcello's gaze is powerful enough to become a conscience haunting the director. Until now the film was about the character, but with Marcello's crucial glance at the camera the film shifts to Bertolucci and to us, while undermining our joint mastery. Marcello's gaze makes explicit that Bertolucci's grounding of Fascism in class identity has been a distraction to turn our attention away from the much deeper uneasiness in heterosexual, homosocial societies, like Mussolini's Italy in the 1930s or Bertolucci's Italy in the 1960s, with unconscious, male homoerotic desire. This fear finds an easy, but problematic, outlet in Bertolucci's binding of homosexuality with Fascism. A masochistic and repressive component is at the heart of Bertolucci's equation. Much more interesting is the handling of homosexuality in Bertolucci's *1900* (1975–1976), where the character of Ottavio, the uncle of a young landowner, Alfredo Berlinghieri (Robert De Niro), never gets involved with the rise of Fascism in Italy. Far from his native land, in Paris, Ottavio befriends Ada (Dominique Sanda), Alfredo's wife-to-be. She drives a fast car and enjoys modernity. Ada's tastes remind us of the promise the Futurist avant-garde must have represented for an Italian "new woman." Ottavio and Ada, representing homosexuality and the proto-feminist side of Futurism, stand out in *1900* as weak but potentially liberating alternatives to Fascism. It is true, however, that Ottavio remains a marginal character in the narrative, and Ada is eventually crushed by her marriage and by her husband's hesitations concerning the rise of the regime.

Only the ending of *The Conformist* breaks the circularity of a narrative where a homosexual becomes a Fascist, while Fascism itself persecutes homosexuals. The actor's gesture of self-revelation is a form of directorial disempowerment more liberating than it is masochistic. In a sense this is a neorealist ending, for the actor's body takes over the character's identity, while homosexual desire wins over a heterosexual mask. Jean-Louis Trintignant does not have to act in character any longer. The subterranean passages of the Colosseum are such a private region that Marcello can stop worrying about his private role. He does not have to be either a Fascist or a communist. After acting in character and playing a social role, the actor's body is all that is left on the screen, just as in a neorealist film where the physiognomy of a non-professional actor tells the whole story with a mixture of directness and ambiguity. It is as if this encounter with the actor's body at the finale of the film were sealing Bertolucci's and our secret admission of having indulged all along in the seduction of Fascism, while hiding the director's and our homophobic prejudices.

# THREE

The
Risorgimento
before
World War II

## UNITY, CONTINUITY, AND NATIONALISM

THE INTERTEXTUALITY of Giovanni Pastrone's *Cabiria* (1914) and Carmine Gallone's *Scipio Africanus* (1937) illustrates Luigi Salvatorelli's claim of continuity between Giovanni Giolitti's and Benito Mussolini's Italy. Renzo De Felice's distinction between fascism as a movement in the 1920s and Fascism as a regime in the 1930s emerges from a comparison of Maciste's athletic body with Scipio's statuesque features. Yet, the image of a statue is but a partial and surface description of the Fascist body politic. Under the marble, something in the 1930s moved toward neorealism. In Alessandro Blasetti's *1860* (1933),[1] the mo-

---

[1] On Blasetti's *1860*, see James Hay, *Popular Film Culture in Fascist Italy* (Bloomington: Indiana University Press, 1987), 165–68; Mira Liehm, *Passion and Defiance: Film in Italy from 1942 to the Present* (Berkeley: University of California Press, 1984), 23–25; Carlo Lizzani, *Il cinema italiano dalle origini agli anni ottanta* (Rome: Editori Riuniti, 1982), 58–59; Pierre Sorlin, "The Italian Risorgimento," *The Film in History: Restaging the Past* (Oxford: Basil Blackwell, 1980), 116–39; Marcia Landy, *Fascism in Film: The Italian Commercial Cinema 1931–43* (Princeton, N.J.: Princeton University Press, 1986), 183–87; Mino Argentieri, "Il cinema italiano e il risorgimento," *Passato ridotto*, ed. Gianfranco Gori (Florence: La Casa di Usher, 1982), 85–94; Lino Del Fra, "Il film storico e il neorealismo," *Rivista del Cinema Italiano* 3, nos. 5–6 (May–June 1954): 67–73; Adriano Aprà and Patrizia Pistagnesi, eds., *The Fabulous Thirties: Italian Cinema 1929–1944* (Milan: Electa International, 1979), 34–49; Elaine Mancini, *Struggles of the Italian Film Industry during Fascism 1930–35* (Ann Arbor, Mich.: UMI Research Press, 1985), 108–13; Alessandro Blasetti, "A proposito di *1860*," *La Rivista del Cinematografo* 7 (July 1966): 419–20; Ettore M. Margadonna, "Cinema," *L'Illustrazione Italiana* 61, no. 15 (April 15, 1934): 560–61; Massimo Mida and Fausto Montesanti, "*1860*," *Cinema* 6, no. 129 (November 10, 1941): 287; Alessandro Blasetti, *Scritti sul cinema* (Venice: Marsilio, 1982); *Cinema e Storia*, vol. 3, *Rassegna Cinematografica "Lido degli Estensi,"* 1959 (Ferrara: Amministrazione Provinciale di Ferrara, 1959), 218.

bilization of the statue becomes apparent due to the fact that the neoclassical-statuesque coexists with the populist-picturesque. These two aspects of film style complement each other, for both idealize the national body politic while pointing to a continuity between fascist and neorealist cinema.

Luigi Salvatorelli in the 1920s and Renzo De Felice in the 1970s were not alone in their reliance on the theme of continuity when discussing the origins of Fascism. Fascism, itself, invoked a continuity with the past, although, given the populist roots of the regime, this continuity was not with the aristocratic-bourgeois oligarchy of Giolitti's Italy. It was rather the continuity between the Risorgimento and Fascism that allowed the regime to justify historically its seizing of power in 1922.

In his *History of Italy from 1871 to 1915* (1928), Benedetto Croce argued that Giolitti's Italy was the successful outcome of the Risorgimento. By contrast, Giovanni Gentile maintained that pre-World War I oligarchic liberalism had failed to unify Italy and that Giolitti did not fulfill the aspirations of the Risorgimento whose legacy Fascism inherited. For Gentile, the project of the regime was to complete the unification Giuseppe Garibaldi had started in 1860 under the auspices of the House of Savoy in Piedmont. For Gentile, the role of Fascism was, after centuries of territorial and linguistic division, to cement the desire for national unity that characterized the Risorgimento.[2]

Giovanni Gentile (1875–1944) was a major proponent of idealist-Hegelian philosophy in Fascist Italy and a major figure in the regime. In 1923, as Minister of Education, Gentile carried out the first important reform of the regime. Mussolini himself remarked that Gentile's reorganization of the national school system, according to a rigid class structure, was the most fascist reform possible. Before Gentile, in Giolitti's Italy, Croce had been Minister of Education, but resigned in 1921 when Mussolini came to power. With these philosophers in charge of the school system, it is not surprising if idealist-liberal and idealist-fascist interpretations of the Risorgimento overlapped and pervaded the popular knowledge, or doxa, mastered by generations of students. With their handling of na-

[2] For a visual overview of military and daily life in the Risorgimento, see Lamberto Vitali, *Il risorgimento nella fotografia* (Turin: Einaudi, 1979).

tional history, the textbooks of the Italian state school system are a social technology comparable to the cinema.

At the end of the 1920s, Benito Mussolini felt that Fascism needed an explicit defense of its value system and a comprehensive statement of its social and political philosophy. This effort of self-validation generated the "Doctrine of Fascism," which appeared in the *Enciclopedia Italiana* in 1932 under the heading "Fascism." The "Doctrine" is divided into two parts; one is entitled "Fundamental Ideas," and the other "Political and Social Doctrine." Both parts appear under the name of Benito Mussolini. In fact, Mussolini only wrote the second part, while Gentile authored "Fundamental Ideas." Gentile's philosophy, Actualism or Actual Idealism, thus provided the theoretical foundation of Fascism as a socio-political system, based on the notion of the "ethical state." According to Gentile, in the ethical state the good Fascist citizen is the individual who embodies the nation, while the nation represents a moral law binding together individuals and generations to come in a tradition and a mission. Gentile translates the Hegelian nation-state into the corporate system, where public and private life depend on an all-inclusive Fascist identity.

Unlike Croce, who, as a lay thinker and a liberal in the nineteenth-century sense of the term, cherished the freedom of the individual and the separation of the public from the private sphere, Gentile speaks against individualism, envisioning the state as a totality.[3] For Gentile, disunity was the germ responsible for political strife during the Middle Ages and the Renaissance. Ironically his image of a germ attacking a healthy organism brings to mind a similar metaphor in Croce's interpretation of Fascism. This similar iconography reflects the fact that Croce and Gentile held a common belief in the unitary nature of subjectivity. And yet, not only do their views on individualism differ, but Croce and Gentile rely on the theme of historical continuity in significantly different ways. With Croce, Fascism is a parenthesis intervening between the Risorgimento and the Resistance; for Gentile, Fascism is the continuation of the Risorgimento. In the 1930s, Croce became an isolated stronghold of antifascism in Fascist Italy. In looking for an example

[3] "Giovanni Gentile," *Enciclopedia Filosofica*, vol. 3 (Florence: Sansoni, 1968), cols. 39–54.

of intellectual opposition to the regime and for an historical precedent of successful, national struggle, the generation of the Resistance turned to Croce's historiography of the Risorgimento.[4]

In the 1930s, the Gentilean themes of continuity and unity accounted for a hostility toward the international scene. National unity required the rewriting of domestic history in a nationalistic vein. The regime played up the struggle against foreign rulers during the Risorgimento to turn attention away from the domestic class struggle. Autarchy, or national self-sufficiency, prevailed, while provincialism fed nationalism. Fascism, however, did not succeed in sealing Italy off from the rest of the world. In search of an entertainment form capable of unifying its composite audiences, Fascism refrained from a ban on Hollywood films until 1940.[5] While in the meantime, select intellectual circles looked with great interest to Soviet realist films.[6]

The official line for the arts was to be "Italian" at all costs. Yet the Fascist culture industry imitated propagandistic devices and generic formulae from "materialist" America[7] and "Bolshevik" Russia. Foreign sources were of interest only as long as they were useful for entertaining and manipulating Italian audiences. Fascist autarchy tolerated under-the-counter international cultural relations. The regime, behaving like a *bricoleur*, was less original than were its claims: its culture industry combined the exploitation of domestic art forms with a curiosity for American consumerism and Soviet populism.

*1860* was produced by Cines, an old Roman production house of

[4] For an overview of competing interpretations of the Risorgimento, see Piero Gobetti, *Risorgimento senza eroi e altri scritti storici* (1926). Introd. Franco Venturi (Torino: Einaudi, 1976); Antonio Gramsci, *Il risorgimento* (Turin: Einaudi, 1966); Walter Maturi, *Interpretazioni del risorgimento* (Turin: Einaudi, 1962); Stuart J. Woolf, "Risorgimento e fascismo: Il senso della continuità nella storiografia italiana," *Belfagor* 20, n. 1 (31 January, 1965): 71–91; Claudio Pavone, "Le idee della resistenza: Antifascismo e fascismo di fronte alla tradizione del risorgimento," *Passato e Presente* 7 (1959): 850–918.

[5] On the number of American films shown in Italy between 1920 and 1940, see "appendix C" in Hay, *Popular Film Culture.*

[6] On the impact of Soviet sociorealism on Italian film culture, see Liehm, *Passion and Defiance*, 38–39.

[7] On violence in America, see Emilio Cecchi, "E Gangsters D'America," in Francesco Bolzoni, ed., *Il progetto imperiale: Cinema e cultura nell'Italia del 1936* (Venice: Edizioni de la Biennale di Venezia, 1976), 117.

great national fame. The art historian, Emilio Cecchi, was the head of Cines and advised the director Alessandro Blasetti during the shooting. In 1933, Soviet films circulated, if only in limited areas such as the G.U.F.s (university film clubs). Meshed with sources from the national tradition, icons of Soviet populism appealed to film circles of young intellectuals more or less supportive of the regime. In the midst of a debate on the direction Italian cinema should take, Soviet cinema kindled a desire for a national-popular film style, for a fresher way of representing regional and daily life, in contrast to the steady diet of kitsch operas for the screen. In literary circles, the Soviet influence blended with a renewal of interest in the work of Giovanni Verga, a nineteenth-century realist writer who depicted rural life in Sicily. After decades ruled by Gabriele D'Annunzio's decorative language, the "germ" of sociorealism developed within the body of fascist cinema to spark a populist taste that led to neorealism.

Millicent Marcus pointedly observes that neorealism lasted approximately from 1943 to 1950 and produced only 21 "classic" films.[8] Yet, well before 1943, in the early 1930s, Blasetti's *1860* participated in the preparation of neorealist style. *1860* was in line with the nationalist dictum of the regime, but it also brought together a constellation of domestic and foreign sources, and recast them along two stylistic registers: the neoclassical statuesque and the populist picturesque.

*1860* moves beyond Gallone's statue. In Blasetti's account of Garibaldi's expedition to Sicily, the phantom of the red-shirted general and the statue of Colonel Carini stand next to two shepherds, Carmelo and Gesuzza. Blasetti's shepherds wear sheepskins, black scarves,[9] and speak in dialect (fig. 18). Blasetti depicts these poor folks as typical Sicilian representatives of the Italian body politic, using the picturesque to integrate their regional difference into the national identity.

Blasetti's use of the picturesque to contain class and regional difference is comparable to Alessandro Manzoni's approach in his his-

---

[8] Millicent Marcus, *Italian Film in the Light of Neorealism* (Princeton, N.J.: Princeton University Press, 1986), xvi.

[9] Vittorio Nino Novarese designed the costumes of *1860*. On Blasetti's views about costumes, see Blasetti, *Scritti sul cinema*, 220–22.

**18.** The sheepskins in Alessandro Blasetti's *1860* (1933). Courtesy of The Museum of Modern Art, Film Stills Archive.

torical novel, *The Betrothed* (1827). Toward the humble Renzo and Lucia, the nineteenth-century realist writer displays a paternalism which Antonio Gramsci ascribes to a "disjunction of feeling." For Gramsci, however, disjunction applies to divisions among classes, not to subjectivity in and of itself as was the case for Bertolt Brecht. Manzoni's approach was, for Gramsci, symptomatic of value-judgments of popular, regional culture stemming from an unconscious sense of class superiority. Manzoni's peasants in Lombardy are "popular 'caricatures,' "[10] and do not achieve the psychological complexity of their wealthier oppressors, Don Rodrigo and L'Innominato.

[10] Gramsci's remarks on Manzoni's paternalism and inclination for the populist-picturesque when dealing with humble folks appear in Giuliano Manacorda, ed., *Antonio Gramsci: Marxismo e letteratura* (Rome: Editori Riuniti, 1975), 45, 276. On Manzoni and the picturesque, also see David Forgacs and Geoffrey Nowell-Smith, eds., *Antonio Gramsci: Selections from Cultural Writings*, trans. William Boelhower (Cambridge, Mass.: Harvard University Press, 1985), 296.

Gramsci's remarks underline class prejudice at the heart of Manzoni's double standard in handling character. While the strong physiognomies of the commedia dell'arte were a sufficient substratum for the depiction of the lower classes, the verbal nuances of the novel fit the higher strata of society. The regional authenticity of Carmelo and Gesuzza may be contrived in the same way that Manzoni's Renzo and Lucia represent local types, but Blasetti's characters are like a breath of fresh air compared to the cardboard Roman generals, Renaissance mercenaries, and medieval knights of the Fascist film industry.

## UNITY, CONTINUITY, AND SOURCES

Blasetti's careful balance of patriotic speeches and local color rescues *1860* from the stifling overtones of shallow Fascist propaganda. *1860* proposes a dynamic but acritical view of national history. This tension between old and new situates Blasetti's film between fascist and neorealist cinema. On the surface, Blasetti's choice to shoot on location and to cast non-actors wearing regional costumes and speaking in Sicilian are elements of novelty. The deep structure of the film, however, is an exploration of national history based on the themes of unity and continuity.

In *1860*, Blasetti fabricated images of the Risorgimento that looked "real" to an audience of the 1930s. The project of *1860* was to celebrate and promote the diffusion of patriotic values. *1860* illustrates the historical consciousness of the Fascist era looking at the past and writing its history anew. Significantly, the Italian print of the film ends with a reunion of former Garibaldini. The old Red Shirts assemble around the Italian flag and greet young Black Shirts parading nearby to the national anthem.

Blasetti's propagandistic ending was cut after the collapse of Fascism in 1943 without harming the narrative. The fact that the parallel between Garibaldi's Red Shirts and Mussolini's Black Shirts did not play a crucial role in ensuring narrative coherence proves the extent of Blasetti's adaptation of Gentile's Risorgimento, draining meaning from Vico's law of the *corsi* and *ricorsi* and turning his concept into sheer repetition as a gratuitous episode left dangling at the end of the film, one easily removable.

The conflict between national unity and selfish individualism constitutes the backbone of Blasetti's travelogue narrative. The newly wedded Sicilian shepherd, Carmelo, reluctantly leaves his wife, Gesuzza. His task is to carry a message of support from the south to Colonel Carini in the north. Stationed at Garibaldi's headquarters in Genoa, the colonel is about to leave for Sicily with an army of volunteers. During Carmelo's adventurous journey by boat, train, and foot, a heterogeneous Italy unfolds. Halfway through the film, Carmelo reaches Civitavecchia, a harbor city near Rome. On the eve of Garibaldi's enterprise, Italy thrives with patriotic fervor. Yet, tensions persist among different political factions, as do vivid manifestations of regionalistic pride among the participants.

Blasetti's visual style acknowledges Gentile's emphasis on the effects of disunity among Italians who, supposedly, would find in Mussolini's leadership the fulfillment of Garibaldi's legacy. Blasetti relies on multiple screen directions and dynamic editing to depict the convergence of groups of people toward a figure of leadership. The leader usually appears at the center of a single image or of an assemblage of shots. The sequence staged on the shore of Quarto illustrates the departure of Garibaldi's "Thousand." It opens with static point-of-view shots of Carmelo witnessing a farewell between a mother and son. Rows of volunteers line up at different heights of the frame. The slow pans, the emphasis on consistent and horizontal screen directions, and the dusky lighting underline the solemnity of this "historic" occasion.

Once an off-screen, anonymous voice announces the imminent arrival of Garibaldi at the nearby Villa Spinola, a sudden change in rhythm and composition occurs. Spatial depth is no longer created through layering of linearly arranged elements such as men or boats. The space, instead, is vertically intersected by the converging movement of several figures running toward the leader.

Garibaldi is obviously the ubiquitous catalyzer of national unity. Yet the mythical leader remains invisible, except for two quick shots. The first time, we get a glimpse of Garibaldi on top of a hill eating bread and cheese; the second time, we see him parading troops before the battle of Calatafimi. During a critical moment of this battle, another choreography of convergence takes place. Various soldiers rushing from left and right and the dynamic editing of shots with opposite screen directions convey the excitement of the counterattack and the charisma of the God-like Garibaldi. His disembodied voice exhorting his men "To win or to die!" acquires the same resonance as Scipio's phantasmic presence.

In contrast to Blasetti's invisible "duce" of the Risorgimento, in *Viva L'Italia* (1960) (Long Live Italy),[11] a late neorealist interpretation of Garibaldi's journey, Roberto Rossellini rejected the heroic approach of fascist cinema and compared the general to a homely Christian warrior.

The painter Renato Guttuso observes that the parallel between Garibaldi and Jesus was a common iconographical solution in nineteenth-century popular culture: "Garibaldi was highly popular. Indeed, some girls in the cloistered convent schools of Sicily went so far as to identify Garibaldi with the figure of Jesus, since he too was handsome and fair-haired."[12] Guttuso's reference to the popularity of Garibaldi in the world of religious boarding-schools for girls finds cinematic confirmation in Vittorio De Sica's *Un Garibaldino al Convento* (1942), a story of forbidden love between a young woman and one of Garibaldi's Red Shirts.

Like Blasetti's in *1860*, the iconography of Rossellini's *Viva l'Italia* adheres to a thesis of historical continuity. This is indicated by the title temporarily assigned to *Viva l'Italia, 1860/Paisà*.[13] This early title makes apparent the popularity of the Crocean interpretation and reveals how the category of continuity justified a parallel between the Risorgimento and the Resistance based on national unity rather than on class division. Both Blasetti and Rossellini rely on visual emblems to link different historical periods. Echoing a popular historical knowledge of the Risorgimento, partly Gentilean and partly Crocean, the two directors concur in stressing how, throughout the centuries, Italy's misfortunes spring from political division and foreign domination.

[11] On *Viva L'Italia*, see Peter Brunette, *Roberto Rossellini* (New York: Oxford University Press, 1987), 224–31.

[12] Dario Durbè, intro., *Pittura garibaldina da Fattori a Guttuso* (Rome: De Luca Editore, 1982), xi.

[13] The final choice of *1860* as a title was preceded by other ideas: *Italia 1860*, *Garibaldi*, *Calatafimi*, *L'Ondata Rossa* (The Red Wave). All these titles are rich in historiographical implications. For opinions, Blasetti turned to the readers of *La Stampa* on May 23, 1933. See Blasetti, *Scritti sul cinema*, 278–79.

After the occupation of Blasetti's Sicilian village, Swiss soldiers remove the clapper from the church belfry to isolate the natives and prevent any request of help from neighboring towns. A bell was the protagonist of an anecdote set in the Renaissance. A promoter of unity among rival city-states, Pier Capponi, confronted the French invaders and threatened to ring the bells of nearby cities in order to gather an army of allies. In Italian popular culture, and more specifically, in Blasetti's *1860* and in Rossellini's *Viva L'Italia*, the bell is an emblem of aggregation. In Rossellini's film, the ringing of the church bells announces the Sicilian patriots' insurrection and calls for support from the neighboring villages.

Both Blasetti's and Rossellini's Sicilian bells evoke Pier Capponi's famous threat to bring together the city-states of Renaissance Italy: "And we shall ring our bells!" Blasetti's iconography, however, lends itself to more than one interpretation. His image resonates with the impulse toward unity against a foreign invasion. Furthermore, the iconographic parallel between French and Swiss invasions confirms Gentile's thesis of continuity between three historical periods brought together by the theme of unity: Renaissance, Risorgimento, and Fascism.

In contrast to Blasetti's heroic allegory of national history, Rossellini's account of Italy's political unification takes on the tone of an evangelical parable. Rossellini's Jesus-like Garibaldi, reaching out to the common people, stems from hagiographic conventions in the *Lives of the Saints*. Just as in *Open City* (1945), in *Viva L'Italia* (1960) Rossellini envisions a militant church of the poor which overcomes differences among social classes and regions. Rossellini translates national unity into Christian brotherhood. As we shall see in greater detail, this joining into a shared identity and shared humanity is also the message of *Paisà* (1946), where the Resistance becomes a sort of new Risorgimento, based on national good will and cross-cultural communication between Italians and Americans, civilians and partisans.

In *Viva L'Italia*, Rossellini stages Garibaldi's triumphant entrance into Palermo in such a way as to recall Christ's arrival in Jerusalem on Palm Sunday. Instead of riding his legendary white horse amidst a cloud of Red Shirts, the blond general sits on a humble donkey and, like Jesus, greets a crowd of enthusiastic children

waving palm twigs. The evangelical subtext also informs Rossellini's depiction of the memorable encounter near Teano between
Garibaldi and the king of Piedmont, Vittorio Emanuele II. Like a
prodigal son returning home after an adventurous escapade, Garibaldi submits to the authority of the Piedmontese king and gives
southern Italy to the House of Savoy in the north.

In the transition from the Civitavecchia sequence to the scene of
Gesuzza's captivity in *1860*, Blasetti implicitly refers to the *questione della lingua*. He stresses that a history of division has led to
centuries of foreign invasions and the proliferation of dialects rather
than the fostering of a common national language. Blasetti edits
shots of portraits of foreign rulers as if they were medallions to be
arranged together, a mode of representation that refers to a bygone
nineteenth-century taste. In the credits of *Un Garibaldino al Convento*, the framing of the main characters in medallions lends an
aura of nostalgia to De Sica's film.

In *1860*, the medallion-montage brings together the portraits of
foreign kings and queens not to signify nostalgia but rather political
oppression and geographical division. Different locations correspond to different rulers. Civitavecchia and Sicily are linked by
clever references to foreign languages and royal portraits. The camera lingers on Napoleon III while French is spoken off-screen. A subsequent pan to Sophia of Bavaria is complemented by German on
the soundtrack. This movement from language to language and portrait to portrait ends with a close-up of the Swiss officer's face,
speaking German, during his interrogation of Gesuzza in the Sicilian village.

The shift from Sophia's aristocratic portrait to the rough face of
the Swiss officer lends itself to at least two interpretations. First, a
nationalist historiography would differentiate foreign invaders only
in terms of their incomprehensible languages. The spatial decontex-
tualization of the portraits downplays any distinction between foreign rulers in Italy. The use of foreign languages does not appeal to
the audience's historical knowledge, but only provokes an emotional response to a frivolous French voice or a harsh German into-
nation.

Second, the lack of an establishing shot, in either scene, stresses
the invisibility of the Italian landscape, a non-entity when com-

pared to other unified, independent European nations. In 1815, at the Congress of Vienna, Prince Metternich observed about the reconfiguration of Europe after Napoleon's downfall: "Italy is only a geographical expression."[14] As a mere convention on the map, the physical existence of the Italian peninsula was just another asset in the possession of a foreign ruler.

In *1860*, Blasetti skillfully orchestrated the use of the Italian language and dialects. He struck a delicate balance between regionalism and nationalism by relying on regional traits to typify minor characters and dramatize Gentile's thesis concerning the need to overcome internal divisions. At the same time, Blasetti underlines the patriotic theme to gloss over the deep split between north and south, or to water down the contrasts of opinion between Garibaldi and Cavour, republicans and monarchists.

Mario Palumbo sums up why Blasetti's film was so successful at the box office: "It was neither too Sicilian nor too northerner."[15] Although *1860* wanted to address a national rather than a regional audience, at times it reveals a sympathetic viewpoint toward the south. This favoring of the southern protagonists—the newly wedded Carmelo and Gesuzza—indicates Blasetti's intention to humanize an abstract view of national history with a regional, picturesque story line.

In the train sequence, the clash of dialects, the conversations among stereotypically regional figures, the layering of voices and folksongs on the soundtrack, the claustrophobic framing of the compartment, convey political and geographical conflicts between Catholics and republicans, northerners and southerners.

During the journey from Civitavecchia to Genoa, Carmelo meets a supporter of the Catholic Vincenzo Gioberti (1801–1852) and a follower of the republican Giuseppe Mazzini (1805–1872). The verbal aggressiveness of the anti-royalist republican clashes with the school-teacher tone and gold-rimmed glasses of the pope's defender. Both of these characters are predictable; their political beliefs tell us all we need to know about their psychology. This approach fits the logic of allegory where concrete people embody abstract ideas.

[14] Prince Metternich, "Letter, November 19, 1849," in *The Oxford Dictionary of Quotations*, 2d ed. (London: Oxford University Press, 1966), 338.

[15] Mario Palumbo, *La Sicilia nel cinema* (Palermo: Ed. Sicilia Domani, 1963), 7.

Since they *are* a political stance, they are "choir-characters." They recall George Wilhelm Pabst's characterizations in *Westfront 1918* (1930) and in *Kameradshaft* (1931). These two films might have been available to Blasetti and Cecchi, who were involved with intellectual circles open to foreign films.

Blasetti's attachment to an Italian literary and visual heritage implements Gentile's nationalism. In *1860*, ideological and stylistic issues overlap. Together they validate a national cultural tradition by virtue of an eclectic use of domestic and foreign sources, ranging from the heroic to the picturesque, such as the Macchiaioli's paintings, Giuseppe Cesare Abba's best-seller, *The Diary of One of Garibaldi's Thousand* (1880),[16] and Soviet sociorealism. Blasetti's style is built upon memorabilia and commonplaces, a pleasant blending of oleographic details and calculated suggestions, such as patriotic graffiti on walls and medallion-like portraits, cactuses, and Saracen ruins. Blasetti was interested in the use of chronicles, anecdotes, regional genre paintings, and costumes, primarily for their local color and their effect of authenticity.

Blasetti's reliance on Giuseppe Cesare Abba's *Diary* and on the Macchiaioli's paintings turns the Sicilian landscape into a mise-en-scène *en plein air* of historical continuity. The landmarks and ruins of previous domination bear witness to the ongoing struggle against the latest foreign invasion. *In Viva L'Italia*, Rossellini proposes a geological view of Sicilian history comparable to Blasetti's. Pierre Sorlin is quick to recognize the connection between landscape and history Rossellini establishes in his film: "In a highly symbolical scene, the Garibaldini, realizing they pass near the ancient temple of Segestum, climb the mountain to contemplate ruins which are now the common property of the Italian people."[17] In true neorealist fashion, the landscape itself is a choir-character, a space housing a national identity. This conflation of landscape and character is reminiscent of the ties between city and physiognomy so frequent in the *maschere* of the commedia dell'arte.

The depiction of vestiges of history left on the land also charac-

---

[16] Giuseppe Cesare Abba, *The Diary of One of Garibaldi's Thousand* (1880; reprint, London: Oxford University Press, 1962). See Gramsci on Abba, in *Marxismo e letteratura*, 167.

[17] Sorlin, *Film in History*, 135.

terizes Blasetti's film. At the beginning of *1860*, imitating Abba's pastiche of Biblical and romantic elments, Blasetti's camera pans from left to right. It is as if a painted scroll were unfolding where "men sleeping in the open, moving over great plains, climbing mountain paths, consorting with a pastoral people, with their sheep and goats, watering at their wells, resting under their olive trees, are living the life described in the Bible."[18] In comparing the Sicilian to the Biblical shepherds, Blasetti tells us that their struggle is as holy and as just as was the Hebrews'. A Saracen tower stands in a mise-en-scène which also includes medieval, narrow archways. This mixture of cultures and styles in the same landscape points to Gentile's teleological argument that the Risorgimento was a preparation for Fascism. Furthermore, Gentile's geological view of history as a series of layers, with moments of unity leading to the regime, seems to strive for a compromise between Hegel's linear historicism and Vico's stratified model in the law of the *corsi* and *ricorsi*.

In representing the Risorgimento, Blasetti confronted a dilemma previously tackled by the Macchiaioli painters: how to revitalize the historical, classical scene with the insertion of elements drawn from daily life and regional genre paintings. In the second half of the nineteenth century, the Macchiaioli were active in Tuscany and, to a lesser extent, in other regions. These painters specialized in open-air landscapes, in vignettes of rural and village life, and in picturesque views of hidden gardens, farmers' markets, military camps, and convent yards.

The Macchiaioli were *the* painters of national history and daily life during the Risorgimento. Emilio Cecchi reminds us how important their role was, by relating the Macchiaioli to other aspects of nineteenth-century Italian culture:

The inspiration of the "Macchiaioli" corresponded more profoundly with the movement of ideas and poetry which inspired the Italian Risorgimento than did any other school of painting during the past century. Only Carducci's lyrics and a few pages by Abba contrive to convey such spiritual aspects of nature as Fattori, Abbati and Sernesi do in their pictures; the sea-green Etruscan scenes, the solitary shores and the "gleam-

---

[18] Abba, *The Diary*, xii.

ing silence of noon." Carducci alone, in his *Rustic Community* and his *Sung Mass*, finds a form suited to express the proud renown of the communes; these works may be compared with the cloisters and interiors of churches painted by Antonio Puccinelli, Abbati and Borrani.[19]

The term "Macchiaioli" derives from these painters' experimentation with contrasts of sharply defined patches of color, or *macchie*, and with black-and-white chromatism, the effects of light and shadow.

The painterly, yet documentary style of Giovanni Fattori, perhaps the most well-known artist of the Macchiaioli, has points in common with Blasetti's historiographical approach. Without contesting the theme of historical continuity, both artists represent the Risorgimento period in innovative though not disruptive terms.

The credits of *1860* unroll over an edifying, classical battle scene. This traditional beginning clashes with the striking appearance of sheepskins. Over the span of a few shots, we move from the highest genre, the historical painting, to the lowest, a regional vignette of an undeniably harsh life style. Within the boundaries of historical continuity, realism is compatible and coextensive with classicism, the generic sketch with the academic tableau. Even the most daring images will, in the end, partake of and conform to tradition. Furthermore, the taming of the daily and picturesque by national history echoes the fate of the south which, at Teano, fell under the authority of the House of Savoy in the north.

The integration of region into nation corresponds to the weaving of the old with the new, climaxing with the parallel between old Red Shirts and young Black Shirts at the end of *1860*. This logic, based on continuity across generations and styles, applies to Blasetti's use of painterly sources such as the Macchiaioli's depiction of the Risorgimento. Within the safe boundaries of artistic tradition, Fattori's paintings marked a change from an old, academic mode to a new, naturalist one. The art historian Norma Broude remarks, "Fattori's break with the costumes and the events of past eras was now at least complete, but the compositional formulae, which he had used in his traditional history paintings in many cases made the

---

[19] Emilio Cecchi, intro., *The "Macchiaioli": The First "Europeans" in Tuscany*, with critical notes by Mario Borgiotti (Florence: Leo S. Olschki, 1963), 6–7.

transition to the *new mode* almost intact. The contemporary bat-
tlescene . . . could attain respectability as a genre only if cast in the
form of a conventional compositional type."[20] Fattori depicted historical events in a neutral, documentary vein. He turned to daily
life for subjects, while these new subjects fell into the compositional schemes of the old historical painting.

Fattori found many of his topics in the Second War of Independence or in the successful actions of Garibaldi's expedition. This is
not to say that Fattori never depicted the horrors of war or the pain
of defeat. In looking at Fattori's *The Battle of Custoza* (1876–1878),
the viewer senses disorientation and discouragement among the
soldiers (fig. 19). Not all the soldiers are looking in the same direction, perhaps because unity and coordination of effort are about to
wane under the pressure of the defeat (fig. 20). On the other hand,
Fattori establishes an area of convergence—a wall of soldiers standing compact while horses die nearby—next to areas with multiple,
if not conflicting, lines of sight (fig. 21). In *The Battle of Custoza*,
Fattori's subject matter is negative and, in this sense, defies the positive aura of the Risorgimento. Yet Norma Broude would argue that
the compositional scheme of *The Battle of Custoza* stays within the
boundaries of tradition.

Blasetti differed from Fattori in his shedding a positive light on
nineteenth-century history; he totally ignored the painful defeats of
1849 and 1866, both of them occurring at Custoza during the First
and the Third War of Independence. Blasetti's search for historical
realism is compromised by his agenda for a positive national identity. By contrast, Luchino Visconti, in *Senso* (1954), offers an unsettling account of the Third War of Independence. On the basis of Antonio Gramsci's interpretation, Visconti challenged Gentile's and
Croce's theses that the Risorgimento was a period of unity among
classes and regions.

Historiographically and stylistically, *Senso* stands in sharp contrast with *1860*. Blasetti's painterly tableaux, with large gatherings
of hopeful soldiers, trepidatious relatives, and obedient animals,
disintegrate in Visconti's haunting depiction of the battle of Cus-

---

[20] Norma Freedman Broude, "The Macchiaioli: Academicism and Modernism in
Nineteenth-Century Italian Painting" (Ph.D. diss., Columbia University, 1967), 208.
Emphasis is mine.

**19.** Giovanni Fattori, *The Battle of Custoza* (1876–1878), detail. Courtesy of Galleria d'Arte Moderna, Florence.

toza (1866). The unusual sight on the screen of the Italian army retreating adds a note of deep embarrassment to the self-explanatory power of dark images. Horror and confusion, smoke and drums made Visconti's Custoza unforgettable, controversial, and unacceptable to the censors of the 1950s. In contrast to Visconti, Blasetti breaks down the battle of Calatafimi (1860) into vignettes of heroic behavior within a human scale. His soldiers charge the enemy as if they were leaping beyond themselves toward glory. In footage of Visconti's battle of Custoza cut by the censors, there are no close-ups and the patriots are shown from behind.

Blasetti must have known Fattori's paintings, though, to my knowledge, there is no straightforward statement where the director acknowledges the Macchiaiolo as a source. Emilio Cecchi, a leading expert on the Macchiaioli, advised Blasetti during the pro-

**20.** Giovanni Fattori, *The Battle of Custoza* (1876–1878) detail. Courtesy of Galleria d'Arte Moderna, Florence.

duction of *1860*, thus making the distinction between intentional reference and unconscious allusion a difficult one to assess.

Both Blasetti and Visconti might have been thinking of Fattori's *bozzetto* of a wagon with horses led by two nuns, entitled *The Battle of Magenta* (1859–1860), for the painting *The Italian Camp after the Battle of Magenta* (1861–1862) (fig. 22). Yet, their handling of this source differs greatly. Blasetti's approach exemplifies a fascist (Gentile) answer to the question of unity among classes and regions in the Risorgimento. Visconti, by contrast, places a Marxist (Gramsci) accent on Fattori's work.

In *1860*, Fattori's carriage, tied to a couple of oxen, is placed on a dusty country road, crowded in the foreground with soldiers. The whitish area at the center of the wagon becomes the *macchia* filled in by the white veils of two nuns. In Fattori's painting, the nuns occupy a similar vehicle, but drawn by a horse. In Blasetti's medium

**21.** Giovanni Fattori, *The Battle of Custoza* (1876–1878), detail. Courtesy of Galleria d'Arte Moderna, Florence.

shot, the nuns sit still. In Fattori's painting, one of them stands on the side of the road, turned toward the battlefield. One can surmise that the two nuns are nurses. Without an active function in Blasetti's narrative, the two nuns are just a passive glimpse of white across the frame.

Blasetti's nuns are as removed from the world as Vincenzo Cabianca's *Le Monachine* (1861–1862) (fig. 23). In this lovely outdoor setting, three dark figures with white veils stand under golden sunshine in a secluded yard, peeping through a little hole into a green valley, as if curious about the larger world outside the convent.

In contrast to Blasetti, in his use of Fattori's *The Italian Camp after the Battle of Magenta*, Visconti stresses the active, social role of the two nuns as nurses. In the Italian print of *Senso*,[21] the refreshing appearance of the white veils precedes a shot of the two nuns helping wounded soldiers at Custoza. In documenting the nuns' ac-

[21] The scene discussed does not appear in the American print.

**22.** Giovanni Fattori, *The Italian Camp after the Battle of Magenta* (1861–1862). Courtesy of Galleria d'Arte Moderna, Florence.

tive role on the battlefield, Visconti rewrites Blasetti's allusion to Fattori's painting. Blasetti was attracted to *The Italian Camp after the Battle of Magenta* for the picturesque potential of the white veils. By showing the nuns at work, Visconti, instead, uses Fattori to allude to the changing perception of religious life in Italian society.

In his discussion of the role of nuns in the paintings of the Macchiaioli Dario Durbè explains that "After all, the theme was widely explored during the nineteenth century, by the Macchiaioli as well as by painters of other regions, and it has to do with a matter of mores, with the conflict between a new lay ethics and the country's religious traditions. From the sublime heights of Diderot's *La Religieuse* to Manzoni's *La Monaca di Monza*, this conflict had descended to a modest subject for daily conversations."[22] Unlike Blasetti's, Visconti's use of the nuns was meant to comment upon new modes of interaction among social classes, lay and religious groups,

[22] Dario Durbè, *I Macchiaioli* (Florence: Centro Di, 1976), 93.

**23.** Vincenzo Cabianca, *Le Monachine* (1861–1862). Collection Giuliano Matteucci, Viareggio.

engaged in competing interests and uneven rewards in the project of national unification.

On a small scale, Visconti's allusion to Fattori's *The Italian Camp after the Battle of Magenta* is an application of Gramsci's view that tensions and contradictions always define historical change: "The viscous forces of certain regimes are often unsuspected, especially if they are 'strong' as a result of the weakness of others."[23] Gramsci's historicism is multifaceted rather than monolithic. It is Viconian, to the extent that Vico, in contrast to Hegel's monolithic historicism, envisions different nations undergoing comparable phases, *but* at different times.[24] Vico's model was compatible with Gramsci's project to understand the processes of history in the light of culturally specific factors. From Hegel to Gen-

[23] Quintin Hoare and Geoffrey Nowell-Smith, eds. and trans., *Antonio Gramsci: Selections from the Prison Notebooks* (New York: International Publishers, 1971), 256.

[24] In the introduction to *Leggere Vico: Scritti di Giorgio Tagliacozzo ed altri* (Milan: Spirali, 1982), Emanuele Riverso explains: "What counts here is that the cycles of history, while displaying uniform traits in the parallel stages of various nations, do not follow each other in a sequence that is the same for all of humankind. His historicism [storicismo] is thus not monophyletic, as Hegel's will be, but rather polyphyletic" (p. 24). I am linking Gramsci to Vico here, via Fernand Braudel, after having read Edmund Wilson, *To The Finland Station: A Study in the Writing and Acting of History* (London: Macmillan, 1972). Wilson discusses the connection between Vico and Jules Michelet, so that I wonder if it is possible to find a Viconian precedent, via Michelet, in Braudel's concept of long duration. In 1824, Michelet translated Vico's *The New Science* and promoted internationally an abridged version of this book.

tile, Vico's continuity lost a potential range of competing rhythms and narrowed into the singular and linear trajectory of a national identity. In Gramsci, by contrast, the duration of "viscous forces" of "regimes"—which we may want to translate into Fernand Braudel's "mentalities" impinges upon the unfolding of surface historical events, such as battles and treaties.

As extensive as allusions to the Macchiaioli's paintings in *Senso* may be,[25] Visconti rejected Blasetti's nationalism by relying upon an international répertoire of references. Alessandro Bencivenni lists several of them: "The music of Brückner mingles with Verdi's, citations from Heine echo the poetry of Foscolo, and pictorial references to Hayez, Fattori and to the Macchiaioli are found side by side with references to Feuerbach, Stevens and Durand."[26] Visconti's international focus is in tune with Gramsci's European perspective, namely his awareness that the Italian Risorgimento was not a revolution like that of the French in 1789. Furthermore, Visconti's international approach was due to postwar practices in film distribution. In 1954, *Senso* could break even with its expensive production costs by radiating on national history the glow of an international art film, for an international market, with an international cast.

Instead of historicizing the conflicts between classes and regions as Visconti does, Blasetti simply delights in the Macchiaioli's decorative effects. Blasetti's images are comparable to the Macchiaioli's paintings especially in terms of lighting. His reliance on chiaroscuro and on compositions with strong contrasts between black and white recalls Fattori's drawing style. As Annie-Paul Quinsac observes, "Fattori is a colorist; chiaroscuro and chromatism are unified in one concept. This happens in the masterpieces of Fattori, which are most often landscapes or studies of animals in a natural setting; they are based upon very strict contour and flat use of pure color, compactly defined in shapes."[27] Working before the advent of color film, Blasetti could depend only on black-and-white stock to dramatize the Sicilian landscape through the chiaroscuro lighting, only approximating the chromatism of the Macchiaioli.

[25] Raffaele Monti, *Les Macchiaioli et le cinéma: L'image du XIX siècle et la peinture des Macchiaioli dans le cinéma italien* (Paris: Éditions Vilo, 1979).

[26] Alessandro Bencivenni, *Visconti* (Florence: La Nuova Italia, 1982), 31.

[27] Annie-Paul Quinsac, *Ottocento Painting* (Columbia, S.C.: Columbia Museum of Art, 1972), 68.

In the literary paradigm of Abba, the colors of Sicily are the green of olives, the white of orange flowers, and the red of the Garibaldini's shirts. Of course, green, white and red are also the colors of the Italian flag. In Italy, orange flowers are used traditionally for weddings. In *1860*, these flowers might appear to allegorize the reunion of Carmelo returning from the north with Gesuzza waiting for him in the south. To expand the theme of unity from a regional to a national scale, the orange flowers are emblematic of the reunion between north and south achieved through Garibaldi's expedition.

Without color, Blasetti had to develop alternative solutions. Peasant women's black veils clash against the dazzling white of the walls. In a narrow alley, the dark shadow of a house cuts the frame diagonally, carving the space crossed by Carmelo on his way to the mainland. Here Blasetti's use of chiaroscuro is reminiscent of Vincenzo Cabianca's technique for *Ombre e Luci* (fig. 24).

As an exception to his nationalist use of domestic sources, Blasetti's close-ups of peasant faces and low angles of patriotic figures set against a blank sky refer to the sociorealist style of Alexander Dovzhenko in *Earth* (1930).[28] Whether about the Macchiaioli or So-

**24.** Vincenzo Cabianca, *Ombre e Luci*. Courtesy of Galleria d'Arte Moderna, Florence.

[28] Blasetti's rural epic *Sole* (Sun, 1929) comes to mind for its sociorealist style. Yet

viet cinema, Blasetti avoided definitive statements about the visual culture he utilized for the making of *1860*. He was proud and adamant about the realism of the film, as if its proto-neorealist orientation could efface its fascist genesis.

Blasetti's use of the low angle produces a different effect when employed in relation to heroic leaders than to populist representations of peasants. The extent to which *1860* anticipated neorealism becomes apparent through a contrast between the self-absorbed gaze of divas in silent melodramas and Gesuzza's anguished expression. Her look, after Carmelo's farewell, and her smile, upon his return, release a genuine freshness. The artificial overtones of Gesuzza's close-ups in low angle are counterbalanced by an acting style based on microscopic facial gestures. Blasetti's tilted camera angle establishes a dynamic relationship between Gesuzza's face and the blank sky, situating the peasant woman in an ideal, bigger-than-life space.

A shot of Colonel Carini from below has a similar static, inhuman quality. The colonel looks like an equestrian statue. Blasetti's low angle conveys the paternalistic, authoritarian attitude of the colonel toward Carmelo, whom he often calls *picciotto*, peasant boy, in Sicilian dialect. In contrast to Carini's, the low angle of Gesuzza's face signals a changing construction of character. Her face vibrates with the allegorical overtones of the Sicilian struggle, while she retains her humanity.

Colonel Carini and the two Sicilian shepherds exemplify the neoclassical-statuesque and the populist-picturesque sides of the fascist style. Neorealism grew out of this second stylistic register. During the involution of neorealism in the 1950s, when this style abandoned social denunciation for light-hearted comedy, it becomes apparent that these two registers differ only in scale and rate of movement. At the end of World War II, the dancers of the commedia dell'arte replaced the statues of opera. Yet, the neoclassical-statuesque orientation of Gallone's cinema and the populist-picturesque approach of neorealism partook of a common emphasis on the relation between figure and ground which the cinema inherited from Italian Renaissance painting.

---

the director maintains that at the time he was shooting *Sole*, he did not know Soviet cinema yet and that his first contacts with Soviet filmmaking took place at Cines, thanks to the Marxist critic Umberto Barbaro, between 1931 and 1932. On *Sole*, see Mancini, *Struggles of the Italian Film Industry*, 101–3.

Giuseppe De Santis was a neorealist filmmaker who continued to work at a time when this type of politically committed cinema had begun to wane. De Santis, in particular, was sensitive to the legacy of the Italian style of painting.[29] Like Blasetti's, De Santis' films combine operatic elements with local color. In *No Peace among the Olives* (Non c'è pace tra gli ulivi, 1949), De Santis tells the story of two shepherds who, like Manzoni's Renzo and Lucia, are persecuted by a local villain (figs. 25 and 26). Besides the allusion to Manzoni's realist, historical novel, De Santis used other literary references to depict rural life in the south and integrate the operatic with the realist mode.

*No Peace among the Olives* could be mistaken for a free cinematic adaptation of a short story à la Giovanni Verga, or à la Elio Vittorini, two Sicilian authors with whom realist language acquires an operatic resonance. In De Santis' *No Peace among the Olives* one can also detect muffled echoes of a hardly known "realist" and regional voice of Gabriele D'Annunzio in *Le Novelle della Pescara*.[30] The operatic pole of D'Annunzio's style by far overshadows his realist one. D'Annunzio is better known for his overwrought language, his decadent sensibility, and his "inimitable" way of living and loving. Like Giovanni Verga in *Mastro Don Gesualdo*[31] and Elio Vittorini in *Conversazione in Sicilia* (1941),[32] De Santis is a neorealist with operatic tastes. In *No Peace among the Olives*, the sheepskin of Raf Vallone and the black clothing of Lucia Bosè blend in with the dramatic music of Goffredo Petrassi, while the rough location witnesses a sweeping melodrama of passion and revenge.

Blasetti's *1860* is an historical film; De Santis' *No Peace among the Olives* is a melodrama. In *1860*, local lives outgrow the daily and the regional to the point that they coincide with the ideal trajectory of national history. In De Santis' film, social injustice loses

[29] On Giuseppe De Santis, see Mariella Furno and Renzo Renzi, eds., *Il neorealismo nel fascismo: Giuseppe De Santis e la critica cinematografica 1941–43*. Quaderni della Cineteca n. 5, Cineteca e Commissione Cinema del Comune di Bologna (Bologna: Edizioni della Tipografia Compositori, 1984).

[30] Gabriele D'Annunzio, *Le novelle della Pescara* (Milan: Fratelli Treves, 1925). I have not been able to locate an English translation.

[31] Giovanni Verga, *Mastro Don Gesualdo: A Novel*, trans. and intro. Giovanni Cecchetti (Berkeley: University of California Press, 1979). In Italian: *Mastro Don Gesualdo* (Milan: Fondazione Arnaldo e Alberto Mondadori, Il Saggiatore, 1979).

[32] Elio Vittorini, *Conversation in Sicily*, trans. Wilfred Davis (London: Drummond, 1984). In Italian: *Conversazione in Sicilia* (Manchester: Manchester University Press, 1978).

**25.** Raf Vallone as a peasant-statue in Giuseppe De Santis' *No Peace among the Olives* (1949). Courtesy of The Museum of Modern Art, Film Stills Archive.

**26.** Lucia Bosè as a peasant-statue in Giuseppe De Santis' *No Peace among the Olives* (1949). Courtesy of The Museum of Modern Art, Film Stills Archive.

its immediate historical connotations, while turning into a catastrophic force of nature. Just as the erotic excesses of the diva drive the male to destruction, with De Santis abuses of power linked to social classes unleash elemental forces in a regional setting. *1860* and *No Peace among the Olives* share a spectacular-allegorical style. Yet these two films differ in that Blasetti humanizes national history, while De Santis transfigures Sicilian life into a Manichean abstraction.

The domestic and foreign sources cited in *1860* create a narrative universe that is provincial and bound to its own past. Dovzhenko's sociorealism, after all, evokes a rural, timeless world, placed outside mainstream international history. The historical context of *1860* is a present of empty rhetoric. The dissonance between the province and the nation emerges briefly during the scene of Carini's admonition to Carmelo when the shepherd temporarily leaves his post as

he is eager to rejoin his wife. The colonel's remarks sound awkward
and unaware of contingent difficulties. The officer displays insen-
sitivity again when he dismisses a sentinel's grievance that he has
to stand duty with a broken, useless gun in his hands.

Blasetti's critique of military leaders, who are as self-absorbed as
divas, is limited to a few squibs that barely undermine Gentile's
blind faith in Fascist unity.[33] The obsession with tradition and un-
realistic ambitions for the future obscures problems of the present.
In *1860*, tradition comes to life through its literary, painterly, and
cinematic manifestations. Yet this exploration discloses a culture
that prefers to look behind, rather than to its fictional image in the
present. In the wake of Gentile's interpretation of the Risorgimento, Blasetti and Fascist cinema exploited national history to de-
flect the gaze of spectators away from the present and reorient it
toward an imaginary body politic, half-statue, half-human.

[33] This crucial exchange of lines in *1860* between Carini and the sentinel goes un-
recorded in the English subtitles of the Museum of Modern Art print. The MOMA
print does not have the fascist ending of the Italian version. The fascist ending is in
the print of the Cineteca Nazionale in Rome.

# FOUR

## The Risorgimento after World War II

### UNITY AND CONTINUITY IN THE RISORGIMENTO

In *Senso* (1954), Luchino Visconti teases out conflicts in the Italian identity due to class, region, and sexual differences. By staging a political betrayal and an adulterous relationship between a Venetian countess, Livia Serpieri (Alida Valli), and an Austrian officer, Franz Mahler (Farley Granger), Visconti shows the victory of private desire over patriotic duty. The discrepancy between a personal, illusory body erotic and a national, imaginary body politic emerges from the way in which Visconti weaves together the spectacular-allegorical styles of opera and neorealism. This weave of different styles, however, is not even between opera and neorealism. In *Senso*, opera prevails over neorealism, though Visconti looks at opera with irony. In fact, Visconti conducts a dialogue with the operatic culture of his aristocratic background the way a son would speak to his own father, with that mixture of respect and rebellion referred to as anxiety of influence.

In the footsteps of Antonio Gramsci, Visconti viewed the melodramatic tradition as the fathering principle of an overly positive view of the nineteenth century. By approving Giovanni Giolitti's leadership of the country born of the Risorgimento, in his *History of Italy from 1871 to 1915* Benedetto Croce had reinforced a specific interpretation of the nineteenth century. Croce viewed the Risorgimento as a phase of civic reawakening on a national scale. In contrast to Croce, for Gramsci the pure ideals of opera had obscured the political stakes and class interests of the movement toward unification. Furthermore, Croce's interpretation of the Risorgimento became a term of reference for the antifascist struggle during the years of the regime, and for the Christian-Democratic Party in the postwar period. From the Risorgimento to Croce's antifascism, the themes of national unity and historical continuity remained so strong that, after the end of World War II, they helped the Catholic establishment influence the popular perception of the history of the Resistance.

The protagonist of this post-Resistance version of the Risorgimento was Alcide De Gasperi (1881–1954), at the head of the Christian-Democratic Party. De Gasperi replaced Croce's lay, liberal values with a Catholic-populist view of the state. In consonance with the atmosphere of the Cold War, De Gasperi's goal was a coalition between the Catholic forces and other lay, democratic parties, including the Socialists. De Gasperi's main objective was to maintain opposition to the Communists. Significantly, the symbol of the Christian-Democrats was and is a cross drawn over a shield.

The Catholic forces were in power when Visconti set out to rethink the Risorgimento in the light of Gramsci's historiography and to reevaluate the Resistance on the basis of the Marxist thinker's controversial interpretation of the nineteenth century. *Senso* encountered governmental opposition and heavy censorship at the production stage, well before its première at the 1954 Venice Film Festival, the year of De Gasperi's death, and two years after Croce's death. In this respect, for Italian cinema, 1954, as much as 1968, was a year rich in historical implications. The release of *Senso* coincided with the exit from the political and intellectual scenes of the two guardians of antifascism, one lay and one Catholic. In the competition in Venice, *Senso* shared a similar fate to Federico Fellini's *La Strada* (1954); *Senso* was defeated by Renato Castellani's *Romeo and Juliet* (1954).[1] Such a defeat was all the more ironic

[1] Mira Liehm, *Passion and Defiance: Film in Italy from 1942 to the Present* (Berkeley: University of California Press, 1984), 345. *Senso* ranked 8th in box office receipts of the season in Italy. For more details on the reception of the film, see Elaine Mancini, *Luchino Visconti: A Guide to References and Resources* (Boston: G. K. Hall, 1986), 46. My analysis is based on the Italian print of *Senso* which I saw in the sum-

since the censors had purged *Senso* of its polemic stance, putting more weight on adultery and, thus, turning the film into a sinful version of Castellani's rather innocent "Romeo and Juliet."

Both *Senso* and *La Strada* stirred controversy as to the direction neorealism should take in the 1950s. Film debates in Italy are usually "political debates." In the wake of the Marshall Plan, an artificial economic prosperity glossed over urgent social problems in this decade. Meanwhile, the operatics of Raffaello Matarazzo's black telephone films replace the denunciation of social injustices typical of neorealist cinema to this point. Opera weighs over neorealism more and more. In *Umberto D* (1951), for example, Vittorio De Sica's neorealist style includes documentary, as well as expressionistic features. From the landlady's boudoir, the music of opera makes comedic microhistory recede into the isolation of Umberto's room where daily gestures must struggle to hold on to their dignity.

The Left, namely the Communist critic Guido Aristarco, attacked *La Strada*. Aristarco accused Fellini of clothing with spirituality and mysticism the rejects of society, instead of denouncing, in orthodox neorealist fashion, the social evils that fostered marginalization. In polemic with Aristarco, André Bazin supported Fellini's exploration of interiority. For the French critic, the soul was a landscape as documentable as Roberto Rossellini's Rome in *Open City* (1945), while Fellini's construction of character was an inside view as legitimate as Aldo Vergano's reliance on external physiognomy in *The Sun Rises Again* (1946).

Not only right-wing, but also left-wing critics endlessly struggled over *Senso*. In short, both camps were unable to reconcile Visconti's melodrama, set in the Risorgimento, with his previous neorealist films addressing contemporary issues. The controversy *Senso* provoked within the Marxist camp alone requires me to outline briefly the historicist tradition of the Italian Left, from the Resistance to the 1950s, from Palmiro Togliatti (1893–1964) to Enrico Berlinguer (1922–1984). At the end of World War II, the Communist Party of Palmiro Togliatti called for unity among democratic forces, in view of the formation of Gramsci's new national-popular culture. The

mer of 1983 in Venice during a festival about Venice on film. The American print of *Senso*, as well as the videotape, are reduced versions of the film. References to the Macchiaioli, for example, are missing. Unfortunately, the "Italian" *Senso* is no longer available for screening at the Cineteca Nazionale in Rome. I was told that this decision had been made to protect the color of the film.

unity of Marxist forces during the Resistance compensated for an old trauma: the division in 1921 between socialists and communists at the Congress of Livorno. Already in 1936, in a report on the Spanish civil war, Togliatti spoke of "gradualism," arguing for intermediate goals which would eventually lead to working class control, rather than proposing direct seizure of power. Togliatti hoped that the postwar democratic republic would create conditions favorable to the working class, that new institutions would emerge which would allow economic and social transformations favorable to the working class.

Togliatti's preference for reform over revolution inspired the Communist Party during the Resistance. In 1944, Togliatti announced the aims of his "new party"—thus forging a collaborationist policy aimed at countering the opposition of various conservative groups, based on his faith in a gradual assumption of power. The communists would work with other groups seeking to bring about progressive democratic government in Italy. The Party Congress officially endorsed Togliatti's strategy in 1945.

The Communist Party participated in the Committee of National Liberation, literally the brain of the Resistance, and in various coalition governments after the fall of Fascism. Togliatti served in a number of ministries and cabinets. The collaborationist policy, however, failed when the communists and the socialists lost the elections of April 18, 1948. The Catholic forces rallied behind Alcide De Gasperi and the Christian-Democratic Party gained the relative majority with 48.7 percent of the vote. Togliatti's "unified popular front" of communists and socialists obtained only 30.7 percent of the vote, with the communists taking the advantage over the socialists.[2] That very same year a neo-fascist attempt on Togliatti's life took place.

Until his death, in 1964, Togliatti continued to propose "gradualism" for communist control, seeking power from inside the sys-

---

[2] In *L'Italia di De Gasperi* (1945–54) (Florence: Le Monnier, 1982), Leo Valiani reports: "The elections held on the 18th of April saw the Christian Democrats win 48.7 percent of the vote, which gave them 306 of the 574 seats in the Chamber of Deputies, i.e., an absolute majority. The Front received only 30.7 percent of the popular vote, with the communists winning far more positions than the socialists. The Socialist Unity list of candidates, which combined Saragat's party with Silone's group, got 7.1 percent, the Republican Party 2.5 percent, the Liberal Party 3.8 percent, the monarchists 2.8 percent, while the neofascists of the MSI—the Italian Social Movement—received 2 percent" (p. 137).

tem rather than attacking it from a position of revolutionary opposition. He kept insisting that there were many different ways to achieve communism. Togliatti also advocated greater independence from Moscow for the Italian Communist Party, after the Stalin scandal. This orientation, called "polycentrism," looked convincing to Togliatti's successor in the 1970s, Enrico Berlinguer, who adjusted it to the times by formulating a plan for an "historical compromise" with the Christian-Democrat Aldo Moro (1916–1978).

In the popular film culture of the 1950s, Peppone (Gino Cervi) was the character who best embodied Togliatti's slogan for unity among the masses in the successful "Peppone and Don Camillo" comedies. Peppone is a naive Communist major of a rural village, while his antagonist, Don Camillo, is a shrewd Catholic priest, delightfully played by the French comedian Fernandel. Peppone and Don Camillo fight each other constantly, but cannot live apart. Their bond of love and hate, as inseparable antagonists in the political allegory of postwar Italy, rehashes the central dilemma in the historiography of the Resistance: the extent to which the "national" cooperation fostered by the Committee for National Liberation glossed over class identity. From popular comedy to the art film, Bernardo Bertolucci in *1900* (1975–1976) tackles the same historiographical dilemma. The political tensions between nation and class, bourgeoisie and peasantry, find a sexual correlative in the unconscious homoeroticism that bonds Alfredo and Olmo, two post-1968 allegorical versions of the positions held by Peppone and Don Camillo in the 1950s.

Bertolucci's *1900* appeared at the Venice Film Festival in 1976, at the peak of the debate on the "historical compromise." Alfredo Berlinghieri (Robert De Niro) is the son of a landowner; Olmo (Gérard Depardieu) is the bastard child of a peasant. As adults Alfredo and Olmo must be enemies, because they belong to different classes; as children they play together in the fields. Their life-long relation takes into account the difficulty of class difference, while it conveys a nostalgia for the national unity of the Resistance days. With the elections of 1976, the Italian Left became the strongest in Western Europe, securing 47 percent of the vote, with the Communist Party alone obtaining 34.4 percent.[3] In such a context, the "historical

[3] This percentage is from Giorgio Spini, *Disegno storico della civiltà*, vol. 3 (Rome: Edizioni Cremonese, 1984), 591. In 1976 the Christian-Democrats maintained the relative majority with 38.7 percent of the vote.

compromise" appears so imminent that we may concede that Bertolucci was alluding to Berlinguer through the name of the Berlinghieri family, and was forecasting that the Communists were about to occupy the seats of the majority for the very first time, traditionally the space for the *padrone*. Yet, the spread of terrorism and execution of Aldo Moro by the Red Brigade in 1978 prevented Berlinguer from carrying out Togliatti's dream of a gradual conquest of power.

Togliatti's stance built upon Gramsci's advocation of a national-popular culture. It is all the more interesting, therefore, that Visconti's turn to Gramsci and the Risorgimento in 1954 was not enough to pacify all left-wing critics. More specifically, the Left did not criticize Visconti's use of Gramsci, but rather the director's operatic style and revisitation of the past. Actually many critics, right- and left-wing alike, concurred that opera and history had been the main staples of fascist cinema which neorealism challenged with narratives set in the present and shot in a documentary mode. Finally, in 1954, Togliatti's Left may not have been quite ready to deal with the contradictory depiction of identity Visconti proposed in *Senso*. Especially in the female protagonist, the Countess Livia Serpieri, class, region, and gender clash and intertwine in a convoluted manner. Livia is an aristocrat who supports the patriots; a Venetian who betrays an Austrian by claiming her regional origin in the city of Trento, an Austrian stronghold; an aristocrat who falls in love with a modest officer; an Italian who brings about the death of an Austrian, while betraying her class and her city. I will argue that Visconti's project was to show, in true neorealist fashion, that structures of long duration linked to region and gender impinge upon a belief in the unitary nature of class and national identity.

Furthermore, in evaluating *Senso* in the 1950s, not all critics understood that the visual pictorialism and careful direction of acting in Visconti's *La Terra Trema* (1948), a film shot on location and with non-professionals speaking their regional dialect, was not incompatible with the ethnography of history Visconti undertook in *Senso*. For this melodrama, the director recruited hundreds of non-professional actors. The extras were young natives from the region of Trento. They played the Austrians in the battle of Custoza, and, in a sense, played their ancestors in the Risorgimento when Trento was under Austrian rule. Visconti personally tried on military uniforms, checking every glove, every gun, with the thoroughness of an anthropologist recreating a geographical environment.

By the mid-1950s, Italy was just recovering from the trauma of World War II. In the midst of the Cold War, the country lived through a phase of restoration. In 1951, Giulio Andreotti, the minister overseeing the film industry, censored Vittorio De Sica's *Umberto D.* Andreotti blamed the film for displaying a negative image of Italy to the world. *Senso* was thus born in a climate of Catholic conservatism. While Gramsci and Visconti sympathized with the Risorgimento of the republican Giuseppe Mazzini and of the democrat Carlo Cattaneo,[4] Alcide De Gasperi's role model in the nineteenth century was Vincenzo Gioberti. The Catholic patriot argued for a federation of Italian states under the benevolent eye of the pope. This is not surprising, for De Gasperi was continuing the work of Don Luigi Sturzo, a Catholic Sicilian priest who founded the Partito Popolare Italiano in 1915. In contrast to the lay, elitist, liberal tradition embodied by Benedetto Croce, before and after World War I, the Partito Popolare was an organization comparable to the socialist movement for its address to the masses.

Like Gramsci, Visconti viewed the Risorgimento as a failed popular revolution. The Piedmontese betrayal of the masses in the south was as condemnable as the one committed by Livia in *Senso*. With the money of Venetian patriots, she helps Franz bribe the military doctors and desert the battle of Custoza. Instead of a popular revolution, like the French in 1789, Gramsci argued that the Risorgimento was a war of expansion, from the industrial north to the rural south, led by the House of Savoy and masterminded by the politician Cavour (fig. 27).

In 1860, Cavour approved of Garibaldi's army, a sort of military avant-garde with volunteers from the democratic bourgeoisie and with enlightened aristocrats. Cavour, however, quickly sensed the revolutionary élan of this avant-garde and neutralized it in the interests of the Piedmontese aristocracy he represented. At Teano, in the south, Garibaldi surrendered the conquered lands and acknowledged Vittorio Emanuele II's authority with the memorable sentence: "I obey."

To purge *Senso* of its Gramscian orientation, the censorship board retailored the character of the Marquis Ussoni, Livia's patriotic cousin, to match Garibaldi's behavior at Teano. The censorship board also eliminated dialogue concerning the replacement of the

---

[4] Carlo Cattaneo (1801–69) played a key role in the insurrection of Milan in 1848. The democratic and cosmopolitan ideas of Carlo Cattaneo inspired Piero Gobetti, Carlo and Nello Rosselli, and the so-called "Action Party" during the Resistance.

**27.** Camillo Benso, count of Cavour (1810–1861). Author's Collection.

volunteer, democratic forces with the regular, Piedmontese army. The censors' cuts certainly obscured Visconti's historiographical stance and, indirectly, fostered even greater polemics and confusion among the critics on the problematic relationship of operatic style and neorealist ideology in *Senso*.

The cuts and changes in the script are so multitudinous and with such overlapping implications that it is necessary to quote Visconti at length:

> Other changes were made to my screenplay. The scene at the General Staff, in which Ussoni asks the captain to allow the volunteer forces to intervene, should never have been cut. The captain replied: "General La Marmora's orders are that you're to stay where you are. It's up to the regular troops to lead the battle." The result was a huge defeat. . . . The events in fact went as follows: Ussoni takes leave of the captain while, at the same moment, we hear the trumpets announcing the General's

arrival. Ussoni meets him in the courtyard but, instead of saluting, puts his cap back on . . . just like that! And that means something, don't you think? And then we see the captain filled with remorse running after Ussoni and telling him to "go through Valeggio in any case". He advises Ussoni to wear civilian clothing, since he doesn't want to see him get killed.[5]

Geoffrey Nowell-Smith confirms that Ussoni's Venetian patriots, "like Garibaldi himself, were a political embarrassment to the Cavour government, and like Garibaldi they were got out of the way."[6] To depict the mutual estrangement resulting from the gap between class identity and national ideal, popular masses and regular army, Visconti set a variety of peasant activities against the turmoil of men, animals, and carriages preceding the battle of Custoza (1866).

In the genre paintings of the Macchiaioli, Visconti found the regional physiognomies and local activities of the times. In *Senso* a group of villagers dry golden maize in the sun and a girl walks her geese along a country road. National history and daily routine, the army and the peasants, seem to cross paths only for the span of this sequence. Two butchers stand in front of slaughtered animals. This bloody sight is an apt metaphor for the useless death of Piedmontese soldiers. The steep human price of Custoza was sadly unnecessary. As Count Serpieri, Livia's husband, remarks, Austria will give up Venice to the House of Savoy, regardless of the military outcome of the Third War of Independence. Aware of the fact that his connections with the Austrian rulers are no longer valuable, Count Serpieri offers his cooperation to Ussoni, whose political beliefs he previously condemned or ignored.

Visconti wanted to show that the outcome of the Risorgimento had little to do with the ideal of national unity. It depended, instead, on shrewd political calculations, indifferent to the senseless sacrifice of human lives. It is no surprise that Visconti's project ran into the opposition of the censorship board. In comparison to the amount of screen-time reserved for Livia's affair with Franz, little footage remains about the backstage dynamics of the battle of Cus-

[5] Franca Faldini and Goffredo Fofi eds., *L'avventurosa storia del cinema italiano raccontata dai suoi protagonisti 1935–59* (Milan: Feltrinelli, 1979), 327.

[6] Geoffrey Nowell-Smith, *Luchino Visconti* (Garden City, N.Y.: Doubleday, 1968), 90–91. Other good monographs on Visconti are Alessandro Bencivenni, *Visconti* (Florence: La Nuova Italia, 1982) and Luciano De Giusti, *I film di Luchino Visconti* (Rome: Gremese Editore, 1985).

toza and Ussoni's journey across the firing lines. Like Garibaldi at Teano, on the wave of heroic aspirations suited for opera but not for life, the Marquis is caught in a process he cannot fully understand or affect. Ussoni's lack of historical vision matches Giuseppe Mazzini's failure to give the Risorgimento the national-popular dimension Antonio Gramsci valued so much (fig. 28). Visconti shows a confused Ussoni running along the lines of the defeated Italian troops, moving toward the future but in the opposite direction of the Italian soldiers' sad retreat.

Mazzini's "Action Party," Gramsci observed, relied on a paternalistic attitude toward the popular masses which it was, therefore, unable to bring in contact with the rest of the nation.[7] Likewise, Ussoni's leadership stops at the role of father-figure to the faithful

**28.** Giuseppe Mazzini (1805–1872). Author's Collection.

---

[7] Quintin Hoare and Geoffrey Nowell-Smith, eds., *Antonio Gramsci: Selections from the Prison Notebooks* (New York: International Publishers, 1971), 97.

messenger Luca, to the local peasants, and to other young, Venetian aristocrats with democratic ideas. On his way to the front, the marquis tries to bridge the gulf between north and south by paternally addressing a young Neapolitan soldier.

By adhering to a view of the Risorgimento where class and region are more important than nation, Visconti embraces an anti-Crocean stance. According to Gramsci, Croce was weary of the popular element latent in the Risorgimento. Croce's *History of Europe* begins in 1815 and his *History of Italy* in 1871, purposefully leaving out a full account of the French Revolution and of the Risorgimento.[8] This is not to say that Croce ignored the Risorgimento, but rather that he avoided a class analysis, while maintaining that Giolitti's Italy carried on the work of unification and the legacy of "liberty."

Popular knowledge of the Resistance of Crocean descent is based on an overly optimistic evaluation of the Risorgimento, a connection well-known to Roberto Battaglia, an historian linked to the Communist Party.[9] Battaglia reviewed a volume entitled *Il Secondo Risorgimento*, published under the auspices of the Italian government by the Istituto Poligrafico dello Stato in 1955, only one year after the release of Visconti's *Senso*. Battaglia writes:

> The fundamental thesis of the book, which seeks to make an "objective" evaluation of the Resistance movement, is that "the Resistance was the culmination and the highest expression of a libertarian tradition whose

[8] David Forgacs and Geoffrey Nowell-Smith, eds., *Antonio Gramsci: Selections from Cultural Writings*, trans. William Boelhower (Cambridge, Mass.: Harvard University Press, 1985), 216. A radical revolution, like the French of 1789, failed in Naples in 1799. Local intellectuals, Vincenzo Cuoco of Viconian background, for example, would have liked to see a new 1789 occur. Edmund E. Jacobitti explains: "The hostility of the people toward the revolution, Cuoco said, came from the fact that the 'common sense' of the people had beeen opposed to the 'reason' of the philosopher-revolutionaries. The revolution had been doomed because its leaders had failed to enlist the support of the masses, failed to provide them with a new 'common sense.' . . . The cornerstone of Cuoco's thesis rested on the idea of the 'two peoples,' the Catholic masses, or *sanfedisti*, and the intellectual élite. The former had been 'educated' by the Jesuits, the latter by the *philosophes* of France." "From Vico's Common Sense to Gramsci's Hegemony," in *Vico and Marx: Affinities and Contrasts*, ed. Giorgio Tagliacozzo (Atlantic Highlands, N.J.: Humanities Press, 1983), 373–74.

[9] On the link between the Risorgimento and the Resistance, the left-wing painter Renato Guttuso says: "The link between Garibaldi and the Resistance is very clear, indeed explicit. The star with Garibaldi's head was in fact the symbol of the Democratic Popular Front during the 1948 elections." Dario Durbè, intro., *Pittura garibaldina da Fattori a Guttuso* (Rome: De Luca Editore, 1982), x.

roots go back to the same *ideas that inspired* the Risorgimento. At the same time the Resistance has also been the point of departure for *a new and positive development* whose essential traits we can by now discern, despite the tremendous hardships of the postwar period."[10]

With *Senso*, Visconti does not argue as does Croce for a positive continuity between two different historical periods. The only way in which the Risorgimento and the Resistance, for Visconti, are comparable is to the extent that both are "failed" revolutions. The Resistance, thus, is a *ricorso* of the betrayal of the popular masses during the Risorgimento. Yet Visconti's evaluation of the Resistance in *Senso* is pessimistic, in contrast to the tone of Battaglia's review. Battaglia sees in 1945 "the point of departure for a new and positive development." In contrast to Visconti's retrospective pessimism, Battaglia's recuperation of the Resistance as a new Risorgimento is not a tribute to Croce, but rather indicates that the Communist historian is closer to Togliatti's optimistic gradualism than was the filmmaker.

Had the censors not intervened, Visconti's view of the Resistance as a *ricorso* of Gramsci's Risorgimento would have been a threat to the Christian-Democrats in power, but also too bitter for the Communist Party. In those days, Togliatti worried about the elections and appealed to voters on a national rather than a class scale, through the celebration of unity in the Resistance. In the meantime, the Left was not ready to develop a post-Gramscian critique of a theme of unity that had been woven into class and regional differences. After all, Italy in 1954 was recovering from 1945, and 1968 was still far away.

According to Geoffrey Nowell-Smith, *Senso* raises a double question: "Did the revolution that might have happened in 1943–47 fail in the same way and for the same reasons as that of 1860–70? Or did it also fail *because* the first one had failed, because the ruling class was allowed to establish a tradition of continuity, and *trasformismo* was allowed from the start to mask the conflicts that, objectively, seem to demand a revolutionary response?"[11] In *Senso*, the parallel between the Risorgimento and the Resistance produces an

---

[10] Roberto Battaglia, "La storiografia della resistenza, dalla memorialistica al saggio storico," *Il Movimento di Liberazione in Italia* 9, no. 57 (1959): 114. Emphasis is mine.

[11] Nowell-Smith, *Luchino Visconti*, 90.

historiographical allegory. The exclusion of Ussoni's Venetian patriots from the battlefield is comparable to the defeat of the democratic-popular front during the elections of 1948. Furthermore, in Visconti as in Gramsci, the historiographical allegory plays the Risorgimento off the genesis of Fascism. Thus Garibaldi's surrender of Sicily to the King of Piedmont sets an historical precedent for Giolitti's exploitation of the south to sustain an uneven industrial growth in the north, with painful consequences for the development of the nation as a whole.

For Gramsci and for Visconti, historical continuity does not intersect with the theme of national unity, but with the hegemony of a ruling class that practices the art of *trasformismo*. Like Count Serpieri, this class shifts its allegiances from Austria to Ussoni, or from the Fascist regime to the postwar Christian-Democrat relative majority (48.7 percent), as soon as the outcomes of the Third War of Independence and of the Resistance become clear.

Visconti's interpretation of the national past acquires a melodramatic coloring, because, as in an opera by Giuseppe Verdi, history from the Risorgimento to the Resistance moves along an ineluctable path, while its old dilemmas reoccur in completely new settings. For Visconti, however, this Viconian view of the historical process is applicable only at the level of class domination and to the theme of betrayed revolution, and not of national unity. We cannot help wondering whether we are witnessing a degeneration of Vico's law of the *corsi* and *ricorsi* to the level of *trasformismo* and resurfacing again all the more Hegelianized in an operatic context.[12] This does not mean that Visconti abandons Gramsci for Hegel, but that the "Hegelian" and linear Vico helps make explicit the fact that the ideals of opera drive forward the political expectations of the patriots. At the same time, since the Risorgimento did not fulfill the promise of its own successful teleology, Vico's cyclical view of the historical process survives to the extent that the patriots are caught

[12] *Trasformismo* means that the substitution of one *élite* for a different, but comparable one (for example from Cavour's and Giolitti's Risorgimento to De Gasperi's postwar Italy) has inhibited or delayed sweeping and long-term social change. Geoffrey Nowell-Smith writes: "There is an implicit parallel between the events of 1866 and those of 1943–45. In each case, by a mysterious process of *trasformismo*, the Italy which emerged from the upheaval was not substantially different from what it had been before. One *élite* replaced another, and the new *élite* came to look suspiciously similar to the old." *Luchino Visconti*, 90.

in the circularity that ties disillusionment to self-delusion and self-delusion to illusion.

## RISORGIMENTO AS MELODRAMA

Visconti turned to Gramsci not only for rewriting nineteenth-century history, but also for an overview of Italian culture. The opening of *Senso* takes place in the opera house of Venice, La Fenice. There, a performance of Giuseppe Verdi's *Il Trovatore* is taking place. In this sequence, Visconti alludes to Gramsci's insight that melodrama is the false consciousness of the Risorgimento. For Gramsci, Verdi's operas were so popular with the high and low classes that they were comparable to Eugène Sue's *feuilletons*.[13]

The music of melodrama was more successful than the written word of the novel because nineteenth-century Italy, Gramsci argued, was still wrestling with *la questione della lingua* in the guise of a high illiteracy rate. Furthermore, as the only type of national culture available to all classes, opera provided its audiences with "a whole range of 'artificial poses' "[14] and "an extraordinarily fascinating way of feeling and acting, a means of escaping what they consider low . . . in order to enter a more select sphere of great feelings and noble passions."[15] Like the cinema in the twentieth century, opera produced an imaginary, bigger-than-life term of identification whose failure to match historical reality is what Visconti exposes in *Senso*.

The narrative universe of melodrama is made of eternal values and pure ideals. The authentic feelings of melodrama are hardly possible in a modern world characterized by mediocre morals and ephemeral commitments. The sordid affair between Livia and Franz does not stand comparison with the noble feelings of Leonora and Manrico in *Il Trovatore*. Likewise, the Risorgimento falls short of the hopes of the popular classes, while the rhetoric of its historiography echoes the voice of a libretto.

By emphasizing music over the word, melodrama charges with pressure the elements of its mise-en-scène to express something

---

[13] For Gramsci on Manzoni, see Antonio Gramsci, *Letteratura e vita nazionale* (Rome: Editori Riuniti, 1971), 96; Forgacs and Nowell-Smith, *Antonio Gramsci: Selections*, 291–94.

[14] Forgacs and Nowell-Smith, *Antonio Gramsci: Selections*, 377.

[15] Ibid., 378.

hovering over the inexpressible. This ineffable dimension, in turn, is symptomatic of an originary fullness of meaning which the fragmentation of modern life cannot quite live up to. After absorbing the intense emotion of music, bigger-than-life gestures receive "a charge of meaning that we might suspect to be in excess of what it can literally support."[16] Pointing back to an original unity between intention and performance, referent and sign, the gestures of melodrama cannot appear but to be at odds with Visconti's divided body politic and mediocre body erotic. Peter Brooks observes that melodramatic gestures tend "toward a terminal wordlessness"[17] which defines melodrama as "the text of muteness: Gesture in all forms is a necessary complement and supplement to the word, tableau is a repeated device in the summary of meanings acted out, and the mute role is the virtuoso emblem of the possibilities of meaning engendered in the absence of the word."[18] The pressure to express turns into muteness, and the emotional movement of melodrama is channelled into a gesture as fixed as that of a statue.

In *Senso*, frequent references to memorable paintings[19] satisfy the penchant of melodrama for the tableau and augment the historicity of its mise-en-scène. But it is Visconti's use of color that especially fits Peter Brooks' insight into the muteness of melodrama. Private passions and public history, melodrama and historiography intersect in color.[20] Their meanings are in conflict, but overlap with such intensity that they need color, a mute or non-verbal element of the decor, to be adequately expressed.

The patriots' money is kept in a little chest. Its deep red color recalls the stage curtain at La Fenice and anticipates the blood of Custoza. The bright yellow of money evokes the beautiful stuccoes of the opera house and the decorations of the Austrian uniforms, while it prepares us for the rows of golden haystacks punctuating the battlefield, in alternation with lines of ant-like, black soldiers.

The tight scansion of red, gold, white, and black in the closed space of La Fenice acquires further relief from the contrast with the

---

[16] Peter Brooks, *The Melodramatic Imagination: Balzac, Henry James, Melodrama, and the Mode of Excess* (New York: Columbia University Press, 1985), 59.

[17] Ibid., 61.

[18] Ibid., 62.

[19] Ibid., 61.

[20] Responsible for the color in *Senso* were G. R. Aldo, Giuseppe Rotunno, and Robert Krasker. Aldo worked on the defeat at Custoza and on the Aldeno sequences; Krasker on La Fenice.

expanses of green fields surrounding the Palladian villa at Aldeno (Villa Valmarana). There the Serpieris retreat to avoid the heated political climate of Venice. The setting of the villa, however, is too Arcadian and the green tones of the meadows too painterly. We soon realize that the peacefulness surrounding Livia's recovery from her affair is not authentic. The fresh sheets, breathing in the sun, anticipate the return of Franz's sweeping white cape.

In the countryside and in Venice, contrasts of color point to the victory of the senses over ratiocination. The dark hallway of the Serpieri palace (Ca' Baglioni) swallows the pastels of the city: the salmon pink of the towers of the Arsenale and the grey-azure of the wet pavement. The marble floors of Livia's house repeat the color scheme of the theatre, a cradle of misleading sexual desires and political duties. Visconti's colors ring against the black-and-white grainy footage of Rossellini's neorealist cinema. In *Senso*, Visconti engages in a virtuoso, musical performance; with color, he orchestrates "the possibilities of meaning engendered in the absence of the word."

In the opening of *Senso*, historiographical and operatic levels powerfully converge. Throughout the film, the theatre is the referent of public history and of private passion. Luigi Chiarini argues that *Senso* fails as "cinema" because it is too theatrical. Chiarini does not perceive that, with Visconti, the spectacle of melodrama turns the spectacle of politics inside out.[21] Chiarini sees *Senso* (1954) as the betrayal of *La Terra Trema* (1948). On the contrary, since neorealism is a reaction against the operatics of fascist cinema, it is precisely neorealism that enables Visconti to undo the spectacle of politics with the spectacle of melodrama.

Put another way, Visconti does not reject neorealism for opera but rather incorporates the lesson of neorealism into his ironic approach to opera, and, by virtue of this irony, uses the ideals of opera to expose the ideals of the Risorgimento. Hence, Visconti's position in *Senso* is partly analogous to the situation of neorealist filmmakers. Just after the war, Rossellini, De Sica, and Visconti himself used fictions that had a newsreel flavor to challenge the illusions and escapism fostered by fascist cinema. With *Senso*, Visconti abandoned documentary for opera. If classic neorealist films such as

[21] For all these conflicting critical opinions, see Guido Aristarco, ed., *Antologia di Cinema Nuovo 1952–1958* (Florence: Guaraldi, 1975).

*Open City* (1945) and *Shoeshine* (1946) had a grain of melodrama in them, especially in their musical scores, with *Senso* opera still carries a grain of the oppositional force of neorealism. The ironic edge of Visconti's approach to opera, however, competes with the undeniable excess of this form the director is tempted to indulge in. Meanwhile, the polemics of the critics have increased the ambiguities of this complex text, while political debates have discouraged a close look at the images themselves.

Echoing Chiarini, the neorealist theorist Cesare Zavattini rejects *Senso*. With its historical setting, *Senso* is a betrayal of neorealism, a cinema attentive to the present. Visconti's operatic style clashes with Rossellini's and De Sica's documentary approach. In disagreement with Zavattini, Guido Aristarco passionately defends *Senso*. Aristarco argues that *Senso* represents an "evolution" of neorealism, not its "negation."[22] Aristarco concludes that Visconti's operatic style is comparable to Balzac's realist style. Aristarco's reference to Balzac is from Georg Lukács.[23] The parallel with Visconti is further justified by the fact that the French novelist also worked in a melodramatic milieu. Aristarco explains that the unmediated neorealist reportage of Rossellini would correspond to the realism of Gustave Flaubert. According to Lukács, Flaubert describes in a detached manner, instead of using narration to delve into the complexities of an era as does Balzac.

Aristarco's reference to Balzac is felicitous. Like Balzac, in constructing his major characters, Visconti moves beyond the one-dimensional allegorical embodiments of theatrical melodrama. Especially Livia and Franz, with Serpieri and Ussoni to a lesser extent, achieve a psychological complexity of novelistic status. With their ambivalent behavior, the two lovers embody the salient contradictions of the Risorgimento. Of course, in evaluating the characters, we also need to keep in mind how much the censors disfigured *Senso* and, therefore, hindered our grasp of individual motivation.

Aristarco's use of the observations of Lukács, however, does not apply to Visconti's minor characters. While their main features are

[22] Millicent Marcus discusses this view of Guido Aristarco in "Visconti's *Senso*: The Risorgimento According to Gramsci," *Italian Film in the Light of Neorealism* (Princeton, N.J.: Princeton University Press, 1986), 172.

[23] The two works by Georg Lukács Guido Aristarco uses for his defense of Visconti's *Senso* are *The Historical Novel*, trans. Hannah and Stanley Mitchell (Atlantic Highlands, N.J.: Humanities Press, 1974) and *Writer and Critic and Other Essays by Georg Lukács*, ed. and trans. Arthur D. Kahn (New York: Grosset and Dunlap, 1971).

strong, they do lack nuances. The bold outlines of these figures stem from a melodramatic rejection of interiority. At La Fenice, Livia listens to an Austrian noblewoman gossiping about Franz. The noblewoman's jewelry displays the power of the empire. Gossip moves across classes, and it is class envy that motivates Franz's landlady. In asking Livia to pay rent for Franz's room, the humble woman acquires the right to address the countess as if she were a prostitute. Unlike a prostitute who receives money from a man, the countess has to pay for her pleasures. Livia's maid, Laura (Rina Morelli), is a stock character. We are never surprised to see her taking care of her lady's secret wishes. Before Livia, Shakespeare's Juliet had had such an ally.

While it is certainly true that Aristarco did much to explain and promote *Senso*, his reference to Lukács, nevertheless, did not capture Visconti's ironic awareness that the Risorgimento *was* melodrama and that, in any case, his cinema cannot represent history as it actually occurred but only the past as opera. For Lukács, instead, the artistic text mirrors social reality and history is representable: "The historical novel therefore has to demonstrate by artistic means that historical circumstances and characters *existed in precisely such and such a way.*"[24] By contrast, for Visconti, since the screen is not a mirror reflecting the world as it is, life is theatre and theatre is life. *Senso*, then, is an "evolution" of neorealism, to use Aristarco's word, not so much in a Lukácsian sense, but in a modernist manner. With Visconti, the interplay between reality and appearance at the heart of the neorealist style escalates into the conflation of history with opera and opera with history. At the same time, history gives in to national passion, while private desire tries to contain history.

Visconti's camera dwells on the features of the stage at La Fenice. Pio Baldelli attributes this attention to detail to the attachment Visconti feels for opera, as well as to the irony with which he exposes its artificiality. Opera is "the father" Visconti loves but also wants to reject. Baldelli describes:

> The framing is static. Now we get a close-up of the carpets, the crudely made tables, the rough backdrops, now of the wings from which some workers, clad in overalls and beret, peep out to take a look around. Then we get a clear view of an assembly of soldiers, played by extras who jostle

[24] Lukács, *The Historical Novel*, 43. Emphasis is mine.

about like puppets. Then we see the actor framed by his shoulders who betrays his clumsiness as he unsheaths his sword, stamps his foot noisily on the tables at the front of the stage and then launches into the antiphon.[25]

Visconti breaks the spell of opera to highlight the role of Venetians as performers in history. Manrico's aria inspires bouquets of flowers with the national colors. Leaflets against the Austrians fly all over the theatre and the stage hands pick them up. Amidst the confusion, the workers leave the backstage area and join the protest under the chandeliers.

The converging of soldiers behind Manrico is not a spontaneous gathering, but follows artificial screen directions. This choreography depicts the Italian body politic achieving unity against a foreign oppressor. The actors' choreography on stage corresponds to the patriots' movements in the upper balconies. While passing subversive papers, men and women work in unison as if their hands and arms belonged to a single body. Yet this unified body politic is an ideal of national cooperation as fake as the angels the camera glides over in the stuccoes of La Fenice, and as short-lived as the passion between Livia and Franz.

By containing the stage with a high angle shot, Visconti shows how the point of view of the popular masses mirrors the opera below. This antinaturalistic, theatrical framing of the high angle occurs again during Franz's courtship of Livia. The high angle shot condemns Livia when she goes to the Austrian headquarters to look for Franz. The countess gives up her reserve, and stoops down to address some soldiers. In the Venetian ghetto, after walking all night, the high angle frames Livia and Franz near a well. They discuss a piece of broken mirror. Livia does not have the gift of self-knowledge. Franz enjoys looking at himself and turns Livia's expression into a mirror of his superego. While he knows his weaknesses, he draws reassurance from a woman's gaze and from the narcissistic contemplation of his own appearance.

Throughout the film, Livia's voice-over narration reveals a lack of introspection, an inability to analyze, and increasing confusion. The countess looks at herself in a mirror only once, at La Fenice, to ready herself for her suitor's arrival. At Aldeno, Franz's reflection

[25] Pio Baldelli, "La demistificazione della storia patria in *Senso,*" *Luchino Visconti* (Milan: Mazzotta, 1973), 132.

invades the mirror on Livia's table. By denying self-knowledge to Livia, Visconti reveals his efforts to expose the artificiality of the body politic, more than to explore the constructed nature of the body erotic. He has not come to terms with his own double standard, according to which Livia's indulgence in the senses leads to isolation and private madness, while Franz's search for pleasure allegorizes the end of an era on the stage of public history.

The high angle shot reinforces that opera is the pervasive referent of Italian culture, just as masculinity is the only term of identification available to Livia. This male bias is also relevant to the director's ironic method of criticizing more forcefully the exclusion of the masses from the Risorgimento. He appears, on the contrary, much less concerned with the marginalization of women from the historical process. At first, through the cousin Ussoni, Livia makes up for her lack of self-knowledge by identifying with a political passion. This route, however, does not gratify the senses. Later, not only is Livia's identity an emanation of Franz's narcissistic personality but her public role loses respectability. This is the price she pays for indulging in the life of the senses.

Franz helps Livia replace the identities of Italian patriot and married woman she has received from Ussoni and Serpieri. With Franz, Livia's new role is that of a lover, indifferent to politics. In an ironic twist, Livia's new self emerges from the portrait of Ussoni the countess herself paints for an Austrian noblewoman. To downplay the cousin's subversive activities, Livia declares that Ussoni is an idle aristocrat, a relative not interested in politics. Meanwhile, people gossip about an adulterous liaison between her and Ussoni. Livia is not just Ussoni's, but also Franz's alter ego. She releases his feminine side. Thus the battle of the sexes acquires a tinge of sexual ambiguity. Franz's military uniform looks too elegant for a man of war, as if the spectacle of fashion is about to undermine the Austrian military reputation.

The tension between femininity and masculinity subtends the iconography of the opening sequence. Bouquets of flowers are held together by red, white, and green ribbons, the national colors. Politics adopt a lady's emblem. The feminine side of Franz becomes apparent when he dwells on the texture of sounds in the room where he meets with Livia; or when, at Aldeno, he comments on the perfume of the ripe harvest. There he also lingers voyeuristically in front of Livia's closet, crowded with gowns as beautiful as the art works decorating the villa. Sound is the form of seduction most closely associated with Franz, whose charm Livia experiences at the opera and whose laughter accompanies her across the deserted alleys of Venice.

In the opera house, Franz and Livia engage in a duet that sets them apart from both the Austrian and the Italian camps. Their isolation underscores the marginality that ties together in every good melodrama the woman with the womanizer. Their common plan is to live a few verses by Heine which Franz recites to Livia: " 'Tis the Judgement Day / The Dead rise to eternal joy, or to eternal pain. / We still embrace, heedless of all, both Paradise and Hell." As exclusive as their affair may be, it follows the events on the stage. In her box, Livia worries about saving Ussoni. Like a reincarnation of the Renaissance "patriot" Ettore Fieramosca, the proud cousin rebukes the Austrians' offensive statement that Italians play the mandolin all day long, and challenges Franz Mahler to a duel. While Livia flirts with Franz to help Ussoni, on stage Leonora offers to the Count of Luna her "fredda, esamine spoglia," to rescue the Trovatore.

*Senso*'s opening sequence presents the irony Visconti uses to rewrite the history of the Risorgimento and to show the frailty of the ideals of melodrama. Visconti's relation to Italian history and melodrama is ambivalent. The director knows that the nineteenth-century aristocratic culture of his class is unable to confront the needs of the popular masses Gramsci is concerned with. On the other hand, Visconti must acknowledge the authority of the past. His intellectual and family roots reach back into the world of melodrama, whose taste and objects, colors and sounds he carefully reconstructs and relentlessly stages. It is well known that Visconti came from a prestigious family: the Visconti of Modrone in Milan. His mother avidly attended the opera at La Scala and his father was a member of that upper-bourgeois, aristocratic oligarchy that led Giolitti's Italy into the twentieth century after the Risorgimento.

Visconti's characters, however, are unable to live up to the heroic standards of melodrama. A comparable inadequacy haunts the director. Visconti's obsessive historicism is symptomatic of an inability to overcome the legacy of the past. Furthermore, Visconti's historicism greatly differs from Croce's. Visconti does not depict history as a promising trajectory aimed at the lofty ideal of "liberty," but as an ill-repaired road full of crevices marked by the discrepancies between the lovers' behavior and the ancient courtly code, as by gaps between public and private identity.[26] As if they were living a degraded version of the tragedy *Romeo and Juliet*, Franz and Livia enjoy their passion only for brief spans of time. At Aldeno, Livia wakes her lover with an alba, an announcement of the arrival of dawn, in the best tradition of medieval poetry. But the referent of this romantic scene is much lower than the operatic stage and, in a sense, erodes, from behind, the myth of Heine's pure love, "beyond history and war." Visconti positioned his actors according to a "Shakespearean" postcard he received from his scriptwriter, Suso Cecchi D'Amico (fig. 29).

Visconti's project of undoing melodrama, of pitching theatrical illusion against historical reality, is operative at the level of decor and narrative development. Doubts spoil Livia's patriotic commitment and she abandons Ussoni for Franz. Like Livia's passion, the Venetians' yearning for "liberty" is a sincere feeling but one represented as unable to foster an analysis of circumstances. Visconti helps us draw a comparison between political ideals and erotic goals when Livia and one of Ussoni's fellow patriots stand next to the statue of an angel holding up a symbolic flame. The flame of politics can burn only in the theatre, while, in the hallway of the Serpieri palace, the flame of Eros is already taking over and obfuscating historical vision.

A center for the diffusion of two traditionally hegemonic arts, opera and the commedia dell'arte, Venice is the perfect and unforgettable stage of Livia's and Franz's affair. In Visconti's *Death in Venice* (1971), a mountebank, with a face that looks like a mask of the commedia, greets the musician Gustav von Aschenbach upon his arrival at the dock of the Lido (figs. 30 and 31). The comedian's heavily made-up, vulgar features become an haunting omen for the artist. Von Aschenbach is torn between the pure, eternal ideals of high art and an increasing awareness of temporality and of the senses. What is ironic, here, is that the musician's attraction to a beautiful young boy becomes a metaphor of the artist's longing for an aesthetic ideal. In other words, eros may replace art, but, as mere figments of his imagination, love and beauty continue to obsess and elude Von Aschenbach until his death.

In *Senso*, the city of Venice becomes a character who witnesses

---

[26] Marcus, "Visconti's *Senso*," 176–77.

**29.** Livia and Franz as Juliet and Romeo in Luchino Visconti's *Senso*
(1954). Courtesy of The Museum of Modern Art, Film Stills Archive.

**30.** The commedia dell'arte in Luchino Visconti's *Death in Venice* (1971). Courtesy of The Museum of Modern Art, Film Stills Archive.

the degradation of pure love into an erotic liaison. The reverberations of the water in the canals tell us that adultery, rather than romance, is taking place in the putrid alleys. Chiaroscuro engulfs Livia and Franz during a long, nocturnal walk, interrupted only by the echo of their footsteps. Like a spell, chiaroscuro binds them again when the light dances on the walls of Livia's bedroom. At Aldeno, the countess reminds her lover that they are not in Venice any longer. Nevertheless, after this duet, Livia agrees to hide the officer. Venice is not just a silent accomplice, but also a condemning judge. In the ghetto, series of dark windows underline the theatricality of the affair. Like huge eyes, the windows subject private feelings to public scrutiny. This turning of passions into spectacle begins to increase our awareness that, in a theatrical city like Venice, what we consider private is always public, that the body erotic is a construct as social as the body politic.

Anton Brückner's Symphony No. 7 in E Major conveys the im

**31.** The commedia dell'arte in Federico Fellini's *Roma* (1972). Courtesy of The Museum of Modern Art, Film Stills Archive.

pulsiveness of Livia's betrayal. The heavy progression of Brückner's music also informs us that the end of the Austro-Hungarian Empire is approaching. The theatricality of Brückner's music corresponds to the transformation of daily objects into stage-like paraphernalia. The heavy, white curtains of Livia's windows and the transparent, white veils hanging over her bed rhyme with the red stage curtain of La Fenice. The stage curtain, a metonomy of the theatre as a public arena, frames the most private corner of Livia's boudoir. When she runs toward a room, as yellow as gold, Livia's betrayal sets in motion a sequence of doors opening onto other open doors. The breaking of barriers between different rooms proves the fragility of the boundary between the passions of melodrama and the passions of life and how easily opera can replace history. Furthermore, the frescoes in the villa depict ideal, mythological landscapes, while Visconti's countryside evokes an ancient painterly tradition that runs from the Renaissance to the Macchiaioli. The exterior landscape is as beautiful, and artificial, as the countryside painted on the walls.

With this confusion between inside and outside, artificial and natural, behavior can be seen as ambivalent and deceptive. When Franz plants the seed of betrayal in Livia's mind, he stands against a fresco depicting two men of different ages. With his arm pointing toward the right, the older man is partly covered by a curtain as heavy as Franz's white cape. In front of this half-hidden figure, a younger man, echoing Franz's figure, stands in front of the curtain. His left arm moves away from the older man behind him. The contradictory direction of the two men's arms ironically underscores Franz's duplicity.

Peter Brooks reminds us that "melodrama requires ... clearly identified antagonists"[27] and boldly sketched polarities. With Visconti, drastic parallels in the guise of narrative reversals make clear how fragile the lovers' illusions about themselves are, and why the patriots cannot perceive their own predicament. Visconti divides *Senso* into four episodes: La Fenice, Venice, Aldeno, and Custoza, echoing the division into four acts of Verdi's *Il Trovatore*. The progression by tableau is in line with the non-verbal orientation of melodrama. Atmospheres prevail over causal links, while emotions rule over logic; music and color rise over the word.

Verdi was the primary source of *Senso*. Visconti's secondary source was a novella by Camillo Boito, a minor writer whose text became a sort of "libretto" in the hands of the talented scriptwriter Suso Cecchi D'Amico, the daughter of Emilio Cecchi, the art historian we have previously encountered at the side of Blasetti during the shooting of *1860*. In regard to the characterization of Franz and Livia, however, Visconti does not rely on a humble libretto; here, high literature prevails over opera. Visconti explains that Stendhal's Sanseverina was the basis for Livia's character.[28] Indeed, *The Charterhouse of Parma* (1839) is an appropriate source to understand why Livia's character has a complexity more novelistic than melodramatic. Unfortunately, Visconti, to my knowledge, did not offer a literary source for Franz, who in any case is a much more complicated figure than Boito's Remigio.

The narrative parallels from tableau to tableau, from the splendor

---

[27] Brooks, *The Melodramatic Imagination*, 17.

[28] On Visconti's interview with *Cahiers du Cinéma*, see Gianni Rondolino, *Luchino Visconti* (Turin: Utet, 1981), 314.

of La Fenice to the horror of Custoza, are powerful reminders that irony is the method the director has utilized. His relation to opera and to the historical culture he questions from the inside is based on a mixture of attraction and rejection. One of the most blatant examples of this reversal is the parallel between Ussoni's stubborn journey across the firing lines and Livia's perilous departure for Verona.

Ussoni's historical blindness and political impotence corresponds to Livia's underestimation of the physical dangers and emotional disillusionments that this untimely trip will have in store. In Verona, the gaudy reds of Franz's apartment, and the walls cluttered with kitsch paintings, stand in sharp contrast to the pristine, neo-classical lines and gold stuccoes of the Austrian headquarters. After surprising Franz with a young prostitute and confronting her identity as an aging, lonely woman, Livia betrays her lover. She turns her betrayal into the political duty of a native of Trento, which, like Venice, was subject to Austrian rule. Thus, she exploits a regional affiliation to overthrow on a personal level her previous betrayal of the national cause.

## THE BODY POLITIC AND BODY EROTIC: THE BATTLE OF THE SEXES AND THE OEDIPAL PLOT

The controversy over the title of Visconti's film is long and indicative of the conservative climate in the 1950s. Visconti recalls, "Initially I had given *Senso* a historical orientation. I had even wanted to call it *Custoza*, but this idea was met with howls of protest from Lux, the minister and the censors. . . . (When we began working on the film they didn't even like the title *Senso*: during the shooting the sign on the clapsticks read *Uragano d'Estate*, 'Summer Hurricane.')"[29] The final choice of *Senso* over *Custoza* was meant to shift attention away from public history to private melodrama, from the body politic to the body erotic, from class and regional identity to the senses, from the betrayal of a political cause to a battle of the sexes (figs. 32a and b). For the censors, the substitution of *Senso* for *Custoza* diminished the Gramscian interpretation of the Risorgimento.

The final settlement on *Senso* as a title was still in line with the

[29] Faldini and Fofi, *L'avventurosa storia*, 326.

**32a.** Aldo Fabrizi as Don Pietro between the body erotic and the corpus mysticum in Roberto Rossellini's *Open City* (1945). Courtesy of The Museum of Modern Art, Film Stills Archive.

sexual politics of melodrama, where public issues feed a personal realm, as if the sexual passion of the diva were swallowing into her orbit the male lover and national history. Eager to meet Franz, Livia confuses politics with eros when she runs to Ussoni's secret address. Serpieri, too, mixes eros with politics when he thinks Livia is using the alibi of a lover to hide her militancy. This misunderstanding between husband and wife is a correlative, in the private sphere, of political *trasformismo*. The count sells his services to the patriots in exchange for protection. While Livia is swept away by passion, Serpieri, too, flows with the tide of history, and shifts from the old to the new order.

The body politic merges with the body erotic during the lovers' nocturnal walk across Venice. They stumble over the corpse of an Austrian soldier. For Geoffrey Nowell-Smith, this accident restores "a sense of real historical context to the scene."[30] Yet Franz, the

---

[30] Nowell-Smith, *Luchino Visconti*, 84.

**32b.** Don Pietro turns the body erotic and the corpus mysticum away from each other. Courtesy of The Museum of Modern Art, Film Stills Archive.

womanizer, removes himself from history because he foresees the end of Austria all too clearly. He joins Livia in an existence outside history, rooted only in the pleasures of the body. This is why Franz rushes to empty the accident of "its political significance," and "offers a strictly erotic interpretation of the problems of the occupying forces."[31]

The substitution of *Senso* for *Custoza* repeats the trajectory from public to private, from the political to the erotic, which is set in motion by Livia's passion for Franz and by the destructive sexuality of the diva in the melodramas of the silent period. Livia, in Verona, is the agent of Franz's destruction, as well as her own. Franz, in turn, seduces Livia through the same promise of escape that the diva, the destroyer of aristocrats, embodies for a petty-bourgeois male spectator envious of the aristocracy. The diva was linked to a struggle among social classes in Giolitti's Italy, for she would often seduce a wealthy nobleman and lead him into bankruptcy. Franz

[31] Marcus, "Visconti's *Senso*," 175.

releases Livia from political unfulfillment by alluring her with the promise of sexual pleasure. And, as the destroyer of wealthy men, the diva is an outlet for lower-middle class viewers who feel that the privileges of the upper classes exclude them from social advancement. So Franz is a sort of diva in reverse, for he leads Livia into political betrayal instead of financial ruin.

With her erotic excess, the diva threatens the established order. And Livia, with her betrayal of the patriots in the name of sexual passion, does challenge the financial power linked to the aristocratic name of her cousin. As a troublesome embodiment of sexual difference and a haunting reminder of castration, Visconti's diva is the negative figment of a male imagination, a destructive alter ego of male authority in the economic and sexual realms. Perhaps for this reason it appears that Livia has no life of her own, her identity linked to either Serpieri's or Ussoni's name. Hence, to reverse the symmetry of the battle of the sexes to expose the diva as a construction, it becomes apparent that the destructiveness of the diva is not a woman's fault, but a man's problem for which a woman is blamed.

Once she realizes that Franz is no gallant suitor, but an emasculated deserter wearing a red robe and drinking wine, Livia resorts to the most powerful father figure at hand. By ordering Franz's execution, the Austrian general punishes a soldier who is a transgressive son and a male weakened by womanizing. Franz's death sanctions the reestablishment of a heterosexual, patriarchal order that Livia's diva-like excessive sexuality had begun to upset. Livia's first betrayal is against Ussoni, her role model, both father figure and love interest. Livia's second betrayal fulfills her Electra complex which the shift from the Italian marquis to the Austrian officer had interrupted. Yet, in both betrayals, sexual passion stands out as a stronger motive than patriotic duty.

The choice of *Senso* for the final title indicates that history interlocks with private life, while the body erotic breaks through the body politic. With Livia as the diva and Franz as the womanizer, in the end sexual passion prevails over class, region, and nation. As a result of the Gramscian orientation of the film, however, class and region, in turn, win over the national dimension sought by Croce's interpretation of the Risorgimento. By showing how contradictory and overlapping the interaction of all these realms is, however, Visconti disrupts Gramsci's belief in the unitary nature of class and regional identity.

What is most ironic is that all the efforts of the censors to make the private sphere prevail over the public do not neutralize the political impact of the film, because, paradoxically, the censors' choice of adultery over history, points at the fact that Visconti, through Gramsci, handles class and region much better than gender. By not engaging in a critique of the diva as a male construction, Visconti underlines the artificiality of the body politic over that of the body erotic. As a result of this imbalance or, better, despite this leaning toward the body politic at the expense of the erotic, the excess of Visconti's operatic style still outdoes his ironic method. It is as if irony had succeeded in shedding light on the patriots' political illusions. Meanwhile, we begin to suspect that the Gramscian reading of the Risorgimento has greater explanatory power in regard to class and region, but is not equally suited to deal with the representation of sexual difference.

Livia and Franz embody, in a Lukácsian sense, the salient contradictions of their age. Furthermore, the woman and the womanizer are at odds with the norms regulating social identity and sexual behavior in their respective worlds. For Visconti, the marginalization of both characters stems from the tension between the body erotic and the body politic, the illusions of the senses taking over the illusions of the Risorgimento. Even though Franz has a latent, feminine side, he controls the narrative. *Senso* leans toward masculinity because this pole is Livia's only term of reference and the privileged site of authorial inscription. Serpieri is the past and the father Visconti, an aristocrat, like Livia, is eager to kill, or at least betray through Livia's betrayal, in order to acquire a new class identity. Yet, the struggle against the father and the past leaves the director with two unsatisfactory alternatives or marginal positions: a democratic, but ineffective impulse à la Ussoni or a decadent attachment to a dying world à la Franz.

Ussoni and Franz, the two men of Visconti's political dilemma, take us back to the fresco at Aldeno with two male figures of different ages standing behind Franz. To say that Visconti's approach to opera is ironic does not mean that *Senso* is a Brechtian critique of nineteenth-century subjectivity, nor that *Senso* relies on counterpoint and disjunction to the point of neutralizing what is, instead, an undeniable indulgence in operatic excess. Yet, the emphasis on the discrepancy between history and melodrama, and the play with the confusion between these two spheres, signals that Visconti is more inclined than Gramsci to conceptualize a split and contradictory self. And yet the director's stereotypical handling of Livia as a woman blinded by passion tells us that he is not quite able to articulate eloquently the splits and contradictions of subjectivity at the level of sexual difference.

The narrative of *Senso* follows an Oedipal pattern, in the sense that in Visconti's film, as in the ancient tale of Oedipus, it is the man and not the woman who rebels against the past, kills the father, progresses in time across the land, and makes history and culture. Franz does not "make" history because he deserts Custoza, but, in the released version of the film, he alone comments on the sunset of the Austro-Hungarian Empire. Originally, Visconti's project was to reverse the movement from macrohistory to microhistory, from public to private, typical of the nineteenth-century historical novel. The director would have liked to have an anonymous young Austrian soldier, as a collective voice, denouncing the senselessness of war and answering the "Viva Verdi" of the opening sequence with "Viva l'Austria" in the final scene. The Italian authorities found this project intolerable. They preferred a grand, patriotic finale. In the released version of *Senso*, Franz declares that the Austrians' victory at Custoza is ephemeral. With his monologue, Franz evaluates the failure of the national culture he lives in and the limits of his class identity. For Visconti, the "progress" embodied by Ussoni is as blind and erratic as Livia's passion for Franz. Lack of historical vision inhibits the involvement of the masses in the Risorgimento, and yet, despite all these obstacles, their participation in history is as unavoidable as Franz's death. It is not surprising if Visconti's historicism, here, takes on a slightly ineluctable ring. This is no allusion to the "Hegelian" Vico, but rather a sort of acknowledgment that Gramsci's national-popular culture will one day be born, no matter how many obstacles inhibit its development.

Unlike Serpieri or Ussoni, Franz understands that the world of the aristocracy, whether Austrian or Italian, is slowly coming to an end. On the way to Aldeno, the packing of the Serpieris' belongings looks more like the definitive dismantling of a life style and less like a temporary move to the countryside. In speaking the last word, Franz mercilessly removes the black veil that covers Livia's fatigued face after the journey. Livia's veil is comparable to one, final stage curtain. Its lifting blocks the possibility of any more confusion between theatre and life. The revelation of Franz's debauchery has a devastating impact on Livia. The body erotic crumbles in front of her eyes, while Franz describes the end of the Austrian body politic. Running delirious in the dark streets of Verona, the countess goes mad, while Franz dies.

All the men in Livia's life are off stage now. Ussoni is not a leader of the Risorgimento any longer, for the democratic forces will play only a subordinate role in Giolitti's Italy. Count Serpieri might still win a seat in the senate of the newly born nation, but his world of class privilege and ancient codes has come to an end. Franz falls in front of the firing squad. It is significant that Livia acquires a pathological identity as soon as she cannot be the female alter ego of any male character. This suggests that while Visconti powerfully represents the end of an epoch, he is at a loss in dealing with the fate of his female heroine. Throughout the film, Livia doubts her own ability to play a role in the historical process, even though her betrayal of the patriots severely damages Ussoni's cause. And now that the battle of Custoza is over, Livia appears to be all the more outside history, engulfed in a melodrama so personal that it degenerates into madness.

Unable to achieve self-knowledge, Livia becomes insane. But Livia's madness is a symptom of that which remains unresolved in the film. Under Visconti's powerful representation of the Risorgimento in the light of Gramsci's interpretation lurks the uneasiness with sexuality typical of Catholic culture. It is this uneasiness that seems to haunt Visconti, who is much more eloquent about history and the body politic than about femininity and the body erotic. An attempt to overcome this limitation perhaps can be seen in Franz's *finis Austriae*, were we to read this monologue as a sort of mea culpa delivered by Visconti himself. An aristocrat, by birth, and a Marxist, by intellectual development, Visconti also lives in a culture where Catholicism colors most values far beyond religious practice. Furthermore, Visconti's situation was complicated by the fact that, in addition to the Catholic church, the Communist Party was hostile to homosexuality. In 1949, for example, Pier Paolo Pasolini, who was an active member of a communist youth organization in Friuli, was expelled because of his sexual orientation. Five years later, nobody but Visconti, a Marxist, an aristocrat, and a homosexual, could have brought together in such a daring way opera, Gramsci, the body politic, and the body erotic, not to mention the labyrinth of class, regional, and sexual identities inhabiting Livia, an aristocrat, a patriot, and a wanton woman.

As a character with both weaknesses and insights, Franz offers Visconti some relief from class guilt. The aristocracy may die, but it is still capable of analyzing in public the historical circumstances of its end. Livia, instead, becomes Visconti's site of shame at the level of his private class and sexual identities. In Venice, with Franz's landlady and with Austrian soldiers, underneath the windows of the ghetto, and at the Arsenale, Livia gives spectacle to her passion. She prefigures Franz's prostitute in Verona. Without ratiocination and too absorbed in the body, Livia, then, embodies that private self of Visconti the Catholic church and the Communist Party would not approve of. Living in a culture where Catholicism is pervasive, despite his Marxist allegiance, the director has, all the same, interiorized the double configuration of the *corpus mysticum* which is that of the Christ-King's two bodies. And he has done so to such a degree that he plays out his dilemmas of social class and sexual background, political conviction, and aesthetic attachments through a pairing of characters rather than through Livia or Franz individually. The pair of Ussoni and Franz embodies the public side, while the pair of Franz and Livia stands for the private side of the "two men" identity Visconti shares with the fresco at Aldeno and, I would add, with Kantorowicz's medieval ruler.

During the Catholic restoration of the 1950s, and in the midst of Togliatti's gradualistic approach, it is not surprising if the Marxist Visconti found it difficult to live with, and necessary to castigate, his aristocratic and homosexual sides, unfortunately at the expense of Livia. Franz may have the last word on public history, but it is Livia who is the key to the director's private, conflicting identity, and, potentially, the most revolutionary character in the whole film. Visconti admits, "Even the idea of *Senso* comes from an image: I had this constant vision of a woman dressed in black who endures the insults of her lover with her face moist from too much weeping."[32] Regardless of its Marxist orientation, the sexual politics of *Senso* thrive on a Catholic mixture of guilt and shame which

[32] Adelio Ferrero, ed., *Visconti: Il cinema* (Modena: Ufficio del Cinema del Comune di Modena, 1977), 59.

Matarazzo's black telephone films crystallized. Of course, with Visconti, sexual passion is a much more contradictory and less stable entity than with Matarazzo. In *Senso*, the ambiguity of the male villain and the pathology assigned by the director to the female protagonist raise strong doubts about the unity of the self. Finally, the charged muteness of melodrama can be seen as a metaphor for the repression of female sexuality and of male homosexuality under a homosocial cover. With Visconti, operatic excess is not the residue of a unified, illusory subjectivity, but a form of irony in disguise, a discourse that speaks of controversial and difficult things through the intensified silence of color.

# FIVE

## The Risorgimento after May 1968

### UNITY, CONTINUITY, AND UTOPIA

IN CONTRAST to Rossellini's anti-operatic style and Crocean stance, with *Senso* Visconti brought Gramsci to the cinema and returned to opera. Born from a phase of involution within neorealism, *Senso* anticipates the composite style of recent Italian cinema. Visconti invokes the legacy of fascist cinema with his operatic style. Yet, in line with a neorealist interest in structures of long duration, Visconti shows that sexual passion destabilizes political identity. It is as if the body erotic were driving a wedge into history, thus exposing the artificiality of the body politic summoned by opera and by the popular knowledge of the Risorgimento of Crocean descent. What remains in the darkness, however, is that the body erotic of *Senso* is a construction that surrenders to a heterosexual, homosocial bias.

In April 1955, *Cinema Nuovo*, under the direction of Guido Aristarco, printed a letter in support of Visconti's controversial *Senso*, written by a young cinéphile, Vittorio Taviani.[1] Twenty years later, with his brother Paolo, Vittorio directed *Allonsanfan* (1973–1974). In terms of narrative structure, color, and music, *Senso* is the Tavianis' stylistic term of reference. The French-sounding title of the film indicates that the aftermath of May 1968 is the context inflecting the Ta-

---

[1] Vittorio Taviani, "Tre Giudizi su *Senso*," in Guido Aristarco, ed., *Antologia di Cinema Nuovo 1952–1958* (Florence: Guaraldi, 1975), 881–82.

vianis' view of the Risorgimento and their conceptualization of history.

While the spectacular visuals of *Allonsanfan* are easily comparable with *Senso*, the historiographical allegory is quite intricate and difficult to unlock for a viewer unfamiliar with Italian politics in the 1970s and without a few, memorable names, dates, and episodes of the Risorgimento. *Allonsanfan* is about the struggle of the "Jacobin" aristocrat Fulvio Imbriani (Marcello Mastroianni) to detach himself from the subversive, secret society of the Sublime Brethren and to return to the comforts of his family, his violin, and his child, Massimiliano. Fulvio betrays and simulates at the expense of Massimiliano's mother, the Hungarian radical Charlotte (Lea Massari), his "brother" in politics, Lionello, and his lover, Francesca (Mimsy Farmer).

Drugged and unwilling, Fulvio finds himself on a boat sailing toward Sicily. Just like a group of radical students, with no weapons and armed only with abstract, revolutionary theories, the Sublime Brethren, led by Tito and, supposedly, by Fulvio, plan to incite the peasants to revolt against the Bourbons.

The arrival of the brethren coincides with a moment of extreme tension on the island. The local population has been angered by the spread of plague and has already assaulted the village bakery. In one, final gesture of betrayal, Fulvio turns to the local priest. By asking to be spared in the confrontation to come, Fulvio tells the priest about the revolutionary intentions of the brethren.

Thinking that these young men wearing red jackets are a group of *banditi*, the peasants join forces with the soldiers and massacre the brethren. Fulvio and Allonsanfan, the son of Fulvio's mentor, Filippo Govoni, are the only ones who survive. Wounded, Allonsanfan tells Fulvio of the successful union of the brethren with the peasants. His delirious words are so powerful that, for a moment, Fulvio believes him. Instead of using his plain white shirt to distinguish himself from his companions in the eyes of the approaching soldiers, Fulvio, the traitor, wears the red jacket of Allonsanfan and dies like the hero of a failed revolution. Fulvio signals with the wrong emblems in the allegory of history and pays with his life (fig. 33).

The historical referent of the Sublime Brethren is the *Carboneria*, a network of secret societies, often with Masonic background, as Filippo's title of Grand Master suggests. Shortly after the Congress

**33.** Dying in Paolo and Vittorio Taviani's *Allonsanfan* (1973–1974). Courtesy of Italtoons, New York.

of Vienna (1815), until Giuseppe Garibaldi's expedition to the south (1860), the *Carbonari* carried out subversive activities against the foreign rulers of Austrian, French, and Spanish descent in control of most of the peninsula.

Italy amounted to a constellation of little kingdoms with different currencies, taxes, and bureaucracies. The expedition depicted in *Allonsanfan* might refer to any comparable attempt made by the *Carboneria* in the south between 1820 and 1860. The spread of plague in the Sicilian countryside might echo the cholera of 1837–1838 in Palermo, described by Giovanni Verga in *Mastro Don Gesualdo*. Yet, the confusion between brethren and *banditi*, the joining of forces between peasants and soldiers, and the brethren's lack of weapons, recall the circumstances leading to the death of Carlo Pisacane (1818–1857) and his small, ill-equipped army in the Cilento, a southern region, in 1857. While Pisacane's companions perished on the battlefield, the patriot committed suicide shortly after this failure. Pisacane's death in desperation seems to match the end of Filippo Govoni in *Allonsanfan*. Feeling that political utopia and his own historical time are at odds, the leader of the Brethren hangs himself.

The Tavianis' may be alluding to Pisacane to rewrite the Risorgimento with reference to the radicalized student groups of May 1968. These groups were called "extraparliamentary" because they operated at the left of the Italian Communist Party and, as such, considered themselves a political avant-garde. They claimed to be a stimulus for the historical Left to rethink its position and priorities.

Four years after Palmiro Togliatti's death in 1964, the intellectuals of these groups replaced the old leader's themes of class unity and historical continuity, with discontinuity and disunity. With disunity these groups denounced a radicalization of the class struggle, while, with discontinuity, they expressed the desire for a radical break with the social order of the past. The extraparliamentary groups saw in Togliatti a predecessor of Enrico Berlinguer, whose positions the New Left considered "reformist," rather than revolutionary, nearly in the derogative sense of *trasformismo*. For Berlinguer, the only way to achieve Gramsci's and Togliatti's national-popular culture was to have the party abandon the seats of the opposition and move to the area of the majority, in a coalition with the Christian-Democrat wing of Aldo Moro.

In *Allonsanfan*, the Taviani brothers fully identify with, but also criticize from the inside, the hard line of the extraparliamentary groups. They look up to Rossellini and Visconti as their mentors and have treasured the lesson of neorealism with its attention to the long duration of deep structures of behavior. By rethinking neorealism in the aftermath of 1968, the two brothers, on the one hand, are interested in the pull of utopia on history. Only utopia can replace gradual changes with radical leaps or moments of acceleration toward a new social order. On the other hand, the Tavianis seem to understand that discontinuity is linked not only to the interaction of history and utopia, but are also aware of the pressures biology can exercise on history. They understand how these pressures drive discontinuities into the historical process. In a sense, the Tavianis seem caught between the need to move beyond 1968 and the ability to rethink neorealism, between an appreciation of utopia and a distrust of revolutionary abstractions. In the end, their interest in the roles utopia and biology play in history has to do with their sense that the contradictory subjectivity Visconti began to explore in true neorealist fashion in *Senso* is also a crucial issue for the militants and filmmakers who lived through 1968.

It was possible to assign to Carlo Pisacane a role comparable to the extraparliamentary groups. The patriot was notorious for having written one of the first treaties of socialist political theory in Italy, and for having more radical ideas than his ally, the republican Giuseppe Mazzini. The Tavianis' political allegory in *Allonsanfan* invites one more historiographical comparison. The struggle between Cavour and Mazzini over the direction of the Risorgimento as a royal initiative or a popular movement, echoes the struggle between Catholics and Marxists over the direction of Italian life after the Resistance. These parallel dilemmas, in the Risorgimento and in the Resistance, are reminiscent of Giambattista Vico's view of history as a series of patterned repetitions or *ricorsi* of different but comparable circumstances.

From an extraparliamentary point of view, the "historical compromise" between Catholics and communists, and the movement of the latter from the seats of the opposition to the space of the ruling class, looks like a selling out of the historical Left after the upheaval of May 1968. The card title at the beginning of *Allonsanfan*, says, indeed, "Negli anni della restaurazione" (In the years of the restoration) thus linking the conservative climate after the Napoleonic era and the Congress of Vienna, to the joint parliamentary leadership sought by the communist Berlinguer through a coalition with the Christian-Democrats of Aldo Moro.

To begin *Allonsanfan* with the word "restoration," instead of Risorgimento, enables the Tavianis to invoke a Gramscian interpretation of the nineteenth century at the level of historiography, and to refer to *Senso* at the level of Italian film history. The word Risorgimento was compromised, on the domestic scene and in international diplomacy, by Cavour's exploitation of the failure of Pisacane's expedition. Only three years after the massacre of Pisacane's group, the progressive Mazzini accepted a sort of historical compromise *ante litteram* and joined the conservative Cavour in the formation of the *Società Nazionale*. It is under the auspices of this middle-of-the-road compromise and coalition of forces that Garibaldi's journey to Sicily became a military success as well as a political failure, or a Piedmontese "royal conquest" of the south, in Gramsci's and Visconti's minds.

The Tavianis' brethren seek a dialogue with the popular masses in the footsteps of Gramsci's model of the "organic intellectual." For Gramsci, Italian intellectuals should be "organically" linked to the audiences they address by using a language which is understandable to all and in touch with social experience. Without such an exchange between the masses and intellectuals, between the language of literature and the language of daily life, no new national-popular culture can be born. Due to the lack of a common written language, opera has been the traditional art form of Italian society as a whole. In other words, the unresolved *questione della lingua* has prevented literature from speaking to the masses. By contrast, opera, which is based more on music than on the written word, has succeeded in addressing large audiences. For Gramsci, Italian intellectuals had traditionally worked in a sphere severed from the life of the nation and spoken a language comprehensible only to the higher classes. From the mid-1930s to the early 1940s, the two Italian writers Cesare Pavese and Elio Vittorini became Gramsci's "organic" intellectuals by seeking to renew, from the inside, the Italian literary language with the introduction of daily speech. Thus Cesare Pavese and Elio Vittorini imitated the more democratic approach to language of the American novelists Melville, Dos Passos, Steinbeck, and Faulkner, whose works they also translated beautifully.

With their expedition, the brethren intend to liberate the oppressed peasants and solve the *questione meridionale*, that is, the painful economic disparity between northern and southern Italy. The brethren's project follows a Gramscian plan: the alliance of the working class in the north with the rural labour in the south. Shortly after their arrival in Sicily, however, the brethren realize how little they know the masses whose liberation they advocate. This sense of an insurmountable barrier between the two is conveyed by the long shot of a stone village, as impenetrable as the dialect the locals speak and the brethren cannot understand. While Tito reads in Italian the brethren's statement of intention, the peasants with the soldiers march against them. During his delirious recollection of the scene, Allonsanfan tells Fulvio that Tito addressed the masses in their native dialect. As we learn from Gramsci, the *questione della lingua* cuts at the heart of class and regional differences and, I would add, accounts for the traditional hegemony of opera and the commedia, two anti-verbal art forms.

## THE TAVIANIS' REDOING OF SENSO IN ALLONSANFAN

The Gramscian subtext of *Allonsanfan* emerges from allusions to *Senso*, which Guido Aristarco carefully outlines:

> The red backdrop that opens at the beginning like a stage curtain takes us straight back to the curtain that rises at the beginning of the other film. Similarly the Villa Imbriani reminds us of the villa at Aldeno; the restaurant where Fulvio celebrates his son's birthday we can link to the Fenice in Venice; Fulvio's insult to Esther's husband, the Austrian official, echoes Ussoni's slight to Franz; the carnival scene with Fulvio and Francesca in the carriage surrounded by a clamour of voices shouting and singing parallels Livia's arrival in Custoza, also in a carriage that has to fight its way through drunken soldiers and the general chaos of people celebrating victory; Livia's betrayal recalls for us Fulvio's own betrayal; Allonsanfan reminds us of Ussoni; when Charlotte gives Fulvio the money needed for the expedition she becomes a Livia in reverse and just as Franz deceives Livia, so too does Fulvio mislead Francesca.[2]

Aristarco lists the intertextual connections of *Allonsanfan* with *Senso*. The critic pays attention to comparable choices of location, comparable narrative situations, and to a comparable tension between character and role, private identity and public image.

In addition to these remarks by Aristarco, other points of contact between *Senso* and *Allonsanfan* emerge. An inquiry into the intertextuality of *Allonsanfan* with its father-text, *Senso*, will clarify the relationship the Tavianis' film entertains with, at first sight, two antithetical traditions, the melodramatic and the neorealist, or with two different stages and sets of performers: the statues of opera in the theatre and the dancers of the commedia in the street. Such an inquiry will also illuminate the role played by sexual difference in the Tavianis' conceptualization of the historical process.

The Tavianis build upon Visconti's awareness that the self is contradictory and that there is a discrepancy between the body erotic and the body politic. Visconti's assignment of a pathological identity to the female protagonist does indicate a heterosexual, homo-

---

[2] Salvatore Piscicelli, ed., *San Michele aveva un gallo: Allonsanfan di Paolo e Vittorio Taviani*, introd. Guido Aristarco (Bologna: Cappelli, 1974), 34.

social bias. On the other hand, through the sexual ambiguity of his male villain, Visconti does direct attention to the difficulty of fitting sexual and public roles, and begins to tackle the latent homoeroticism of the Oedipal complex with his ambivalent interrogation of the past.

In *Senso*, the static tableau gives prominence to the relation of figure with ground, of the individual with its self-image of duplicity. Private ambivalence allegorizes social contradiction. It would seem that *Senso* sets the clock of film history back and reverts to the days when neorealism had not yet released movement from the monolithic statues of Fascism. Furthermore, nineteenth-century melodrama appears antithetical to the documentary grain of postwar cinema. According to Peter Brooks, melodrama expresses a yearning for pure ideals which are impossible to achieve in a post-sacred, modern universe. Hence to compensate for these unattainable goals, melodrama seeks to arrest what is mobile and contingent into a fixed moment or extreme condition.

In *Senso*, the fact that Livia and Franz are unable to live up to the standards of Leonora and Manrico, points not only to a discrepancy between stage and life, but also between acting and being. By contrast, in the characters of fascist cinema, the private always coincides with the public, while ordinary individuals overcome their inadequacies by identifying with the compact image of the leader in the corporate state.

*Senso* is a neorealist film because it does not use melodrama in the escapist way that fascist cinema does, to avoid an interrogation of reality. The so-called white telephone films produced in the 1930s replaced the difficulties of daily life with Manichean abstractions, mindless intrigues, self-absorbed characters and luxurious decor. On the contrary, *Senso* relies on melodrama to make explicit the gap between unattainable goals and oppressive circumstances, to explore the discrepancies between the public and the private, the daily and the historical. It is just these discrepancies that the movement and the behavior of Rossellini's and De Sica's non-professional actors shed light on. It is, however, the worn-out statue in an indoor tableau, and not an agile dancer in the open air, that is the correct metaphor to describe Visconti's deceiving, impotent body politic in Ussoni, and sinful, excessive body erotic in Livia.

The statues of *Senso* never pretend to be pure marble, nor to experience the lofty ideals of opera. In an essay entitled "Cinema Antropomorfico,'' published in *Cinema* on June 10, 1941, Visconti rejected the artificial characters of fascist cinema:

> They live as if already dead, oblivious to the passing of time, of the reflection of objects long since perished, of that faded world of theirs where one moved about with impunity on floors made of cardboard or plaster. Where the backdrops would shake at the slightest murmur of an opening door. Where rose bushes made of tissue paper would flower forever and styles and periods magnanimously combine and intermingle. To speak more clearly, this was a world where stylized liberty Cleopatras in *toupè* vampirized (and whipped) shadowy hunks of Mark Antonies in whalebone busts.[3]

Like Visconti's Mark Antonies, the statues of Fascism would like an audience that takes them seriously. By contrast, Visconti knows all too well that Livia and Franz can only wear the faded colors of the frescoes at Aldeno or the dusty robes piled up in the costume room of La Fenice.

*Senso*, then, is such a misunderstood film because, as early as 1954, Visconti was moving beyond Gramsci's and Togliatti's belief in the unitary nature of class identity, while setting forth the hybrid vein of recent Italian cinema. Ahead of the critical debate that tried to make sense of it, *Senso* weaved together the legacies of fascist and neorealist cinema. Twenty years later, Bertolucci, Wertmuller, Scola, and the Tavianis are still working in this composite mode.

In the footsteps of *Senso*, the narrative of *Allonsanfan* develops by tableau. In *Allonsanfan*, however, the tableau is not built around the relation of figure and ground, but that of figure and group. The collective of the Sublime Brethren is an image as ubiquitous as the music of Ennio Morricone, the discontinuous rhythm of which accompanies the unexpected appearance of the group every time Fulvio thinks he has succeeded in escape.

On the basis of this dynamic of individual and group, the tableau suggests that one is indispensable to the other. Fulvio and the brethren move away from and after each other, engaging in a chase that articulates the attraction and rejection between fathers and sons during May 1968, while also characterizing a systematic circularity whose irony we cannot help but notice since it is antithetical to the revolutionaries' yearning for a break with the past (fig. 34).

---

[3] Adelio Ferrero, ed., *Visconti: Il cinema* (Modena: Ufficio del Cinema del Comune di Modena, 1977), 32. Originally these remarks by Visconti appeared in *Cinema* 119 (June 10, 1941): 386.

**34.** Marcello Mastroianni as Fulvio and the Sublime Brethren in Paolo and Vittorio Taviani's *Allonsanfan* (1973–1974). Courtesy of Italtoons, New York.

Like a rebellious son, Lionello threatens to drown Fulvio. With a similar attitude, Allonsanfan attacks the leader Tito on the boat to Sicily. But Lionello, Tito, and Allonsanfan also look up to Fulvio as their role model, the bearer of the legacy left by the Grand Master Filippo Govoni. Fulvio, instead, secretly plans to abandon the group and flee to America, the land of a people who have, in the wake of the French Revolution, severed themselves from their origins and from the Ancien Régime.

Fulvio's situation is intensely melodramatic, just like Livia's and Franz's. They are unable to love like Leonora and Manrico; and Fulvio is unwilling to live in hiding and in pain, like his mentor, the Grand Master. Furthermore, Fulvio's situation is complicated by the fact that, while he does not want to act as father in public to the Sublime Brethren, he is eager to do so in private with his child Massimiliano, named after another of Fulvio's political mentors, Robespierre.

Ironically, Fulvio's refusal to act as father to the brethren is in consonance with the desire of his fellow comrades to break away from the authority of the past. In turn, Fulvio's attachment to his son points to the latent homoeroticism of his homosocial culture, just as the brethren's longing for a father figure does. It is precisely this set of overlapping contradictions, or comparable dilemmas, between irreconcilable antagonists that the Tavianis explore in *Allonsanfan*, a film with a revolutionary title set in the years of the restoration. In so doing, the two brothers amplify Visconti's awareness of the discrepancy between fluid, private roles with rigid, public ones.

In neorealist cinema, the behavior of the non-professional actor constructs character. While looking at the brethren advancing as a group toward his family villa, Fulvio comments on a few of them individually. At a distance he recognizes Gioacchino, Ugo, and Lionello from the way they, respectively, ride a horse, walk, and hop. Fulvio's observation of a silent longing for death in Lionello's hop, recalls the neorealist assumption that movement, more than dialogue, reveals identity, that external manifestations mirror an internal state of being.[4]

Neorealism concentrates on ordinary, casual movement to explore the realm that belongs to the daily or private and does not fit neatly, or remains hidden underneath, the records of public history. In *Senso*, the incongruity of the body erotic with the body politic depends on a neorealist insight into the uneasy fit of the private with the public realm. From Fulvio's point of view, the brethren's problem is too much of a fit between these two spheres.

Fulvio comments on the stifling congruence of public and private when he describes the three brethren advancing as a group. Gioacchino, Ugo, and Lionello appear characterized by too much coincidence between inside and outside, behavior and identity. It is as if the congruence between sign and referent sought by the neorealist image had reached a stage of formalized self-assuredness. The unstable documentary aura triggered by a non-actor's physiognomy

---

[4] André Bazin's remarks on subjectivity and objectivity in the neorealist image could be used to describe a comparable relationship between appearance and being for the construction of character in the commedia dell'arte: "a mental landscape as objective as a straight photograph and as subjective as pure personal consciousness." *What Is Cinema?*, vol. 2, trans. Hugh Gray (Berkeley: University of California Press, 1971), 98.

signifying an historical moment or a geographical environment freezes into cliché. The brethren are dancers of the commedia on their way to become statues of opera.

The fact that the brethren live their lives the way they move is exactly what Fulvio, torn between private desires and public duty, finds intolerable. Movement can flourish only in areas of discrepancy, where there is room for change to take place and contradiction to express itself. If Visconti's statues in *Senso* look intentionally fake, in *Allonsanfan* dancing takes on the stiffness of a compulsory routine.

The Sublime Brethren think of themselves as a single body, standing compact and ahead of the oppressed multitude in the south. When the brethren perform a southern dance, the *saltarello*, hopping in unison behind the peasant Vanni, they announce their intention to leave for the south, regardless of contingent setbacks; they express the unarrestable movement of the historical process; they grant, unknowingly, a collective breath to Lionello's individual hop towards death.

In revealing the homosocial substratum and unconscious homoerotic component that exists beneath their obsession with father figures, the communal dance of the brethren constitutes a denial of sexual difference, as well as of political disagreements. The dancers fix themselves into statues. It is this blockage into a single-minded position or political dogma that Fulvio rejects and avoids until the very end, constantly shifting from the role of traitor to that of revolutionary.

Ironically, Fulvio ends in a sort of "no man's land," in the political sense of the metaphor, neither right-wing nor left-wing. Fulvio chooses his son Massimiliano over the brethren, and thus cultivates, in isolation, his private homosocial, Oedipal economy. Furthermore, Fulvio blames the brethren he betrays for the same rigidity the extraparliamentary avant-garde disliked in the historical left of Berlinguer. While criticizing the Communist Party for its conservative-reformist stance, the New Left, like the brethren, overvalued the dimension of the group, as a result of its search for a revolutionary identity and historical role.

In line with the impure melodrama of Visconti's *Senso*, Fulvio reinterprets the neorealist equivalence of movement and identity, acting and being, into a life-long simulation. "I am a born actor," he tells Tito before returning to the family villa disguised as a Capu-

chin monk (fig. 35). To throw light on the difficult dynamics of individual and group, the Tavianis degrade the neorealist dictum of
acting as being into the artifice of an aristocrat with the talent of a
mountebank, of a Capuchin monk heading for a life of pleasures.

In *Allonsanfan*, as in *Senso*, color is not a mere accessory of the
decor, but an element of primary importance. In consonance with
the weak status of the word in melodrama, the Tavianis, like Visconti, do not build meaning through contrasts and parallels based
on the dialogue. Rather, they structure the movement of the text
around color. Like music and gesture in stage melodrama, color in
film contains a special charge. It points to what Peter Brooks would
describe as "immediate, primal spiritual meanings which the language code, its demonetization, has obscured, alienated, lost."[5] In

**35.** The Capuchin
monk in Paolo and
Vittorio Taviani's
*Allonsanfan* (1973–
1974). Courtesy of
Italtoons, New
York.

[5] Peter Brooks, *The Melodramatic Imagination: Balzac, Henry James, Melodrama,
and the Mode of Excess* (New York: Columbia University Press, 1985), 72.

responding to the loss of a sacred dimension in the modern world, stage melodrama relies on music and gestures. In addition to sound and acting style, film melodrama relies on color to stage psychological and social struggles in modern life. Color speaks to the potency language used to have in prehistoric times, when a word was the thing it referred to and no separation existed between speaking and experiencing, acting and being. Language, then, had magic powers.

For the filmmaker Sergei Eisenstein, color was a sort of primal language, an utterly non-verbal form of eloquence adding a plastic edge to the objects and people we see on screen. Eisenstein assigned to color the same attributes the primitive logos must have had: "in early stages of evolution the *same* concept, meaning or word equally represents two *opposites* that are mutually exclusive."[6] Color points back to this lost unity of signifier and signified, while its power to compress or charge meaning leads to an effect of compartmentalization. The rejection of nuances and the polarization built into a primal language explains why color is so suited to the binary logic of melodrama and allegory.

The Tavianis' use of red, green, white, blue, black, and gold fully exploits the oppositional meanings that can be attached to a single color. The two brothers develop parallels and contrasts through music as well. Music shares with color a vocabulary of descriptive terms, such as: orchestration, tonality, vibrance. In particular, the *saltarello* of the brethren stands in relief against the *Dirindin din din* of Fulvio's family. And Ennio Morricone's staccato beat for the brethren seems even more compelling when played against Francesca's slow song on Charlotte's grave.

Red means revolution in the north, blood on Allonsanfan's forehead in the south. Blue is the color of utopia and hallucination. It belongs to Allonsanfan, whose beautiful features we first see set against the open sky in an eye-level shot. Fulvio's hallucinatory encounter with Lionello, the "brother" he has let drown in the lake, requires passing through a threshold, namely a window, open onto a blue sky and the imaginary night. Giovanna, the girl who reads Filippo's last letter to the brethren, wears red and blue. As one of the few bystanders with the skill of literacy, she belongs to a time still to come.

---

[6] Sergei Eisenstein, *The Film Sense* (New York: Harcourt Brace and Co., 1942), 125. Emphasis is mine.

Black, white, and grey are the colors of Tito and Vanni. Both assume a difficult role of leadership: Tito takes his companions to death; Vanni initiates his own, personal revolt against the soldiers, without much support from the other villagers. Like Allonsanfan and Giovanna, the child, Massimiliano, belongs to the realm of fantasy and utopia. He is first associated with a deep blue sky at dusk. Yet, in conformity with the Oedipal scenario that pervades *Allonsanfan*, Massimiliano is also an extension of Fulvio's fatherly self and, as such, wears black.

Green is used to strike a contrast between two locations emblematic of class and regional difference: the supple meadow in front of Fulvio's patrician villa and the dry plain where the peasants massacre the brethren. In combination with white and red, green completes the color scheme of the Italian flag. And Fulvio becomes a living image of the flag, right before his death. Black is the color of the father and signals the alignment of biological with historical continuity, moving from Filippo to Tito, from Filippo to Massimiliano, from Filippo to the brethren as a group.

White is the emblem of terminal situations, such as birth or death. The peasants wear white, as does Charlotte when she dies on a patch of green near a road with a few blue reverberations. The brethren wear white robes with red borders when they kidnap Fulvio after his release from prison. By contrast, during Fulvio's recovery at the villa, white means rebirth. "Make me beautiful," the former revolutionary, now a *viveur*, says to his barber as he sits, all clothed in white, in front of a mirror with a golden frame.

With the transfer of clothes, color is used to trace shifting alliances, not just between fathers and sons but also between men and women. Fulvio gives his golden coat to Lionello, who becomes his tormenting conscience during the blue dream. Fulvio and Charlotte leave Fulvietto alone on a country road, with Fulvio's golden scarf around the child's neck. A new bond between Fulvio and Francesca replaces the old one with Charlotte. This liaison becomes apparent by virtue of the golden coat Francesca wears on her shoulders. Allonsanfan's red jacket is fatal to Fulvio. He literally dies because he wears the wrong clothes.

Like Visconti's in *Senso*, the Tavianis' orchestration of color activates a checkerboard of comparisons and rhymes, historical oppositions and emotional overtones. In comparison to Visconti, the Tavianis accentuate the links between color and psychology even further. In *Allonsanfan*, colors are never stable. Rather, they seem to change according to shifts in lighting and emotions. On the boat to Sicily, Fulvio's blue coat turns black when he opposes the sons he does not want, the brethren.

In mobilizing color through lighting, the Tavianis place color at the interface of illusion and reality, subjectivity and objectivity. It is an awareness of the contradictions of subjectivity that the Tavianis see as missing from the political stance of the brethren and of the extraparliamentary student groups. In turn, an excessive attention to the demands of his own will to pleasure leads Fulvio to underestimate the interpellation of history on his private identity.

Color makes explicit the fact that the dilemma of illusion and reality affects both antagonists: Fulvio and the brethren. Furthermore, the Tavianis' use of the point-of-view shot conveys the fragility of the barrier between subjectivity and objectivity. The interchangeability of these two spheres produces a "no man's land," nevertheless shared in an Oedipal, homosocial fashion by Fulvio and Allonsanfan. Liehm remarks:

> Some scenes are shot with a subjective camera (from Fulvio's point of view); others are rendered objectively. The Sublime Brethren . . . are seen through Fulvio's eyes as a group of fanatic madmen, incarnating the mystical faith in a cause. On the other hand, Allonsanfan, the youngest and the most rational member of the sect, is portrayed with an objective camera as the only one who realizes the real possibilities of a revolution.[7]

Liehm suggests that the dynamics of objectivity and subjectivity, public and private, become more explicit if we turn again to color, the element of the Tavianis' decor most charged with the imbrication of these two dimensions.

The Tavianis' use of color, as opposed to Visconti's, explicitly follows Goethe's color theory. In contrast to Newton, who studied color exclusively as a physical phenomenon, Goethe was interested in its psychological and social implications. Goethe argued that: "These colors, which are not fixed upon the surface of an object but can be seen only under special circumstances, I should like to call absolute colors, and those that are so fixed, body colors."[8] This dis-

---

[7] Mira Liehm, *Passion and Defiance: Film in Italy from 1942 to the Present* (Berkeley: University of California Press, 1984), 310.

[8] Rupprecht Matthaei, ed., *Goethe's Color Theory* (New York: Van Nostrand Reinhold Company, 1971), 20.

tinction of Goethe's is literally put into practice by the Tavianis in the sequence of Fulvio's first dinner with the family. He sits with sister Esther (Laura Betti), brother Costantino, and nephew Fulvietto. An orange sunset warms the walls and the faces around the table. A change of lighting takes place with the arrival of the candles. Esther turns to violet; Costantino to cabbage green; and Fulvietto to gold, Fulvio's favorite color. These are the inner tonalities Fulvio associated with his relatives and himself before joining Robespierre, the hero of a great revolution the Risorgimento failed to live up to.

Fulvio does not like his gold to be confused with vulgar yellow, Esther adds. In Goethe's theory, Eisenstein explains, yellow is the color of traitors, while gold is for saints and heroes. This detail confirms that colors to the Tavianis are not objective, stable physical phenomena, but can be ambivalent like identity, an effect of ever-shifting perceptions tied to psychology and sociology. Esther remembers that Fulvio was always unable to assign blue, the color of happiness and utopia, to anyone in the family.

These "absolute colors," as Goethe put it, are colors of the mind. They are unbound (from the Latin, *absoluti*) because they are free from the constraints of physical reality or from fixed associations, such as red with revolution, dictated by official history or party dogma. These colors are projected from Fulvio's point of view, at the head of the table, onto his companions. These colors of the mind speak to the sensual pleasures Fulvio is eager to experience with his return to the womb-like space of the family, a pre-historical and pre-linguistic domain. Fulvio seeks to return to a lost childhood whose ineffable unity with the mother and ideal purity, only melodrama, and color, can refer to, yet never achieve.

Fulvio's family is like a womb from which the child and the revolutionary have been severed upon their entrance into the domains of language, duty, and history. By withholding the reverse shot during the dialogue at the dinner table, the Tavianis underscore the trauma of Fulvio's separation from the family. The two brothers keep the camera on Esther, Costantino, and Fulvietto. With the exception of brief and self-contained close-ups of Fulvio in chiaroscuro, the Tavianis hardly show an easy exchange of looks between him and the relatives. Fulvio remains in the darkness of the room, as if he were struggling behind an invisible, but painful threshold, before his return to the realm of desire and the safety of the family womb. Overcoming this threshold set between desire and duty, the maternal and the paternal, implies for Fulvio a reinvestment in the senses, whose demands he has ignored for the sake of his commitment to politics. The rediscovery of a new private identity occurs when Fulvio wakes up in his bedroom after an illness (fig. 36). The arrival of a wave of desire emerges from the use of fluid camera movements. The Tavianis use an alternation of dissolves and cuts to describe the erratic flow of Fulvio's intensified perception of colors and sounds.

The light buzz of a green bug on the white curtain, the soft purring of a cat across the bed, precede golden and orange rays of light, in motion, on the ceiling. Accompanied as these rays are by a female and a male voice from the nearby terrace, they are reminiscent of beams of light during the projection of a film. Fulvio reawakens in the middle of the night. In the candle-lit room, his eyes turn to a children's theatre box, to his violin, and to a picture of a vessel sail-

**36.** Reawakening as rebirth in Paolo and Vittorio Taviani's *Allonsanfan* (1973–1974). Courtesy of Italtoons, New York.

ing toward America. These three images illustrate the newly found identity Fulvio had acquired a few hours earlier, waking like a child and hearing his parents' voices. The melodramatic sense of life as theatre, the love for music, and the longing for an unbound movement toward a utopian land come back to Fulvio in the darkness of the room.

In depicting Fulvio's rebirth, the Tavianis refer to the cinema perhaps with the intention of allegorizing Jacques Lacan's "mirror phase." In Lacan's psychoanalytic narrative, the separation of the male child from the mother and the arrival of the father is a traumatic event. Until then, the child delights in drawing identity from an ideal unity with the mother's body whose image appears as if reflected in a mirror. The father's arrival breaks this pre-historical, imaginary harmony, while his language becomes the new term of reference for the child. In conjunction with the father's arrival, the child learns to construct identity through an arbitrary system of linguistic symbols, inflected in such a way to produce an awareness of sexual difference. After realizing that the mother's body is not like the father's, the child predicates this awareness of sexual difference into a fear of castration. For Lacan, when the male child sees the mother nearby in the mirror, an "imaginary" phase is taking place. This stage of the imaginary ends with the entrance into language, a system of symbols that marks the beginning of a new phase Lacan calls the "symbolic" stage.

Interestingly, in the Tavianis' version of Lacan's mirror phase, Fulvio's rebirth is more of a pre-Oedipal fantasy and less of an Oedipal trauma. The father's language does not quite separate the child from the mother's body, for the male and female voices Fulvio overhears mingle and are beautiful to the point of being unintelligible as language, more like music. In the Tavianis' mirror phase, by melting into music the language of melodrama can temporarily help Fulvio abandon politics and duty, and return him, instead, to family and desire. Yet, at the moment of reawakening, this family appears so incredibly soothing that Fulvio is living through a utopian fantasy and not dealing with an historical reality. Fulvio's rebirth is a fleeting magic moment, one that comes close to fulfilling the central aspiration of melodrama: to recover a lost unity. Furthermore, if the male and female voices on the balcony stand for the parents', their perfect harmony implies a heterosexual ideal. This ideal, in turn, is at odds with the pre-Oedipal, homoerotic economy the child-Fulvio experiences in the fantasy of a fusion with the mother's body. These voices, instead, belong to Fulvio's brother and his wife. After escaping from the brethren, for the first time in the film Fulvio can fantasize about the voice of his own brother without the anxiety of a loss of self and can make this familiar male voice blend with a feminine counterpart. These voices, therefore, do not belong to the parents of Lacan's allegory. Rather they are projections of Fulvio's split self and mark an instance of reconciliation between his masculine and feminine side. This momentary fusion is as strong as the pre-historical bond between signifier and signified that melodrama tries to summon through color.

## HISTORY AS DISCONTINUITY AND THE FEMININE AS UTOPIA

In *Senso*, the processes of history become tangible through the self-conscious, past-bound life style of Franz and the erratic movement toward the future of Ussoni. Visconti's mixture of decadence and blind progress reappears in the Tavianis' view of history as a process of labyrinthine reversals, between the leaps of utopian thought and the pull of biology.

This view of history as an uneven maze emerges from the temporal disorientation of the characters themselves. After Fulvio's death, Lionello admits that only he understood that the brethren arrived on the political scene either too soon or too late. On the way to Sicily, Tito expresses his own sense of displacement in regard to the expedition, by saying: "I wish it were already next year's May to find out if all this makes any sense." Not making sense, then, becomes a metaphor for the historical process, and a description of the music used in the credits, where we hear the disjunctive proliferation of sounds typical of a rehearsal preceding an operatic performance.

In theorizing history as a discontinuous process, the Tavianis take a stance against a Marxist historicism based on continuity. Sebastiano Timpanaro explains that this tradition considers "nature's determination over man as exercised primarily at the dawn of human history; it is conceived as a kind of prologue or pre-historic antechamber, . . . 'natural man' is increasingly overshadowed by 'historic man,' in whom eventually he is absorbed and wholly transcended."⁹ During the dream sequence, Lionello becomes the spokesman of Marxist historicism and argues that Fulvio's return to the senses is a regression into biology.

The Tavianis' interest in biological man can be put in relation to Sebastiano Timpanaro's work on Giacomo Leopardi. Like the brethren, Leopardi, a major Italian poet, lived "in the years of the restoration." Sebastiano Timpanaro finds in Leopardi's poetry a powerful reminder that the oppression of mankind does not come only from the socio-economic sphere but also from nature, illness, the body. For Leopardi, biology is a realm with an historicity of its own. The processes of biology have the long duration neorealism explored with daily life. Biological time unfolds at an "incomparably slower pace, . . . [with] an automatic and unconscious character to which it would be mistaken to attribute any purpose or providential design."¹⁰ While Timpanaro speaks of the "oppression exercised by nature over man," in *Allonsanfan* the turn from history to biology is a difficult, but, at times, more positive experience than Leopardi's materialist pessimism allows. This turn requires the crossing of the threshold, from the symbolic back to the imaginary, and puts historical beings back in touch with the maternal, feminine side which the allegiance to duty and the language of the father inhibits.

During the sequence of Fulvio's awaking, the Tavianis invoke Vico's first stage of mankind as an antidote to Leopardi's sense that biology is an evil kind of history that produces oppression. By associating Fulvio's return to the maternal body of the family with utopia, the Tavianis refer to Vico's sense that childhood is a time of free imagination outside the constraints of history and adulthood.

The Tavianis locate utopia in biology, a pre-historical realm, but in his famous poem *La Ginestra* (The Broom), Giacomo Leopardi views nature as a cruel stepmother. The Tavianis' location of utopia in biology is, however, unsatisfactory. Despite the positive aura sur-

---

⁹ Sebastiano Timpanaro, "The Pessimistic Materialism of Giacomo Leopardi," *New Left Review* 116 (1979): 12. Also on Timpanaro and Giacomo Leopardi, see Robert Dombroski, "Timpanaro's Materialism: An Introduction," *The Journal of the History of Ideas* 44, no. 2 (April–June 1983): 311–26. On Leopardi, the historical Left and the New Left, also see Sebastiano Timpanaro, *Antileopardiani e neomoderati nella sinistra italiana* (Pisa: ETS Editrice, 1982). For a sense of the non-Hegelianized Vico in relation to Leopardi's materialism, see Vincenzo Maria Amari, "Vico, Leopardi, Nietzsche: A Comparative Study of the Problem of Nihilism" (Ph.D. diss., Columbia University, 1979).

¹⁰ Timpanaro, "Pessimistic Materialism," 11.

rounding Fulvio's rebirth, the placement of utopia in pre-history, in biology, retains a patriarchal perspective to the extent that it reinforces the traditionally oppressive association of nature with women. This suggests that the Tavianis are interested in utopia more in order to theorize history as a discontinuous process and less for the sake of releasing femininity from the constrictive label of "difference," one that immobilizes women with the authority of a scientific definition.

The Oedipal orientation of the Tavianis' film is so strong that stepping over the threshold between the maternal and the paternal, in the end, is more threatening than tempting. Yet, to live always under the authority of a strong father figure is painful for men and women alike. In *Allonsanfan*, this predicament is further marred by a haunting perception of sexual difference. To this problem the brethren respond with the unconscious homoeroticism of the *saltarello*. Like children caught by surprise, with this folk-dance they defend themselves from the dangerous questions of a woman.

During the carnival, an anonymous woman interrupts the brethren's secret meeting and pretends to be in labor. The brethren see this false mother as an inquisitive phallic mother. It is as if the pain caused by the separation from childhood had spilled over into adulthood, and turned the mother from a lost object of love into an intruding one of hate. Furthermore, the woman's fake birth pains climax in the sudden appearance of an ugly, black puppet, thus making a mockery of Fulvio's rebirth at the villa. Here the Tavianis adopt Leopardi's sense of nature as a cruel stepmother and abandon Vico's view that poetry flourishes before the entrance into history. In this case, the carnival is the setting for a return to the freedom of childhood depicted in a negative light, as an impossible possibility. By contrast, Allonsanfan's utopian union between the peasants and the brethren carnivalizes in a direction opposite the false birth sequence. Allonsanfan's delirious words reverse the outcome of the expedition, from duty back to fantasy, from history to utopia.

Guido Aristarco argues that Allonsanfan's narrative functions as an Archimedean stance, from which to deal with the anguish of history. Allonsanfan's monologue is a term of reference for a positive political strategy in the face of structures of long duration slowing historical change to the rhythms of biology.

History can be so full of anguish as to make utopia look not just impossible, but even undesirable. This negative coloring of utopia prevents men and women alike from overcoming stereotypical sexual personae and fixed family roles. Fulvio and Francesca end up in the palace of a young nobleman. There they pursue the pleasures of the senses during the carnival. With his notorious talent for simulation, Fulvio declares to Francesca that he let her lover, Lionello, drown to spare her from a future of hardship as a militant. Hesitating for a moment at Fulvio's declaration of love, Francesca steps outside the bedroom and meets the inviting glance of the young nobleman. His alluring smile lurks in the darkness. Even though the nobleman is there for her, in the domain of fantasy, Francesca is unable to discard the rules of behavior operative in the patriarchal culture to which she belongs. She, therefore, fulfills her Electra complex by choosing the father, Fulvio, as a lover, instead of the young nobleman.

In comparison to the masculine Charlotte, Francesca is less subject to the demands of militancy and, therefore, closer to utopia, if not for her own sake then at least in relation to Fulvio. Furthermore, Francesca, unlike Charlotte, does not become the mother of a child from Fulvio and, consequently, is not caught in a pattern of continuity between father and son. As her rejection of the nobleman demonstrates, Francesca does not give up the father, thus remaining trapped in a type of history that only acknowledges male identity. Yet, by not becoming a mother, the timid Francesca comes closer to utopia than the revolutionary Charlotte. This is ironic if we consider that the Hungarian radical devoted her life to a political cause and, in a sense, played a more active role in the historical process than did Francesca. That Francesca is closer to utopia than Charlotte becomes clear in the sequence of Fulvio and his new lover in the bedroom, with the same alternation of cuts and dissolves used for the Jacobin's reawakening at the villa. Furthermore, that Francesca opens the way to utopia for Fulvio becomes apparent when these two characters join the carnival. As a ritual characterized by "gestural freedom and effervescence of dance and movement,"[11] the carnival stages a temporary crossing of the threshold between duty and desire, history and utopia. As a woman, living on the margins of history and political activity, Francesca maintains a privileged access to the utopian dimension mobilized by the power of the carnival to turn things upside down.

[11] Robert Stam, "Mikhail Bakhtin and Left Cultural Critique," in *Postmodernism and Its Discontents*, ed. E. Ann Kaplan (London: Verso, 1988), 136.

The colorful and vulgar masks of the carnival recall the characters of the commedia dell'arte. The provocative motions of the carnival resemble Esther's uninhibited dance on the steps of the villa, at the quick pace of *Dirin Din Din*. While Esther's sexually allusive movements celebrate the newly found pleasures of family life, the carnival allows for a brief entry into the "sphere of utopian freedom."[12] In the midst of the carnival, Francesca is most comfortable and laughs freely. Fulvio, instead, looks worried and puzzled. It is Francesca's laughter that enables him, temporarily, to shake off the burden of militancy and greet the carnival.

The Tavianis attempt to work through the constraints of political duty and rethink the relations of history and biology for the sake of utopia, but not of femininity. Fulvio's dissatisfaction with political dogma finds an outlet only during the brief season of the carnival. The overall accent of the film remains on the generational tensions that tie Allonsanfan to Fulvio and the Tavianis to Visconti. In *Senso*, sexual passion upsets public history. In *Allonsanfan*, a few feminine figures manage to project from the dominant, Oedipal grain of the film. Allonsanfan, the voice of utopia, has the soft skin of a woman and the visionary gaze of a prophet. If utopia seems to die on the dry, green grass of Sicily, stained with red shirts, it also lives on in Giovanna, the girl who reads Filippo's last letter, and in the wide open eyes of the peasant girl accidentally shot by Vanni. With the exception of Allonsanfan, the male spokesman of history as discontinuity, the two female characters associated with utopia are as minor as the expedition undertaken by Carlo Pisacane. His death, however, remains a testimony of how powerful dreams can kindle the imagination of the future and, eventually, jolt the slow and deep structures of the historical process.

[12] Stam, "Mikhail Bakhtin," 134.

# SIX

The
Resistance
after World
War II and
after May
1968

## THE EUCHARISTIC BODY OF NEOREALISM

GALLONE's Scipio embodies inhuman ideals. The Fascist statue is compact and timeless. This monument refers to an opaque essence, an idea without inner light. The characters of *Open City* (1945), *Paisà* (1946), and *Voyage to Italy* (1953) reveal, in contrast, that the neorealist body of Roberto Rossellini's cinema is frail and transitory. At the end of World War II, the male statue began to move again, and became vulnerable. In *Open City*, the Nazis interrogate the communist partisan Manfredi. He looks like a suffering Christ (fig. 37). Manfredi's tortured body strikes a note of contrast with the metallic armor in the Nazis' office.[1] This armor recalls Gallone's artificial characters and Filippo Tommaso Marinetti's glorification of war as the expression of an all-powerful technology of masculinity.

In contrast to the marble heroes of fascist cinema, the body in Rossellini's neorealism is a human organism inhabited by the antithesis of sheer biology, the soul, as if a Christian spirituality had developed next to a pagan attachment to the earth. In representing the impact of official history on daily life and anonymous people, neorealism adopted the microscopic scale of the commedia dell'arte and turned away from

[1] Robert Burgoyne makes this point in "The Imaginary and the Neo-Real," *Enclitic* 3, no. 1 (Spring 1979): 26.

**37.** Figura Christi in Roberto Rossellini's *Open City* (1945). Courtesy of The Museum of Modern Art, Film Stills Archive.

the monumental setting of opera. With its attention to physiognomy and behavior, neorealism put movement into the statues of fascist cinema. By contrast, in holding onto national unity and historical continuity, Rossellini's *Paisà* and the popular perception of the Resistance upheld by the Catholic establishment in the postwar period are based on Benedetto Croce's interpretation of Italian history.[2]

In *Open City*, Rossellini's children are fatherless and, in a Rome reduced to rubble, walk alone toward an uncertain future (fig. 38).

[2] On neorealism and the Resistance, see Roy Armes, *Patterns of Neorealism* (South Brunswick, N.J.: A. S. Barnes, 1971); Massimo Mida and Giovanni Vento, *Cinema e resistenza* (Florence: Luciano Landi Editore, 1959); Alfonso Canziani, *Gli anni del neorealismo* (Florence: La Nuova Italia, 1977); Robert P. Kolker, *The Altering Eye* (New York: Oxford University Press, 1983); Pietro Pintus, *Storia e film* (Rome: Bulzoni, 1980); Cesare De Michelis, "La resistenza nel cinema degli anni facili," *Cinema 60* 3, nos. 23–26 (May–August 1962): 87–91; Sergio Solmi, "Il film della resistenza," *Filmcritica* 9, nos. 47–48 (April–May 1955): 131–32. On Rossellini and Croce, see Tag Gallagher, "NR = MC²: Rossellini, Neo-Realism, and Croce," *Film History, An International Journal* 2, no. 1 (1988): 87–97.

**38.** The fatherless children of Roberto Rossellini's *Open City* (1945). Courtesy of The Museum of Modern Art, Film Stills Archive.

The absence of fathers certainly suggests the beginning of a new era in Italian history, but does not propose a view of the historical process as discontinuous. Rossellini's call for unity in difference reinforces the theme of continuity. Indeed, the themes of national unity and historical continuity are bound together and implement each other. This is why, speaking from opposite camps, Croce and Gentile end up echoing each other in their stress of continuity in unity.

Rossellini's weaving of historiographical themes into the narrative design of his films is by no means representative of neorealist cinema as a whole. Aldo Vergano's *The Sun Rises Again* (1946) is an example of a neorealist film that performs a class analysis of the Resistance and defies Croce's sense of national unity. Vergano's characters, however, are allegorical embodiments of monolithic class identity. The bourgeoisie is always evil, while the representatives of the working class are inherently good.

With Vergano, class prevails over nation, while a Gramscian belief in the unitary nature of consciousness lives on. By contrast, Rossellini's communist partisan Manfredi in *Open City* embodies the nation as a whole, not just the working class. Inasmuch as the physiognomies of Rossellini's characters are as stereotypical and, at times, as Manichean as Vergano's, it is also true that behavior, with Rossellini, acquires more nuances and begins to turn the unpredictable rhythm of the street into a spiritual search. Finally, in contrast to Vergano's one-dimensional class identity, in *Senso*, Luchino Visconti begins to challenge Gramsci's belief in the unitary nature of consciousness.

The integration of an old historiographical discourse with a new comedic scale suggests that neorealism was split between continuity and change. The ties of neorealism to a Crocean interpretation of Italian history resurfaced during the involution of this film style. Thanks to the economic boom of the late 1950s and early 1960s in the aftermath of the Marshall Plan, escapist comedies crowded the screens, while a superficial optimism prevailed. The fluid life of the street returned to the rigid molds of picturesque statuettes. These embodiments of populist types in postwar Italy were as artificial as their counterparts in the 1930s.[3]

The cooptation of neorealism in the 1950s existed already *in nuce* within Rossellini's *Open City* and *Paisà* in the 1940s. With his depiction of the Resistance, the director did not question the national unity Croce ascribed to the Risorgimento. Yet, Rossellini's films shocked their audiences at home and abroad, primarily because they greatly differed from those of the regime. Fascist cinema promoted an abstract, death-like essentialism. On the contrary, Rossellini's life-long search for an essential image—one that would be vibrant with daily life, but also spiritual enough to transcend it—has little to do with Gallone's reified, kitsch emblems.

In *Paisà* and *Voyage to Italy*, the bodily, concrete side of daily life participates in a deep sense of religiosity. This is not to say that Rossellini dwells on scenes of religious rituals, but rather that the struggle for survival in *Paisà* and the conjugal crisis of *Voyage to Italy* interlace the characters with life and death, body and spirit.

In the Florentine episode of *Paisà*, invisible hands pull a rope and send a jug of water placed on a small cart across the street. While

[3] On pink neorealism, see Mira Liehm, *Passion and Defiance: Film in Italy from 1942 to the Present* (Berkeley: University of California Press, 1984), 141–45. A reader fond of Italian popular culture will enjoy learning that, as late as 1954, opera held a monopoly on the pop-music scene. Claudio Villa, the star of melodic Neapolitan music in the record industry, dominated the market.

the air is still with death, history is in the making, and ordinary objects keep moving with a life of their own. At the end of *Voyage to Italy*, Ingrid Bergman loses herself in a crowd of Neapolitans. The encounter with the threatening body of another culture helps her find again spiritual comfort in her marriage. Rossellini is interested in fluid currents of invisible change under the surface of daily life; his images seem to outgrow the borders of the frame as if the movement onscreen were an extension of off-screen reality.

Rossellini's neorealist image is so documentary-like that it seems to incorporate the tactile quality of the referent in its weightless shadow. In the wake of Fascist spectacles, the director continued to allegorize different aspects of the national self. The characters' bodies are sites for the negotiation of abstract values with concrete experiences, of the spiritual with the biological. Unlike fascist cinema, Rossellini does not depict inhuman essences through lifeless marble. On the contrary, Rossellini's neorealism is based on what André Bazin calls "the amalgam."[4] With this chemical metaphor, Bazin describes the interaction between the cinematic apparatus and non-professional actors.

Rossellini cast non-actors because their physical appearance was emblematic of a social type. According to Bazin's amalgam, the body of Rossellini's neorealism does not just look back to the commedia dell'arte. As the term "amalgam" suggests, the metaphor of the Eucharist fits the Italian director's and the French critic's Catholic sensibilities. In fact, *Paisà* and *Voyage to Italy* are about the transubstantiation of life into cinema and, reversedly, of human interiority into daily behavior. As the critic and filmmaker Jacques Rivette points out, despite these intimate links with lived experience, Rossellini's cinema rises above the populist *bozzetto* and endows the marginalized aesthetics of documentary with spiritual resonance.[5]

Brunello Rondi, Robert Warshow,[6] and Peter Brunette express awe of Carmela Sazio, the non-professional actress Rossellini paired with an American soldier, Joe from Jersey, in the Sicilian episode of

[4] André Bazin, *What is Cinema?*, vol. 2, trans. Hugh Gray (Berkeley: University of California Press, 1971), 22–25.

[5] Jacques Rivette, "Letter on Rossellini," in Jim Hillier, ed., *Cahiers du Cinéma, The 1950s: Neo-Realism, Hollywood, New Wave* (Cambridge, Mass.: Harvard University Press, 1985), 192–204.

[6] Robert Warshow, *The Immediate Experience* (New York: Atheneum, 1979), 252–53.

*Paisà.* These critics' remarks reinforce each other. Rondi, for example, anticipates Brunette's observations, by saying: "Carmela Sazio's bloated, ungainly body, that tangled mass of hair, those eyes set amidst long, dark stares and the beauty that one suspects hidden beneath those features, the rage, the profound, passionate, opaque grief of that inner expression, that mangled speech, equal, in and of themselves and also because of the way they are narrated, a most intense figurative construct."[7] When Rondi talks about "the beauty that one suspects hidden beneath those features," he is not saying that Rossellini uses a non-professional actress to show a beautiful girl emerging from an ugly cocoon. Carmela's beauty is not hidden in order to tease the viewer. The screen presence of the Sicilian girl has nothing to do with a Hollywood notion of sex appeal (fig. 39).

With amalgamation, Bazin means that neorealist chemistry and

**39.** The Sicilian girl in Roberto Rossellini's *Paisà* (1946). Courtesy of The Museum of Modern Art, Film Stills Archive.

[7] Brunello Rondi, *Il neorealismo italiano* (Parma: Guanda, 1956), 142.

Carmela's beauty stem from the encounter between the apparatus and the body of a non-professional actress, between cinema and life with all its ambiguities.[8] It is as if Rossellini's Eucharistic transubstantiation were adding new dimensions of the spiritual and the physical to the negotiation of public and private, of concrete and abstract, which the modern, lay body politic sustains in the mold of the medieval *corpus mysticum*.

In dealing with the vicissitudes of Italy as a modern state, Rossellini thinks of society as an extended church. In *Open City*, with Manfredi, the atheist communist partisan, and Don Pietro, the Catholic priest supportive of the Resistance, Rossellini implies that the alliance of Catholics and communists against Fascism is comparable to the Christian brotherhood of the church against all evils.

Rossellini's characters are "blocks" of human experience. Their external behaviors allegorize their inner predicaments, while they remain alien to the nuances of psychological interiority. All their dimensions, whether individual or social, are played more on the surface of their bodies, and less among lines of dialogue or in complexities of mind. Gestures and postures are emblems of the characters' values and roles.

In *Paisà*, for example, a Black G.I. watches a spectacle where a Sicilian puppet battles with a dark-skinned Saracen. Excited by the action, the soldier confuses illusion with reality. He jumps on stage and inserts himself in the performance. His huge body bends down toward the audience in a puppet-like posture. The episode is ambiguous, open-ended, while the relation of the soldier's body with his self-image articulates the individual and social meanings of racial identity.

Like neorealism, the commedia dell'arte explores the duration of deep structures by turning individual characters into embodiments of social contexts. Amédée Ayfre seems to allude to this method when he explains that, in neorealism, personal and social, objective and subjective elements, intersect in a "bloc événementiel," or in a "bloc de durée."[9] Ayfre's "bloc," in my view, is the body of the commedia in Rossellini's neorealism, allegorizing the transubstantia-

---

[8] On ambiguity in Bazin, see J. Dudley Andrew, *André Bazin* (New York: Oxford University Press, 1978), 106.

[9] Amédée Ayfre, "Néo-réalisme et phénoménologie," *Cahiers du Cinéma* 3, no. 17 (November 1952): 9.

tion of interiority into social identity and documenting a microhistory of national behavior.

The Eucharistic transubstantiation of appearance into being reminds us of how the commedia uses the body as a window on the character's soul. This method for disclosing interiority, however, makes up for the commedia's inability to achieve introspection through subtle verbal means. In regard to Carmela Sazio, the Sicilian girl of *Paisà*, Peter Brunette writes: "The very presence of the girl—slovenly and directly sensual in a way no real actress would ever chance—gives an edge to her encounter with Joe that makes the film seem bracingly out of control."[10] The Bazinian amalgamation between a non-actress and the cinema acquires an epiphanic edge, leading Brunette to speak of sexual energy between Carmela and Joe. It is not the possibility of erotic tension between Carmela and Joe from Jersey, but precisely the use of a non-actress that makes Rossellini's film seem "bracingly out of control."

Rivette's commentary may seem to deny that Rossellini's construction of character is rooted in the commedia dell'arte: "Rossellini's work 'isn't much fun'; it is deeply serious, even, and turns its back on comedy; and I imagine that Rossellini would condemn laughter with the same Catholic virulence as Charles Baudelaire."[11] Rivette's observation that Catholicism does not cherish irreverent laughter is not difficult to accept, and receives further support from the absence of a carnivalesque dimension to Rossellini's films. The absence of laughter and slapstick, however, does not preclude the deeper analogy between the microscopic scale of neorealism and that of the commedia dell'arte. While Fellini and Wertmuller enlarge the comedic features of their characters, Rossellini and De Sica show that a private or a social condition lingers on in the interstices of routine gestures or casual behavior.

Rossellini's neorealism and the commedia share an insight into the coextensiveness of the small and the universal, the daily and the eternal, the spiritual and the physical. In *Voyage to Italy*, Ingrid Bergman's visits to the caves of the Sybilla, to a mausoleum of skulls, and to a volcanic spring of ebullient mud, reassert the invisible forces that underpin daily phenomena, while life goes on in the pregnant women of Naples. To Bergman, in the role of Mrs.

[10] Peter Brunette, *Roberto Rossellini* (New York: Oxford University Press, 1987), 72.

[11] Hillier, *Cahiers du Cinéma: The 1950s*, 201.

Joyce, a tourist from England, the staging of the Mediterranean body, in its cycles of regeneration and decay, is a disturbing experience that leads her to confront her own existential anguish.

The transubstantiation of life and cinema Rossellini depicts extends back to ancient rituals which still thrive in Italian modern life. The miracle of ordinary things, prodigies that go unobserved, a constant undoing of matter into spirit and spirit into matter, all appeal to Rossellini, who searches for transcendence in what is contingent, and who, in *Voyage to Italy*, *Stromboli* (1949–1950), *The Miracle* (1948), and *The Flowers of St. Francis* (1950) explores the tension between body and soul, the pull of the earth and the emotion of God.

While pointing to the absence of superficially comedic elements such as laughter and slapstick, Rivette is sensitive to the Eucharistic component of Rossellini's neorealism. In writing about *Voyage to Italy*, Rivette explains why Ingrid Bergman can experience "the incarnation of this idea,"[12] only among the ruins of Pompeii or in the streets of Naples:

> There is no longer any question of symbols here, and we are already on the road towards the great Christian allegory. Everything now seen by this distraught woman, lost in the kingdom of grace, these lovers, these pregnant women who form for her an omnipresent, haunting cortege, and then those huddled corpses, those skulls, and finally those banners, that procession for some almost barbaric cult, everything now radiates a different light, everything reveals itself as something else; here, visible to our eyes, are beauty, love, maternity, death, God.[13]

"Beauty, love, maternity, death, God": these words mark the stages of an essentialist search. Yet Rivette's remarks also survey an unsettling earthiness: the mothers Bergman sees everywhere in the streets of Naples; the huddled corpses of man and wife she painfully confronts at Pompeii when her marriage is breaking apart; and, finally, the tangible oozing of blood that Neapolitans cherish once a year during the "barbaric cult" of San Gennaro (fig. 40).

The conjunction of ideal and material elements, of body and soul, has its roots in a popular folklore, split between paganism and Christianity, that presides over the genesis of the commedia in classical antiquity and lives on in the neorealism of Rossellini. In *Voy-*

[12] Ibid., 99.
[13] Ibid., 200.

**40.** Archaeology in Roberto Rossellini's *Voyage to Italy* (1953). Courtesy of The Museum of Modern Art, Film Stills Archive.

*age to Italy*, in *Paisà*, and in *Open City*, the Fascist statues come to life. The sculptures of a Neapolitan museum leap toward Ingrid Bergman, who, puzzled, sees in the marble the display of emotion she has been avoiding in her marriage.

Working in the wake of *Voyage to Italy*, Vittorio and Paolo Taviani acknowledge the coextensiveness of pagan and Christian elements in Tuscan regional culture and transfer this tension of body and soul, daily existence and official history, to their retelling of the Resistance in *Night of the Shooting Stars* (1982). Rossellini's neorealism had a tremendous impact on the Taviani brothers. It is commonplace to say that *Night of the Shooting Stars* is the *Paisà* of the 1980s. The question is how and why the Tavianis renegotiate Rossellini's amalgam of spirituality and biology, of cinema and life. An intertextual approach must also attend the Tavianis' handling of national unity and historical continuity, and their conceptualization of history as it differs from Rossellini's.

The intertextual relation of *Night of the Shooting Stars* with *Paisà* consists of appropriation and rejection. If *Allonsanfan* had allowed the Tavianis to play out their anxiety of influence in relation to Visconti's *Senso*, *Night of the Shooting Stars* offers them the opportunity to investigate their relationship with Rossellini, another important father figure whose cinema affected their intellectual development. Rossellini and the Tavianis work off a common set of strong parameters: spectacle, allegory, and body. While Rossellini moved away from opera in favor of the commedia, the Tavianis weave together the legacies of these two hegemonic art forms. Furthermore, the Tavianis replace unity and continuity with disunity and discontinuity. In so doing, the two brothers reject a Crocean doxa at the level of film history and *Paisà*, and a Gramscian doxa at the level of Palmiro Togliatti's historicism. Most sensitive to the New Left, the Tavianis well understand the meaning of Togliatti's death in 1964, shortly before the outburst of May 1968. In fact, they insert newsreel footage of the communist leader's funeral in their film, *The Subversives* (1967).

Like Croce, Rossellini believes in the unitary nature of consciousness. This view of the individual self corresponds to an image of society based on a Catholic sense of "coralità." In *Paisà*, Rossellini describes the difficulty, but also the possibility, of communication across social roles in struggle with one another. From the streets of Florence to the marshes of the Po Valley, the Resistance becomes a national and an international experience, and, as such, fosters community between a British nurse and a dying partisan, an American officer and a Venetian fisherman, a Black G.I. and a Neapolitan child.

In antithesis to Croce's holistic individualism, for the Tavianis the self is not a homogeneous entity, and unity does not inhabit the Italian body politic. In *Night*, they show how families and villages divide under the pressure of antagonistic political factions and how individuals themselves are caught between the leaps of the imagination and the pain of history, the flight of fantasy and the instinct for survival.

By emphasizing the disunity of the self and the splitting of communities, the Tavianis reject continuity between the Risorgimento and the Resistance, on the grounds that neither one of these periods is characterized by unity at the level of nation or class. For the Tavianis, the unity of the Resistance is not an historical experience but the phantasmic childhood of postwar Italian history, which, in *Night*, they remember with nostalgia. By comparing the unity of the Resistance to a childhood that never was, the Tavianis identify with the popular historical knowledge of the New Left and reject the historicism of the historical Left. Yet the Tavianis still depend on Giambattista Vico's sense that national history undergoes phases comparable to the ages of the individual. With the Tavianis, the Resistance is a utopian moment reserved for those who are too young or too old, and therefore stand on the margins of official history and adulthood.

May 1968 was a season of generational tensions. In keeping with this climate of rejection and attraction toward the past and father figures, the Tavianis have an ambivalent relation with the film history that precedes them. For the Tavianis the father is neorealism, but it is also Fascism: a much more difficult stylistic legacy to overcome. In *Night*, the reevaluation of neorealism does not ignore the stylistic legacy of fascist cinema and opera. The Tavianis blend operatic macrohistory with comedic microhistory, possibly a statement that the institutions and the style of Fascism do not entirely disappear with the Resistance.

Neorealism and Rossellini are the fathers with whom the Tavianis grew up and whom they must supersede by allowing their anxiety of influence to assume both positive and negative guises in their films.[14] In *Night*, for example, Galvano Galvani (Omero Antonutti), the ominous father of *Padre Padrone* (1976–1977) and of *Good Morning Babylon* (1987), is a positive figure of Biblical proportions. Like Moses leading the Jews across the Red Sea, Galvano appoints himself leader of a group of villagers from San Martino.

[14] On the father, the Tavianis explain: "Yes, we are truly interested [in the father], but to be precise, as biological element, in the sense that the son must avenge himself on the father, but only in instances in which history, specifically through the renewal of generations, creates in the new generation a new set of circumstances and new ideas." Guido Aristarco, *Sotto il segno dello scorpione—Il cinema dei Fratelli Taviani* (Messina-Florence: Casa Editrice G. D'Anna, 1977), 207. On neorealism as father, the Tavianis say: "Our relationship with neorealism is a love-hate, father-son relationship. Born of a beloved and admired father, we then denied him with the ungrateful violence of sons who realize themselves in the measure to which they destroy the parent. The denial, however, remains always a form of relating. Our formation, our choice (that is, to make films) is bound to love for the cinema in general and for neorealism in particular." Millicent Marcus, "The Taviani Brothers' *Night of the Shooting Stars*: Ambivalent Tribute to Neorealism," *Italian Film in the Light of Neorealism* (Princeton, N.J.: Princeton University Press, 1986), 361–62.

The group searches for the Fifth Army across the yellow and green Tuscan countryside.

The figure of the father is too powerful to apply to the leader Galvano alone. The theme of fathering resurfaces across a chain of events. To be sure the need to become a father partly motivates one of the villagers, Corrado, to join the ranks of the partisans. Corrado adopts his own father's name, Giovanni, as a fighting pseudonym. Corrado, thus, fills in for the son, Giovanni, he himself could not father because his newlywed wife, Bellindia, dies in the Fascist massacre of the cathedral of San Martino. The name of the father lives on through the son, so that another father and another son may die. Corrado avenges the death of the unborn Giovanni by killing the bloodthirsty son of the Fascist Marmugi.

In *Night*, national unity disintegrates as a result of the conflicting roles played by class and regional identity in the historical process. Yet, the Tavianis' critique of national unity in Croce and Rossellini, and of class unity in Gramsci and Togliatti, stops at class and region, while not addressing the question of sexual difference. In *Night*, continuity turns to discontinuity with class and region. With regard to sexual difference, however, historical discontinuity reverts to biological continuity and to a heterosexual, homosocial genealogy. During childhood and old age, women have access to utopia, but as adults they bear the burden of reproduction and appear to live outside history, a male domain.

In several interviews, Paolo and Vittorio Taviani admit that *Paisà* is the father-text of *Night*. In the wake of the neorealist transubstantiation of cinema into life, and biology into spirituality, the Tavianis' films are intensely corporeal, but also sensitive to the abstractions of a utopian imagination. It is as if the two brothers only half-understood the formula of Rossellini's amalgam and the centrality of the Eucharistic transubstantiation in their mentor's cinema.

In *Night of the Shooting Stars*, for example, the Eucharist occurs three times: after a country wedding with bread and wine, before leaving on a dangerous journey with bread and tomatoes, and before the explosion of the cathedral in the village of San Martino. In the first case, it is no sharing of the body of Christ but irony on the body erotic. The father's bread is a benevolent mockery of his wanton daughter, already pregnant on her wedding day. In the second case, there is no light-hearted desecration. The communion in the cellar simply marks the splitting of the community. Galvano's group eats, before leaving behind those who choose not to leave the village. In the third case, the sense of atonement that usually defines Catholic ritual is missing as soon as one little girl discloses the most prosaic of realities. She tells her friend she cannot swallow the holy host.

In *Night of the Shooting Stars*, the Eucharist occurs in secular, daily terms, nearly veering toward the pagan: love-making outside wedlock, eating to gain strength and survive, the children's perspective on ritual. With the Tavianis, the Eucharist does not stand for Catholicism in the narrowest sense; it takes place outside the church and marks social division. These repetitions of the Eucharist, however, turn *Night* into a litmus test for Rossellini's neorealism. By representing the Eucharist, *Night* makes *Paisà* say, in 1982, what it could not say in 1946 about the dancers of the commedia replacing the statues of opera.

The Eucharist does not just stand for Rossellini's transubstantiation, or Bazin's amalgam. The Eucharist marks the moment when the *corpus mysticum* becomes available to the community, and, in so doing, the Eucharist also implies an historiographical stance. In *Paisà*, the neorealist body is Eucharistic because it "celebrates the unity of the [national body politic conceived of as a] *corpus mysticum* and of the group participants in it."[15] It is as if the Resistance had temporarily made possible the transubstantiation of class into nation, of the individual into the collectivity, and thus overcame internal divisions.

## UNITY AND CONTINUITY IN THE RESISTANCE

In Rossellini's *Paisà*, the inhabitants of Sicily, Naples, Rome, Florence, Emilia-Romagna, and the Po River Valley interact with the Allies who are slowly moving up the Italian boot. The physiognomy of and dialect spoken by each Italian character refer to social backgrounds instantly recognizable to a domestic audience. In the Sicilian episode, for example, after the landing of the Americans the villagers gather inside a church. There class differences become quickly apparent through clothing and through the hostile manner in which a local bourgeois comments on the arrival of the Fifth Army.

[15] Marcus, "The Taviani Brothers," 386–87.

In neorealism, gestures and behaviors document an historical experience. Onomastic labels fit types, just as the masks of the commedia dell'arte bring to mind the idyosyncracies of a region or city.
Joe from Jersey can only be the good-hearted, wholesome American;
Carmela is Carmela Sazio, the native Sicilian girl. By contrast, with
the Tavianis names do not always match characters in such a predictable fashion. In joining the ranks of the partisans, some villagers
adopt pseudonyms which are more a projection of their fantasy
selves than a documentary description of their identity.

The villagers' appearance allegorizes a class or a regional origin,
but the Resistance enables a few of them to detach their names
from their bodies and leap into utopia. Giuseppe Verdi's *Requiem*,
a music of death, becomes a man's name for his newly born identity. The fair-haired Nicola decides to call himself Bruno, which
means the dark-haired one. In turn, Bruno changes his name to Nicola. This onomastic exchange sanctions the bonding of the two
friends. It is nearly a marriage between males who, later on, will die
side by side. Four other villagers take on the names of Leone, Or-
ango, Pelo, and Gufo. In so doing, they transform themselves into
the half-human and half-animal creatures of fairy tales, while their
features take on cartoon-like expressivity.

The imaginary identities assumed by the Tavianis' partisans find
a literary equivalent in Italo Calvino's *The Path to the Nest of Spiders* (1947). This novel is set in the northern region of Liguria and
deals with a child's perception of the Resistance. Calvino's characters have the hybrid features of fantastic creatures in folk tales, half-
real, half-imaginary. Pin, the protagonist, has "red and black freck-
les" clustering up "around his eyes like a swarm of wasps," while
the village thief, Pietromagro, remains unforgettable for his "face
covered in short black hair like dog's fur, eyes ringed with yellow
round the pupils, and hand upraised."[16] Calvino's realism puts the
reader in contact with the imagination of regional folklore, while a
child's eyes transfigure a history whose horrors are all too real.

From the involution of neorealism to May 1968, the documentary
style of *Paisà* loses its aura of neutrality, and, retrospectively, seems
to have participated in the project of postwar restoration. This project amounted to the containment of class and regional differences

[16] Italo Calvino, *The Path to the Nest of Spiders* (1947), trans. Archibald
Colquhoun, pref. author, trans. William Weaver (New York: The Ecco Press, 1987),
2.

through the production of a composite, but homogeneous, term of identification. In the attempt to replace unity with disunity, the Tavianis do not follow Rossellini's one-to-one correspondence between physiognomy and social identity. With the Tavianis there is no such easily decipherable match between onomastic label and physical appearance.

For the two brothers individual behavior is partly, but not exclusively, predicated on social roles. Instead of names consistent with the bodies to which they refer, a contradictory overlapping of physiological reactions and social identity informs the Tavianis' construction of character. According to this perspective, each character is simultaneously the embodiment of a class, of a region, of a sexual type, and a biological being as well, facets of identity that hardly ever fit together neatly.

After the massacre in the cathedral, for example, we see Bellindia's mother pushing a wheelbarrow containing her daughter's slain body. With a muffled cry of "I'll do it alone," she rejects the bishop's attempt to help. Is the mother behaving under terrible stress or does she accuse the bishop for not preventing the Black Shirts' and the Nazis' use of the cathedral?

Such an accusation is possible if we consider the opposition of the Church to the reenactment of the massacre in *San Miniato, Luglio 1944*, a documentary made by the Tavianis with Valentino Orsini in 1954.[17] To be sure, the Tavianis prevent us from locking a character's response into one, single interpretation, for history is made of intersecting levels of experience, ranging from the physiological to the psychological to the sociological.

This same view of human behavior as a compound of multiple aspects, some closer to culture, others to biology, reappears during the execution of the Marmugi father and of his fanatical young son.

[17] On *San Miniato July 1944*, Marco De Poli writes: "In 1964 they made, together with Orsini and Cesare Zavattini, their first documentary, *San Miniato July 1944*, a reconstruction told through the words of the protagonists of the massacre committed ten years earlier by the Nazis in the local cathedral. The religious and civil authorities blocked the project, and the documentary, if finished, did not attain the censor's stamp of approval." "Paolo e Vittorio Taviani," *Belfagor* 30, no. 1 (January 31, 1975): 73. In addition to this article, see on fathering, biology, and history, Marco De Poli, *Paolo and Vittorio Taviani* (Milan: Moizzi Editore, 1977). On the Tavianis' relation to the Catholic church, Marcus offers a prudent, but valuable interpretation: "Nor do the filmmakers condemn the bishop for the gullibility which makes him, like his parishioners, a vain believer in the moral power of institutions to prevail over wartime criminality." "The Taviani Brothers," 387.

Corrado's shooting of the fifteen-year-old bears an ideological explanation, but not exclusively so. Beside political punishment, it is also the act of someone who is avenging the deaths of his unborn son and newlywed wife. The Marmugi father grinds his head into the dust in desperation at having lost his child. "Kill him, don't you see how much he is suffering!" says Corrado's companion. The Marmugi father looks less like a Black Shirt and more like an animal gone mad. His suicide, therefore, is not so much an ideological choice, but a symptom of psychological devastation. No longer a human being, nor a Fascist, but only a beast annihilated by pain, he inflicts upon himself the treatment reserved for crippled horses.

The Tavianis' rewriting of the Resistance has some points in common with the position of Mario Cannella, a film historian close to the New Left. According to Cannella, Togliatti failed to understand that Gramsci's unity and continuity for the sake of class, rhyme with Croce's unity and continuity for the sake of nation. These Gramscian themes, therefore, are unable to anticipate and prevent the victory of Catholic forces in the election of 1948. Despite its participation in the Resistance, the postwar Catholic party can be partly seen as a *ricorso* or a *trasformismo* of Giolitti's pre–World War I lay, bourgeois leadership. Cannella blames the historical Left for subordinating a critique of Gramsci to the glorification of the Resistance as a national experience, comparable to a Risorgimento of democratic forces.

Cannella's essay first appeared in 1966 in *Giovane Critica*, a left-wing journal published in Catania, Sicily. This essay participated in a process of historiographical revision, and led to new perceptions of Fascism and of the Resistance that invaded popular culture in 1968. Furthermore, Cannella linked the containment of neorealism to the themes of unity and continuity to such a degree that already in 1966 he seemed to set the stage for the opposition of the New Left to the "historical compromise" between Catholics and Marxists in the 1970s. To the New Left after 1968, this plan appeared to be one more example of *trasformismo*, rather than a significant step toward a truly new social order. Of course, Aldo Moro's and Enrico Berlinguer's project never came to fruition, and some popular magazines argued that the kidnapping and assassination of Moro by the Red Brigade (March 16, 1978) was carried out with the intention of sabotaging the "historical compromise," by destabilizing the political climate once and for all.

According to Cannella, historical continuity feeds *trasformismo.* The postwar establishment preferred to be associated with the Risorgimento than with Fascism. The analogy between the Risorgimento and the Resistance posits Fascism as a parenthesis, thus absolving the ruling class of any contamination with the regime. Cannella writes, "The widespread interpretation of fascism as a momentary 'perversion' or 'deviation,' as a parenthesis in the history of Italy, naturally favoured such positions: things had to be renewed, brought up to date, adapted, but *within the same terms of reference as a tradition which had proved its validity in the course of the two previous decades.*"[18] The view of Fascism as a parenthesis, or as an alien virus attacking the otherwise healthy body politic of the Italian liberal state, traveled from the desk of Benedetto Croce to the script of Rossellini's *Open City*. In *Open City*, Marina (Maria Michi), a drug addict and a collaborationist, is an embodiment of Giovanni Giolitti's Italy temporarily infected by the fascist disease (fig. 41): "Marina's corruption by promiscuity and drugs in *Open City* leads her into a kind of lascivious exhaustion, an exhaustion that will become generalized onto the whole German people in *Germany, Year Zero*; here, however, the impetus of the corrupters' forward movement keeps the disease projected outward onto the Italians they cynically use."[19]

Peter Brunette argues that *Paisà* is a film about unity in difference.[20] The historiographical implications of Brunette's reading explain the ending of the Sicilian episode. Carmela avenges the death of Joe from Jersey, but she dies on the rocks, having been shot by German soldiers. Joe's platoon leaves the site unaware of Carmela's sacrifice. The girl is only a poor native both for Germans and Americans: "A dirty Eye-talian." Shortly before her death, Carmela equates Americans with Germans, since all these soldiers are invaders of her homeland. The equivalence drawn between the two armies, turns the Sicilian girl into an allegorical embodiment of Italy as a nation. She stands for the body politic crushed on the rocks by

[18] Mario Cannella, "Ideology and Aesthetic Hypotheses in the Criticism of Neo-Realism," *Screen* 14, 4 (Winter 73/74): 12.

[19] Brunette, *Roberto Rossellini*, 46. Rossellini's adoption of Croce's view that 1945 was a year zero becomes clear in the title of two films: *Germany, Year Zero* (1947) and *Italia Anno Uno* (1974), a tribute to Alcide De Gasperi's leadership.

[20] Peter Brunette, "Unity and Difference in *Paisan*," *Studies in the Literary Imagination* 16, no. 1 (Spring 1983): 91–111.

**41.** Maria Michi as Marina and the fascist virus in Roberto Rossellini's *Open City* (1945). Courtesy of The Museum of Modern Art, Film Stills Archive.

one enemy after another. Carmela is both Sicily and Italy. While the equivalence between the land and the woman is trite, her body serves as a site of reconciliation between region and nation.

The image of Carmela's body crushed on the rocks acquires meanings that outgrow the boundaries of *Paisà*. Italian schoolchildren learn that political history is a violent agent that alters the physiognomy of national geography. Carmela, then, stands allegorically for a whole nation subject to a foreign invasion. In *Paisà*, the Resistance is comparable to a textbook version of the Risorgimento. In moving from the classroom to the screen, the geopolitical image of Italy changes repeatedly, in 1815, 1848, 1860, 1915, and again after 1943, with the constitution of the Republic of Salò and the appearance of the Gothic Line.

It is historiographically significant that the map punctuates *Paisà*. Brunette grounds the theme of unity in difference in the image of this geographical body that is repeatedly invaded:

a temporal movement that meshes with the equally relentless linear, spatial movement upward on the map, insists upon a sameness, a unity to the Italian experience. . . . Yet the chronological movement, which seems to describe merely different temporal points in a homogeneous space (Italy), or different "aspects" of a homogeneous, single national experience, cannot disguise the fact that the spaces, the regions of Italy, insist on their heterogeneity in each episode just as strongly as ever. The clearly proclaimed regionality of the map thus defeats in advance its simultaneous proclamation of unity.[21]

The surface of Italy appears violated by the advancing arrows of the Fifth Army, from Sicily to the Po Valley.

Brunette's claim of unity in difference echoes Pietro Pintus' discussion of spectatorship in *Paisà*, which he considers a travelogue for a national audience:

*Paisà* to us today appears to be a great travel survey through Italy, a newscast in six parts on the conditions of the country during the advance of the Allies. A newscast executed with great commitment and expense like a great television production of our days. Let's not be deceived by stereotypes and legends: *Paisà* was the most expensive movie among those that were produced in 1946, and it had definite ambitions as a discourse directed to the nation. The tendency to go beyond regionalism we find in neorealist cinema is in fact the same tendency we find in television, and, as in television, this tendency is tinged by linguistic, ideological, and productive humanism.[22]

Pintus' analogy between the transregional spectatorship of *Paisà* and the rhetoric of television well summarizes the interclassist ideology of Rossellini's neorealism.

On the basis of scholastic training, an Italian audience will relate the outline of political geography in 1944, to its previous versions in the Risorgimento. In this case, the American arrows on Rossellini's map will also acquire an ambivalent meaning. The Allies are not liberators, but invaders, even though more welcome than previous ones. Rossellini's map reinforces assumptions crucial to postwar popular perceptions of history linked to Croce's interpretation.

[21] Brunette, *Roberto Rossellini*, 62.
[22] Pintus, *Storia e film*, 27–28.

By stressing continuity, this popular knowledge posits that the national identity survives undisturbed beneath a map with a changing surface. The deep core of the Italian identity remains intact despite different invasions, and emerges uncontaminated after exposure to a foreign army or to an alien virus such as Fascism.

With Rossellini, cooperation among different classes matches attempts to overcome the cultural barrier existing between Italians and Americans. According to an initial script approved by Admiral Stone, *Paisà* was meant to commemorate the deaths of American soldiers. Since the Italian film industry was in shambles, Rossellini relied on the financial backing of MGM. Each episode was to start and end with a white cross on an American grave. In the final version, before the Neapolitan episode, the camera pans across the plain of Paestum and intercepts two white crosses, standing in the lower part of the frame. In keeping with the interests of American propaganda, Italian regional diversity was to be a mere backdrop against which to stage clichés of "courage in a foreign land."

At first, the scriptwriter Sergio Amidei had proposed to Rossellini a heroic double-plot of unfulfilled love and desperate death in Val D'Aosta. In this northern mountain setting, the characters were supposed to be a towering blond American, a partisan's sister, and her two-meter-tall comrades. By relying on less than a *canovaccio*, Rossellini, at the last minute, decided to avoid Val D'Aosta and shoot, instead, in the Po Valley, an area familiar to him from childhood. Futhermore, the initial script contained a seventh episode, later eliminated. This additional episode, entitled *The Prisoner*, narrated the encounter of a dumb Italian driver and an American pilot. Unable to be understood, the Italian driver saves the American pilot's life with the help of gestures. In the midst of which the Italian dies under German fire (fig. 42).

In the episode set in the Po River Valley, the American Dale fights the Nazis side by side with the local fishermen. Roberto Battaglia notes that the contributions of "foreign partisans" in the so-called International Brigade are acknowledged in the earliest, but also most anecdotal, accounts of the Resistance.[23] Battaglia goes on to say that this intercultural cooperation that seeps to film from

---

[23] Roberto Battaglia, "La storiografia della resistenza, dalla memorialistica al saggio storico," *Il Movimento di Liberazione in Italia* 9, no. 57 (1959): 80–131.

**42.** Gestures instead of words in Roberto Rossellini's *Paisà* (1946). Courtesy of The Museum of Modern Art, Film Stills Archive.

partisans' memoirs of the late 1940s, dims the indigeneous, popular character of the Resistance. Were these regional features to become too apparent, the issue of class might also surface. And too much attention to regional and class differences would call into question the belief in the theme of unity that shapes the national identity.[24]

From the beginning of *Night*, the Tavianis equate history with storytelling. Their project in *Night* was not to tell the true story of the Liberation, but to show how history is made up of different stories—some of them tied to historiography and some to popular folklore, some to personal memory and some to the cinema.

The flashing of Rossellini's map comes with an objective, male, voice-over narration. By introducing a convention of war documentary into a fiction, Rossellini lends authenticity to the six stories that unfold from region to region. The Tavianis abandoned Rossellini's impersonal, male narration in favor of a warm, feminine voice-over, evoking a distant night of Saint Lawrence. The adult Ce-

[24] Ibid., 93.

cilia narrates episodes that she did not always witness as a child. This mixture of an adult's and of a child's perspective, of firsthand and word-of-mouth accounts, denies the history of the Resistance an objective singularity and recomposes it into a plurality of stories and subjective experiences.

The Tavianis' history is an unreliable story. *Night* is "replete with stylistic 'pointers' which disrupt our suspension of disbelief."[25] One of the centers of consciousness belongs to the child, Cecilia. Only a child's perspective, halfway between primitive *bricolage* and the plenitude of Vico's age of poetry, can accommodate the heterogeneous sources of *Night*: " Within that repository of popular thought, World War II history finds analogues in folk religious observances and pagan myth, whose precepts are no sooner announced in the film than they immediately become the basis of Cecilia's childhood perceptions."[26] The Tavianis stretch neorealist microhistory to cosmic proportions, without either monumentalizing or downplaying the pictorial vividness of the events recounted. When Cecilia's grandfather recites the *Iliad* under an oak tree, all of a sudden World War II appears for what it was: a devastating speck of human experience afloat in the layers of pagan and Christian time, of regional folklore and national history.

The fairy-tale atmosphere of the Tavianis' film conveys the quickness with which the history of the Resistance acquired a utopian coloring. According to Roberto Battaglia, its early historiography is mostly regional and folkloric just like *Night*, a film explicitly set in Tuscany and with a title pointing to half-pagan, half-Christian superstitions: the wish-fulfilling power of shooting stars on August 10.

The regional scale of *Night* is in line with the microhistory neorealism opposes to the monumental, operatic macrohistory of fascist cinema. This regional focus, however, goes against the grain of Rossellini's *Paisà* in an historiographical sense. *Night* differs from *Paisà* in that it avoids the theme of international communication. Marcus comments on how the intercultural solidarity of Rossellini

---

[25] Marcus, "The Taviani Brothers," 362.

[26] Marcus, "The Taviani Brothers," 367. On the neorealist screen turning from objective window to subjective mirror, see Ben Lawton, "Italian Neorealism: A Mirror Construction of Reality," *Film Criticism* 3, no. 2 (Winter 1979): 8–23; Guido Fink, "*Neorealismo* Revisited," *Twentieth-Century Studies* 5–6 (September 1971): 72–82. On the Tavianis and fantasy, see Nuccio Orto, *La notte dei desideri: Il cinema dei Fratelli Taviani* (Palermo: Sellerio Editore, 1987).

has literally no object to latch onto, since "the Americans are totally absent,"[27] in the sense that they are present only in the imagination of the villagers.

## DISUNITY IN HISTORY

By narrating the vicissitudes of a socially heterogeneous group, the
Tavianis challenge the theme of national unity.[28] Thus the Resistance is portrayed as not just a struggle against an external, foreign
enemy, but an internal war as well. In playing family off of class
and region, neighborly relations off of political camps, the Tavianis
touch on a controversial area of Resistance historiography. Roberto
Battaglia cites the historian Massimo Salvadori voicing the crucial
question: civil war or class struggle? or maybe both? "It is a matter
of classes. But there were fascists in all classes, even if more in
some classes than in others; and likewise there were antifascists in
all classes, from peasants to miners, from industrialists to aristocrats."[29] Do Salvadori's speculations on the opposition to the regime of aristocrats and industrialists constitute a rehashing of an
interclassist or antifascist national unity, an interpretation partly
due to Croce, partly due to Togliatti? In the Tavianis' *Night* this
historiographical dilemma emerges from their use of color.

The night they secretly leave town, the villagers wear black gar-
ments. But the color black is worn as well by former friends and
relatives who are their enemies, the Black Shirts. Rather than se-
crecy as for the first group, the color signifies violence for the second group. Black also punctuates the yellow wheat field where the
villagers confront the Fascists. Black travels across factions, thus
underlining that history is not made up of separate entities clashing
in the vacuum of an operatic stage, but of elbow-to-elbow daily life.
Within the cozy space of the village of San Martino, the personal
sphere may or may not coincide with the political, just as sexual,

[27] Marcus, "The Taviani Brothers," 370.

[28] *Night* can be seen as the Tavianis' response to Italo Calvino's invitation: "When
they begin to make films about the Resistance again . . . I say—the film I would like
to see made is a film that portrays the different attitudes of the Italians toward the
partisans' struggle—with that same formula adopted by Maupassant in *Boule de Suif*
and by Ford in *Stagecoach*—a hodgepodge of various types of people . . . who find
themselves by chance travelling by the same means." "Viaggio in camion," *Cinema
Nuovo* 25 (April 1955): 293.

[29] Massimo Salvadori as cited in Battaglia, "La storiografia della resistenza," 110.

class, and regional features, when attached to an individual, may overlap in a contradictory manner.

The mobility of the color black in *Night* finds a parallel in the relationship between Galvano Galvani, a representative of the popular classes, and Signora Concetta, a representative of the upper bourgeoisie. The tension between rich and poor weakens in relation to a romantic attraction dating back to youthful days. Daily contact fostered by the struggle for survival prevails over an abstract notion of class difference. Perhaps this quotidian dimension of forced or unusual class contact explains the temporary social pact of the Resistance. As the journey progresses and the dangers increase, Concetta renounces the signs of her class: her earrings, her veil, her hat. Meanwhile her relationship with Galvano grows less and less cold, until it returns to affection on the last night of their journey.

Despite its romantic overtones, the conclusion of *Night* is no happy ending à la Hollywood. The Tavianis depict the embrace of the working class with the bourgeoisie as the utopian projection of an unfulfilled desire for unity that flares across Italian history, from the days of the Resistance to Berlinguer's plan for the "historical compromise." Galvano's and Concetta's romance is a utopian moment in a Viconian sense. It reunites two people who live on the margins of history and adulthood. Love between Galvano and Concetta is possible only in a village with a heavenly name. Sant'Angelo is so removed from the processes of history that the Americans do not even bother to liberate this little town on top of a hill.

## DISCONTINUITY IN HISTORY

To the theme of continuity, from the Risorgimento to the Resistance, the Tavianis juxtapose a conceptualization of history based on discontinuity, with leaps from biology to history, and from history to utopia. For the two brothers, there is no teleological trajectory from the struggle for independence in the nineteenth century to the fight against Salò and Nazism in the twentieth century. Croce's and Togliatti's linear historicisms are as misleading as the straight road the villagers follow in their search for the Americans. The road shoots into infinity and into the vanishing point of the villagers' desires. The road also accentuates the depth of centered compositions where people walk without knowing where to go.

For the Tavianis, the history of the Resistance is not Croce's straight road leading to "liberty," nor Togliatti's gradual path. On the contrary, history is uneven and erratic, because, on the one hand, it interfaces with biology and, on the other, with a utopian imagination. At the beginning of *Night*, two images of thresholds refer to the leaps from history to utopia, and from biology to history. In Cecilia's bedroom, the window opens onto an artificial-looking landscape: a village asleep under a starry sky. The window is the threshold between reality and fantasy, history and utopia. The bluish lighting and the spell-bound atmosphere of Cecilia's bedroom charm us like another fairy tale we all love, which also begins with a window as a threshold to fantasy: *Peter Pan*. With this soft beginning, the two brothers inform us that blue is the color of romance and of the imaginary. They use this lighting again for Sant'Angelo, a village on the margins of history in the land of utopia.

The image of a second threshold illustrates the interface of biology and history. In the opening sequence set in the Tuscan countryside, the distant sound of an American cannon, followed by a sudden, nearly metaphysical wind, shakes the branches of a pear tree. History upsets the rhythms of nature and the arrival of the Fifth Army makes the pears fall. The camera follows a pear, aimlessly rolling on the grass, until it cuts to a grave-like shelter. Corrado emerges from underneath the ground. The tree is perhaps the tree of life threatened by war, but the pear is certainly a magical object. It marks the boundary between life and death, biology and history, and between Corrado and Bellindia.

While death surrounds him, Corrado is a modern Lazarus experiencing resurrection. It is as if the presence of his explicitly pregnant and soon-to-be wife had summoned him back to sunshine and fresh water. If he, the man, comes from the realm of death, history, and culture, Bellindia, the woman, is associated with biology, life, and nature (fig. 43). As a result of these predictable and problematic associations, she is the bearer of an unrestrained, male sexuality, of an instinct for survival that stands up against the challenge of World War II and against a Nietzschean view of history as death.

## BIOLOGY, HISTORY, AND UTOPIA

Biology, history, and utopia are the key terms of *Night of the Shooting Stars*. At the end of World War II, when everything seems about to change overnight, utopia no longer appears far away, but exists, together with biology, on the margins of adulthood and history.

**43.** Woman in Paolo and Vittorio Taviani's *Night of the Shooting Stars* (1982). Courtesy of The Museum of Modern Art, Film Stills Archive.

Utopia inhabits the eyes of Cecilia, a child gifted with an irreverent, and therefore revolutionary, imagination.

By associating utopia with childhood, the Tavianis repropose the opposition between poetry and history that Nietzsche does not borrow, but rather shares, with Vico. In the wake of Vico's theory of history as a process patterned on the ages of humankind, the Tavianis' utopia, like biology, belongs to a pre-historical, child-like realm, to that phase of experience that precedes the adulthood of individuals and nations and which, in a Nietzschean sense, has not yet been spoiled by the evils of an abuse of history.

In embracing this Viconian perspective, the Tavianis rekindle the memory of other famous neorealist children: Italo Calvino's Pin in *The Path to the Nest of Spiders* and Elsa Morante's Useppe in *History: A Novel* (1977).[30] Like Cecilia, Pin and Useppe have the gift of

---

[30] Elsa Morante, *History: A Novel*, trans. William Weaver (New York: Knopf, 1977). In Italian: *La Storia* (Turin: Einaudi, 1974).

"discovering and naming daily—yet also wondrous—surround-ings."[31] Morante's novel *History* is set in Rome at the end of World War II and proposes a truly Nietzschean attack on history. Unlike Morante, the Tavianis do not hate history so long as fantasy helps us leap into utopia. For Calvino and the Tavianis, without the imag-ination of folktales history would turn into a nightmare of Nietz-schean coloring. This is why, with the sunshower at the end of *Night*, the two brothers treat us to a spell-bound, utopian moment, an imaginary window through which to fantasize about the promise the Resistance did not fulfill: a love story between the bourgeoisie and the working class in the village of Sant'Angelo.

In *Night*, history scars the body with emotional and physical pain and leaves indelible traces in the memories and behaviors of the characters. Corrado, for example, is unable to remember his father's name, Giovanni. The fifteen-year-old Marmugi obsessively repeats: "È vero, babbo! è vero, babbo!"[32] The name of the father is a fixa-tion for a Black Shirt crawling on the ground, in agony: "Mussolini, Mussolini." When Nicola and Rosanna lose control, in reacting to the sight of a black cloth or to the sudden noise of an airplane, brother and sister perform jerky movements. Their behavior comes from spatial disorientation in familiar surroundings and resembles that of animals who become frenzied inside their cages.

By zooming to the villagers' ears as they listen to the dynamiting of their houses, the Tavianis emphasize that the incorporation of an historical, public event takes place on an individual and physiolog-ical level. The historical evidence of the explosion can hardly be found in archives. The documents, instead, are these ears which are forever changed by one, unforgettable blast.

The body is subject to history but can also resist its effects, espe-cially if the psyche, the protective armor of a utopian imagination, holds up against war. After being hit by sniper fire, Mara transfig-ures German soldiers into *paisans* from Brooklyn. As a Sicilian, Mara does not fit in Tuscany and reminds us of Rossellini's Car-mela Sazio. Mara's fantasy of being at home becomes real in the instant that precedes her death. In her agony, she sees the *paisans*

---

[31] Gregory Lucente, *Beautiful Fables: Self-Consciousness in Italian Narrative from Manzoni to Calvino* (Baltimore, Md.: The Johns Hopkins University Press, 1986), 251.

[32] "Isn't it true, daddy! Isn't it true, daddy!"

holding a "souvenir bottle" with tiny plastic snowflakes falling around a "miniature Statue of Liberty."[33]

The horror of death loses its impact again, thanks to a wish ful-fillment fantasy, when Cecilia witnesses the killing of her grandfather in the wheat field. In front of the stupefied girl, Bruno turns into a Homeric warrior avenging the death of the old man. Mara's American dream parallels Cecilia's comic book version of the *Iliad*. For the child, the Homeric poem is not a classical text, but a fairy tale she learned from her grandfather.[34] The Tavianis suggest that, just as Mara's and Cecilia's imaginations can push away the arrival of death, the utopia of regional *filastrocche* can prevail over pain and fear. The *filastrocca* of Cecilia's mother is the life-preserving inheritance that the child as an adult will pass on to her son.

## FROM HISTORICAL DISCONTINUITY TO BIOLOGICAL CONTINUITY

By exploring the interface of biology and history, the Tavianis mo-bilize a linear view of the historical process into a discontinuous experience. Yet they do so only with regard to class and regional identity, while failing to address the issue of sexual difference. No-where in *Night* does there appear any effort to rethink the role of women in the Resistance. Shortly before an air raid, Rosanna and Cecilia's mothers sit by the river. They still wear around their necks the keys to their family homes destroyed by explosions. The Tavianis' iconography of women, river, and keys allegorizes the un-locking of chastity belts and the continuation of life, despite the threat of history. Ilvo, one of the villagers, makes advances to Ce-cilia's mother. His interest in her is purely sexual, not romantic. Ilvo's behavior calls attention to his quasi-animal drive to survive and live to the fullest. For a moment the urges of the body erotic prevail over the demands of the body politic.

For the two brothers, men make history, while women are bearers of children. The ending of the film reasserts the association of women with nature and, in so doing, replaces a view of history as discontinuous with the continuity of biology. But this shift from discontinuity to continuity, at the level of sexual difference, comes

---

[33] Marcus, "The Taviani Brothers," 369.

[34] On the stylistic affinities of *Night* with comic books, see Richard Corliss' re-view, *Time*, February 21, 1983, 80, as cited in Marcus, "The Taviani Brothers," 365.

as a surprise. Only at the end of *Night* do we discover that a sleeping baby lies on the bed beside the mother.

The discovery is as unsettling as the spatial disorientation the Tavianis ascribe to the villagers, for whom history is a stressful process. Up to this point we assume that Cecilia is telling her story to a male lover, who, like us, is enraptured by the texture of her voice and by her explicit invitation to listen: "Wait, don't sleep my love, I wish to find the words to tell you about. . . ." These words of Cecilia's precede the appearance of the title on the screen. The flashing of the credits coincides with, even seems to grow out of, the trajectory of a shooting star. Cecilia's words do not belong to her but to the Tavianis, the poets of historical filmmaking. As poets, they invoke the Homeric muse before telling their story and ask for help in finding the "right words." They exploit the seductiveness of Cecilia's voice to lure the men and women of their audience into the spell of a night of Saint Lawrence and to place them in the position of an ideal male spectator.

Appropriately, the Tavianis rely on an emotional response to voice and music as they begin to tell a story about the subjectivity of history. They use Cecilia's voice to develop an alternative conceptualization of history, but not of woman. Cecilia's voice-over narration simply indicates that the Tavianis do not assign objectivity and truth to history. A history without authority does not call for an authoritative source. Hence, the two brothers do not need the God-like, disembodied, male narration Rossellini uses in *Paisà*. Once the spell is over, and the story has come to an end, the earthly limitations of Cecilia's voice, and even her luring us into an assumption, become apparent. In mainstream, narrative cinema, the voice-over is often male and disembodied. Here Cecilia's voice rejoins a maternal body.[35]

In the opening sequence, set in the countryside, two women help Corrado get ready for his wedding ceremony. The young one wears Corrado's hat while he washes his face. The old one holds his white shirt on a hanger. The tasks performed by the two women confirm that the story is spoken by Cecilia, but that it is not for her. Tavianis' *Night* is a male text dressed in a female voice. In opposition,

[35] Kaja Silverman, "Dis-Embodying the Female Voice," in *Re-Vision, Essays in Feminist Film Criticism,* ed. Mary Ann Doane, Patricia Mellencamp, and Linda Williams (Frederick, Md.: University Publications of America and The American Film Institute, 1984), 131–49.

the young woman mimicks Corrado by temporarily wearing his hat. Even if the Tavianis underline that woman, the bearer of life, can defy history as death, in the end her role is not to fulfill her desire but to sustain a heterosexual, homosocial genealogy. A young woman may wear a man's hat, but despite this disguise her fate is to grow old next to him, holding his shirt.

The old woman who holds Corrado's shirt prefigures Signora Concetta's strength. Shortly after the battle in the wheat field, Concetta bears on her shoulders the full weight of Galvano's body. He is helplessly hanging from a tree. Galvano's rescue discloses that the male leader is not so self-assured and independent as we might expect. He needs the help of Concetta to stand on his feet. Galvano cries after the explosion of his house. He sits alone and confused in the deserted square of Sant'Angelo. He is unable to make sense of the return to normalcy, and unwilling to give up the interclassist romance of the Resistance.

Galvano is not the only man whose feet hurt after a long march. When Nicola joins the villagers at Corrado's wedding, his feet are as badly damaged as Galvano's. In folktales, the narrative agent who travels is always male and his reward is the love of the female princess and the conquest of new territory. The man is the traveller, while the woman is both the landscape and the goal of the journey, or the ground of representation and its telos. Man is the agent of culture, history, and death, who conquers nature, the land, and the female.

In *Night*, the villagers do not always know where they are going. Men's feet hurt. Galvano and Nicola suffer as they move forward to make history. Are the Tavianis undermining the association of men with culture? The two brothers' narrative fits the patriarchal framework typical of folktales, a framework that demands the marginalization of women, while it also is responsible for the oppression of the men it supposedly empowers. Still, in *Night*, the question of sexual difference is subordinate to a Nietzschean view of history as death. The antidote to the evils of history is the equation of female sexuality with biological continuity.

In assuming that the listener to Cecilia's story is a male lover, we place ourselves on the side of romance, hence of utopia. As soon as we see the baby, we discover, instead, that the Tavianis' folktale does not have the magical brevity of a utopian moment, but the patterned reoccurrence of a biological cycle. While in a classic Hollywood film romance and sexuality overlap, in *Night*, where adult sexuality means biology and history, sexuality is antithetical to romance and utopia. Thus, romance and utopia belong to childhood and old age; biology and sexuality to a child who becomes a woman. In fact, only the little Cecilia survives, grows up, and gives birth to a new generation after the Resistance.

Cecilia narrates to the sleeping baby her experience of the Resistance. In contrast to Cecilia, Galvano and Concetta are not agents of continuity. By virtue of their old age, like the child Cecilia, they can leap beyond history and meet in the land of utopia. Yet the love of Galvano and Concetta lasts only one night. The following morning, the entrance of their hostess with a baby in her arms ironically underlines that, as a couple, they are childless. To be more precise, Galvano and Concetta are childless in relation to Italian political history. Their love is fruitless because the end of the Resistance witnesses a *ricorso* of bourgeois hegemony. Their romance of unification between the working class and the bourgeoisie, however, lives on, on the right through popularizations of Croce's historiography, and, on the left, through Berlinguer's "historical compromise." For this reason, Cecilia's baby is Concetta's baby too.

The Tavianis' baby does not look like Rossellini's or De Sica's neorealist children: emaciated, dirty, and bundled up in military clothes. Cecilia's sleeping child is as blond as an American baby, beautiful and perfect, but also motionless and artificial. Cecilia's baby is the fruit of the love affair Italian culture has undertaken with America through the literary translations of Cesare Pavese and Elio Vittorini, and through Hollywood cinema. That Cecilia's partner is "the Americans" emerges from a magical object that is also a figure of reversal: the soldier's prophylactic becomes the little girl's balloon.

*Night of the Shooting Stars* works through the trauma of killing fathers and the trauma of sons who have been killed too soon, too violently. The extreme case is that of Giovanni who dies in the womb of his mother Bellindia. The fathers can and have to be superseded by an alternative telling of history. But even if the father dies, fathering must go on. Fathering is the male anxiety at the heart of this film, its homosocial imperative, tinged by an unconscious homoeroticism. In the role of mother, Cecilia is a means to this end. By falling in love with Bruno, Rosanna strengthens Nicola's bonding with his beloved friend. In other words, Cecilia is to Paolo and Vittorio Taviani what Rosanna is to Nicola and Bruno.

Although the death of Corrado's son does not occur at the very beginning of the film, this event is the founding trauma the narrative has to exorcize. That the inhibition of fathering is the founding anxiety of the story surfaces from the decor of the credit sequence. Under the metonymic chain window, starry sky, small village, and *Peter Pan*, one more association is possible—one based on sacred iconography rather than on a pagan fairy tale. The landscape lying outside the window of fantasy looks like the perfect backdrop for a *presepio*, a nativity scene. Christianity blends with pagan superstitions: December 25 is the referent of August 10. And the shooting star is the comet that leads us to the baby we discover beside Cecilia, at the end of this travelogue of the Resistance.

If it weren't for the sensuous voice hinting at the proximity of a male lover, from the referent of Cecilia's words alone ("amore mio") it is not possible to guess the gender of the baby. In Italian, the possessive adjective "mio" would still be in agreement with the masculine noun "amore," even if the baby were a "bambina." As brief as this ambiguity may be, it does momentarily open the text up to a reading that could undermine a view of history as the passing on of a legacy from father to son. Furthermore, the possibility to replace a homosocial genealogy with a bond between women emerges from the gift old Concetta gives to young Cecilia at the end of the Resistance: a beautiful pair of earrings. "Amore mio" and the jewels are only two isolated instances of the potential weakening of a strong patriarchal chain. Female spectators cannot help but fantasize about history becoming a utopian narrative of female identity.

Were we to abandon this fantasy and surrender to the dominant grain of the narrative, we would instead conclude that Cecilia's baby is a *bambino*, who at the end of the film replaces the void left by the unborn Giovanni—that Cecilia brings to completion Bellindia's pregnancy. When the *bambino* becomes the recipient of Cecilia's story, the model addressee of the film is engendered as male. Female spectators must wear a man's hat and experience the seduction of a female voice as if they were men.

The gender of the baby is historiographically significant. In Rossellini's Eucharistic body, regional and class differences find a site of reconciliation, subordinate to national unity, to Christian "coralità." Hence Rossellini's Eucharistic body allegorizes a composite, but homogeneous national self, whose gender is not called attention to, but is tacitly assumed to be male. Rossellini's national addressee yearns for Crocean "liberty," and becomes female when, with Carmela, it embodies the Italian body politic crushed by a foreign army. In the Tavianis' *Night*, instead, the sexing of the national body politic is still male, but, in comparison with Rossellini's, more explicitly so, for such a monolithic sexual identity clashes with a contradictory view of subjectivity at the level of class and regional backgrounds.

In the wake of the commedia dell'arte, and of neorealism, the body is a document for the Tavianis. On the other hand, with their vivid pictorialism, they reject the documentary authenticity of Rossellini's cinema. *Night of the Shooting Stars* is a stylistically composite text. It integrates the aesthetic legacies of the two founding fathers of postwar Italian cinema: Visconti's penchant for grandiose spectacles and Rossellini's interest in the minutiae of behavior. In *Night*, operatic macrohistory meets comedic microhistory.

### OPERATIC MACROHISTORY, COMEDIC MICROHISTORY

In *Paisà*, the script is neither literary nor binding. It amounts to a tentative outline of locations and types. The script develops and changes during the shooting. In discussing the production of *Paisà*, Peter Brunette remarks that episodes were "developed after characters had been chosen."[36] Brunette's observation confirms that Rossellini's film was planned as a microhistory of national behavior. For Brunello Rondi, the faces, gestures, and movements of non-actors in *Paisà* carry history *in* them, while carrying *forward* the story. Better than any other Italian critic, Rondi recaptures the corporeal and spiritual dimensions of Rossellini's cinema, and deserves to be quoted at length. Describing the grace of the monks' movements, Rondi writes: "The wonderful shots of the monks kneeling to give thanks for dangers overcome, . . . those movements in the passages, those rituals almost, that slow reassembly of an age-old dance. . . . are faces of what is 'human, too human'; without trepidation, Rossellini unveils this aura of little school, of primitive little 'clan.' "[37] Rondi's descriptive strokes, "kneeling," "dance,"

[36] Brunette, *Roberto Rossellini*, 368, n. 2.
[37] Rondi, *Il neorealismo italiano*, 152.

"movements in the passages," "slow reassembly," succeed in the difficult enterprise of depicting *verbally* a life style based on the *language* of the body, but, at the same time, as *anti-verbal* as the commedia dell'arte (fig. 44).

Rondi also describes the thud of the partisans' dead bodies falling into the water: "One shot dwells, with the camera aimed low, on the *surface* of the water; the splashes made by the partisans' bodies, hands bound, being dumped in, follow one after another, identical, *monotonous*. Nothing else: only this terrible fixation, this dead *duration*, this low camera angle, truly uncommon for 'an ending shot,' and the closing of the water over the last body."[38] Here Rondi recreates the weight of Rossellini's images. The flat description of death matches the shapeless volumes of bodies falling into the water. Rondi also lists the key components of Rossellini's style: "sur-

**44.** The monks in Roberto Rossellini's *Paisà* (1946). Courtesy of The Museum of Modern Art, Film Stills Archive.

[38] Ibid., 158–59. Emphasis is mine.

face," "monotonous," and "duration," in antithesis to depth, varia-
tion, and climax of classic Hollywood narratives.

Rondi captures the vulnerability of Rossellini's characters as they
run across deserted streets and empty corridors in Florence: "a very
intense moment is in that *tracking shot* inside the empty gallery of
the Uffizi, with all the statues in packing, and in that pervasive
sense of the world coming to an end."[39] An ironic contrast emerges
between a peaceful, monumental past and World War II chaotically
unfolding in the present tense. The statues of the Renaissance observe with indifference anonymous people struggling to survive.

The Tavianis follow Rossellini's example and develop episodes
around the behavior of non-actors. Cecilia and her friend Renata
rely on gestures and grimaces to communicate with two American
soldiers who come from nowhere, like some wondrous creatures. A
similar style of expression characterizes the interaction of a huge,
Black G.I. with a little *sciuscià* in Rossellini's Neapolitan episode.
The communication between these two characters, who speak different languages and belong to different worlds, is entirely based on
how they move: "It is in the gestures of the black man who slips
the sweaters off the little boy's neck; that small body that squirms
free of the enormous sweaters is viewed with pity and pain that are
no less moving for being filled with modesty."[40] Rondi notices that
the story of the G.I. and the *sciuscià* develops out of the difference
in size between the characters. To this I would also add that it is
the tension between moving figure and shattered ground that brings
these two individuals together. The huge soldier and the small boy
look equally lost among the rubble of destroyed Naples. The harmony between body and architecture typical of Italian Renaissance
painting appears irretrievable after World War II.

If the Tavianis learn from *Paisà* (1946), Rossellini, in turn, seems
to anticipate Calvino's blend of fantasy and realism in *The Path to
the Nest of Spiders* (1947) and, thus, paves the way for the Tavianis'
interest in the magical quality of daily life. The folk tale of the Pied
Piper is the subtext of the long walk the Black soldier and the child
undertake together, across the desolation of Naples. Rondi writes:
"That *sciuscià* who compels the black man to follow him, almost
casting a spell over him with the sound of his harmonica, is a situ-

[39] Ibid., 149.
[40] Ibid., 146.

ation that, without detaching itself from the purest realistic tone, takes on a fabulous touch that, it seems to us, fulfills the longed for blending of neorealism and fable."[41]

In Rossellini's *Paisà*, in Calvino's *Path*, and in the Tavianis' *Night*, ordinary objects sit on the border between history and utopia, reality and fantasy. In *Paisà*, the American chaplains give canned goods and Hershey bars to the Italian monks. These modern treats come from America, the land of utopia and bounty. In the kitchen of the ancient monastery, powdered eggs and instant milk glow with mystery. So does the shiny, black pistol Calvino's Pin steals from a German soldier. Likewise, a special aura lingers on the Camel cigarettes Galvano finds on the grass while he wonders whether the Americans really exist.

In *Night*, the allusions to *Paisà* lose the documentary quality of grainy, newsreel-like footage. The Tavianis' style is anti-naturalistic. Their colors have such an intense glow that the Tuscan countryside seems to lie halfway between a postcard and a hallucination. Space takes on the shape of a stage, stretching across the façade of a church, or amounting to the perimeter of a square. Backdrops look unashamedly artificial, as if made of cardboard. With wipes, zooms, and highly directed tracking shots, the Tavianis call attention to the presence of the apparatus of cinema and its power to shape perception. The lighting is hardly ever diffused in an even manner. It is theatrical rather than naturalistic. It dramatically isolates individuals and groups. In the underground shelter, during the air raid, the group follows screen direction with sculptured effects, comparable to the ones achieved by Fritz Lang in his shaping of crowds for *Metropolis* (1927).

The Tavianis' handling of color, space, camerawork, lighting, and screen direction is more theatrical than operatic. At first it is possible to assign the operatic label only to the dialogue, or to the explicit citations of famous pieces of music. A villager performs Verdi's *Requiem* in the cathedral and a German soldier sings Wolfram von Eschenbach's "Hymn to the Evening Star" from Wagner's *Tannhäuser*.[42] Through an alternation of solos, especially Galvano's and

---

[41] Ibid., 145. On the fantastic in neorealism, see Peter Bondanella, "Neorealist Aesthetics and the Fantastic: *The Machine to Kill Bad People* and *Miracle in Milan*," *Film Criticism* 3, no. 9 (Winter 1979): 24–29.

[42] I am indebted to Millicent Marcus for the identification of the pieces of music used in *Night*.

Cecilia's, and a polyphony of voices, such as the arguments in the shelter, or the externalization of private thoughts before the explosions, the Tavianis' dialogue explores, in an operatic fashion, the interaction of individual and group. But opera pervades *Night* in more subtle ways than musical citations or dialogue stylistics.

In opera, music prevails over the libretto. Likewise, in *Night*, music from German and Italian opera, and from American culture, in addition to Nicola Piovani's original sound track, dictate the tempo to which the Tavianis' historiographical rewriting unfolds. The operatic conception of *Night*, in fact, becomes most apparent when we realize that different types of music point to different ways of experiencing history. The "urgent staccato"[43] of Nicola Piovani, for example, is an acoustic translation of how discontinuous but compelling the movement of history can be. Through sound, the Tavianis replace the teleological trajectory of Croce's and Togliatti's historicism with a jagged rhythm that now leaps toward utopia, now falls back into biology.

The music from Wagner's opera allegorizes the sunset of German power for the villagers, while American patriotic music announces the dawn of American-history-made-in-Italy. To Italian ears, the "Battle Hymn of the Republic" means America, and not much else, while its sound is enough to mobilize and dupe an entire crowd. Eagerly awaiting "gli Americ(h)ani," one young Tuscan scans the empty horizon from a tall post and declares "I see them." For a brief moment, the Italian perception of a utopian American freedom becomes a reality for these villagers caught between Fascists and Nazis. By contrast, the reality of the German defeat looks like a ghostly apparition. From afar, the villagers spot a German platoon moving slowly through the middle of the valley, enveloped in a Wagnerian aura and accompanied by the surreal song of a thousand cicadas.

The Tavianis mesh an operatic telling of history with a neorealist observation of behavior. In the context of recent Italian cinema, this approach is common practice. Ettore Scola undertakes a comparable project. However, the Tavianis' weaving together of operatic and comedic motifs differs from Scola's. The regional physiognomies and magical objects of *Night*—shiny eyes, glowing cheekbones, thick bread, rough clothing—are so full of life and sun, blood and dust,

---

[43] Marcus, "The Taviani Brothers," 366.

that we cannot help but think of the Tavianis' post–May 1968 neo-realism as an opera *en plein air*.

Scola's world, instead, is made of closed, indoor spaces, such as the apartment of *A Special Day* (1977) (fig. 45) or the ballroom of *Le Bal* (1983). In *Le Bal*, the affinities between Scola's types and the masks of the commedia are emphatic. Yet Scola's use of a comedic scale marks the last and, perhaps, most exhausted stage of transub-stantiation between life and the cinema. Were they asked to leave the ballroom of French history and step outside, Scola's bodies would quickly melt. This is also the fate of a few, ancient Roman frescoes. During the excavation of the subway, in Fellini's *Roma* (1972), they disappear at the touch of fresh air.

**45.** Dance in Ettore Scola's *A Special Day* (1977). Courtesy of The Museum of Modern Art, Film Stills Archive.

# SEVEN

Antifascism
after May
1968

## UNITY AND CONTINUITY IN ANTIFASCISM

THE GENERATIONAL conflicts of May 1968 hover over *Spider's Stratagem* (1970), a film produced in 1970 by R.A.I., the Italian state television network.[1] More specifically, the late 1960s and the early 1970s were years of great interest in the past, but also of rebellion against the authority of fathers. Within this Oedipal climate, Bernardo Bertolucci set out to explore the ambiguities of antifascism. The filmmaker interrogates the neorealist style of postwar Italian cinema and challenges the theme of historical continuity, which is operative in the right-wing as well as in the left-wing postwar historiography of antifascism. Postwar popular historical knowledge inherited the theme of continuity from the liberal philosopher Benedetto Croce's interpretation of antifascism. Croce argued that antifascism was an experience that cut across social classes and compared it to the Risorgimento as a nineteenth-century movement toward national

---

[1] "Italian television produced *Spider's Stratagem* and, exceptionally, it broadcast it twice during the same week: Sunday, October 25, 1970, and the following Friday; the film was critically acclaimed at the Venice Film Festival that very same year." Francesco Casetti, *Bernardo Bertolucci* (Florence: La Nuova Italia, 1978), 60. On directing *The Conformist* and *Spider's Stratagem* back to back, Bertolucci remarks: "I made *Spider's Stratagem* immediately before *The Conformist*, but even though there were only a few short months between them, my psychological situation was different . . . and that is why these two films are so different. I made *Spider's Stratagem* in a state of melancholic happiness and great serenity and *The Conformist* in a tragic state of great psychological upheaval." Amos Vogel, "Bernardo Bertolucci: An Interview," *Film Comment* 8, no. 3 (Fall 1971): 28.

unity. The theme of continuity was equally important for Palmiro Togliatti's political stance in the postwar period. The communist leader's project was to historicize the identity of his party by drawing a connection between the democratic forces of the Risorgimento and the antifascist movement. In contrast to Croce's national emphasis, however, Togliatti highlighted the class unity of the Resistance. Furthermore, Togliatti argued that the Resistance had produced an historical role for those popular masses whose containment and betrayal in the Risorgimento Gramsci decried.

From the boulevards of Paris to the piazze of Italy, generational tensions went hand in hand with a radicalization of the class struggle, which climaxed during the labor disputes of *Autunno Caldo* in 1969. Beside the theme of historical continuity, May 1968 put under scrutiny the unity of the national body politic. *Spider's Stratagem* would lead one to conclude that the national unity of the struggle against Fascism was temporary and that Togliatti in the postwar period held on to an outdated historicism. Sheltered from the flow of time, Tara is the small town of *Spider's Stratagem*. There, communist antifascists practice the art of a Nietzschean abuse of history. As a homogeneous *corpus mysticum*, Tara's body politic allegorizes the alliance between southern rural peasantry and northern urban proletariat that Gramsci thought could prevail over regional divisions.

In *Spider's Stratagem*, what Bertolucci does not address is the question of sexual difference. Bertolucci's inability to rethink the role of women in the historical process is due to the fact that, for the Italian director, May 1968 was primarily a crisis of male identity, a turmoil between fathers and sons, rather than between husbands and wives, or fathers and daughters. Hence Bertolucci depicts femininity as the threat of castration which the patriarchal community of Tara, a small town, can overcome only through a male genealogy. As a community, Tara puts on a strong heterosexual façade, thus hiding an unconscious and latent homoeroticism. Furthermore, in Bertolucci's film, men and women engage in a battle of the sexes, the haunting symmetry of which emerges from the dialectic the director establishes between two art forms: sculpture and dance. Sculpture and dance do not correspond to male and female character, but are the two conflicting halves of the protagonist, the Fascist traitor Athos Magnani, whose death in the role of an antifascist hero his son, also named Athos, investigates thirty years later (fig. 46).

The father is an antifascist on stage, but a Fascist behind the scenes; a hero for his mistress Draifa and for Tara as a town, but a traitor for his three best friends, Costa, Gaibazzi, and Rasori; a dancer while he is still alive, he becomes a statue after his death, which he orchestrates like a Fascist vendetta in the local opera house. Convincingly, Robert Kolker argues that *Spider's Stratagem* is the "most modernist"[2] of Bertolucci's films, a modernism based on identification rather than distance. This kind of modernism works as a stratagem: in revealing the deception, it traps. Athos' private discovery that his father was a Fascist traitor, leads to his own entrapment in the public memory of an antifascist hero. Within this

**46.** The father's monument in Bernardo Bertolucci's *Spider's Stratagem* (1970). Courtesy of The Museum of Modern Art, Film Stills Archive.

[2] Robert Kolker, *Bernardo Bertolucci* (New York: Oxford University Press, 1985), 105.

pattern of love and hate, Bertolucci acknowledges the power of his *allusions*, in order to call attention to them as *illusions*. The pull of origins, whether the political reputation of a father or of cultural sources, is strong enough that the best way to represent the shape of time in Tara is not through a backward-moving line, but a self-contained curve. In the town of historical continuity, ordinary movement is reduced to a fixed moment. There the past is inescapable, as much as the referent is inaccessible. The logic of Bertolucci's modernism is based on closure, circularity, and effacement.

Kolker's label of modernism is appropriate but takes into account only Croce's and Togliatti's interpretations of antifascism at the level of historiography, and the experience of neorealism at the level of film history. By contrast, "modernism" is not a good description for the role played by sexual difference in Bertolucci's conceptualization of the historical process. In rephrasing the question the son still asks of the father at the end of the film, when he already knows the truth—"But what was Athos Magnani's plot after all?"—we should perhaps ask, instead: What is the sexual stratagem behind the political stratagem? Indeed, in *Spider*, there are two stratagems, one that appears on the surface of the action and another that underlies it. The surface stratagem is political and modernist and uses history as story; the deeper stratagem is sexual and postmodern and produces a homosocial rerouting of the Oedipal conflict. In *Spider's Stratagem*, opera and the commedia dell'arte, sculpture and dance, architecture and photography, illustrate the political and sexual ambiguities of male identity, as well as its oscillation from document to monument, from neorealism to postmodernism. Bertolucci's use of painting, too, relies on heterosexual masculinity as a term of reference, to the extent that it is about the exclusion of women from the historical process.

## ANTIFASCISM AND COMEDIC MICROHISTORY AT A STANDSTILL

In Tara, an imaginary place in Emilia-Romagna, the region of Giuseppe Verdi, the scale of opera applies to the story of a single man who becomes a role model for the whole community. The use of commedia dell'arte, as well, allows Bertolucci to depict the collective physiognomy of a small town.

In the footsteps of Roberto Rossellini's *Paisà* (1946) and Luchino

Visconti's *La Terra Trema* (1948), Bertolucci casts non-professional actors to play the inhabitants of Tara. These non-actors are certainly neorealist characters. Their bodies convey the history of their town much in the manner that the masks of the commedia dell'arte are inextricably bound to social stereotypes, to the vices and virtues of a city. Arlecchino belongs to Bergamo; Pulcinella to Naples; and Pantalone to Venice. In turn, the town itself, Tara, is a sort of character, just as Rome is the protagonist of *Open City* and Venice of *Senso*.

As a modernist filmmaker, Bertolucci looks back at neorealism with the mixed feelings of a son. By using the postwar style as "the basic cinematic source for the film,"[3] the director acknowledges the cultural authority and the heroic status neorealism deserves as a father. Yet Bertolucci is also aware of its treacherous side. Tara, too, is a deception; for Bertolucci shot *Spider's Stratagem* in Sabbioneta, one of the ideal cities of the Renaissance. This geographical detail alone undermines the authenticity of Bertolucci's non-actors who speak and behave like natives of Emilia-Romagna, when the film was shot in the nearby, but completely different, region of Lombardy.

The masks of the commedia dell'arte tell us little about the history of a region or of a city, but much about their popular self-image. Despite its humble origins and modest stage, the commedia gets no closer to lived experience than opera does. In the commedia, the coincidence of appearance and being is as contrived an effect as any technique in opera, where the display of great emotions masks the shallow artificiality of their production.

At the beginning of Jorge Luis Borges' *Theme of the Traitor and Hero*, the literary source of *Spider*, the narrator admits that his tale could easily travel from one setting to another and take place in different countries: "Poland, Ireland, the Republic of Venice, some state in South America or the Balkans."[4] While the plot remains the same, details anchoring it to an environment must change for the sake of verisimilitude.

In neorealism, local color conveys the interpenetration of character and region. It is as if, in the footsteps of Borges' narrator, Bertolucci had adopted a comparable method by interlocking details of environment with the actors' physiognomies. For Bertolucci, how-

[3] Ibid., 107.

[4] Jorge Luis Borges, *Ficciones* (New York: Grove Press, 1962), 123.

ever, neorealism does not produce a documentary truth. Rather, this style conveys the degree to which the viewer is willing to suspend disbelief and to be lured into the narrative.

The characters of *Spider's Stratagem*, like all neorealist characters, are allegorical and signify beyond themselves. Athos' death occurs in 1936, during the so-called "consensus" period. 1936 was also the year of the Ethiopian Campaign, when antifascism was mostly an activity pursued by expatriates like Professor Quadri in *The Conformist*.

Through the ambivalent figures of Professor Quadri and Athos Magnani, Bertolucci questions the origins of the antifascist movement. Beside antifascism, in *Spider*, one more referent goes under scrutiny. The inhabitants of Tara are not allegorical emblems of the opposition to the regime in the 1930s. Rather, they embody a larger postwar Italy engaged in the cult of the Resistance.

In the 1950s and the 1960s both Catholics and Marxists promoted a celebratory view of the Resistance. Each camp claimed involvement in the partisans' movement to present itself as the product of the struggle against Fascism. During national holidays or before general elections, at the Christian-Democrat *Festivals dell'Amicizia* or at the communist *Festivals dell'Unità*, the Resistance lives again with photographic exhibits, rock and roll concerts, and films for the whole family. In the piazza and on television, politicians address the public with a perfunctory mention of their antifascist past and subsequent involvement in the Resistance.

*Spider* ends with a ceremony in honor of Athos Magnani as if he were a hero adopted by the postwar historical Left. Bertolucci thus depicts the practice of turning the Resistance into a spectacle. A group of young boys wearing red scarves around their necks, just as Athos used to do, join the audience listening to the son's speech. All the men of Tara hold on to identical black umbrellas, while they stand under a scorching sun. This series of black umbrellas suggests that Tara, as a body politic, unifies itself in the image of Athos' statue for the sake of class and regional identity. The son describes this unity by quoting the last words of Jean-Paul Sartre's *Les Mots*: "A man is made of all men. He is equal to all of them and all of them equal him."[5] Sartre's line summarizes well the logic of unity-in-difference typical of the medieval *corpus mysticum*.

---

[5] This line from *Les Mots* echoes the famous slogan of the four musketeers: "One for all, all for one." The reference to Alexandre Dumas' musketeers is further justi-

The paradox of black umbrellas in the hazy sunlight lends a surreal edge to the scene which undermines the solemnity of the occasion. Faced with this mise-en-scène of inappropriate objects for
the sake of conformity, an audience with a minimum knowledge of
Italian political history is likely to remember that black is also the
color of Fascism.[6] This very same audience, looking at the boys' red
scarves, perhaps would ask if the traditional red of the Communist
Party is appropriate for the descendants of a Fascist traitor. The fact
that, at the level of the mise-en-scène, red is exchangeable with
black, and vice versa, does not mean that communists are Fascists
and Fascists are communists, but that the popular historiographical
claims produced by these two groups are isomorphic, for they both
cling in different ways to the themes of unity and continuity in the
postwar period. The son decides to remain silent and the appearance
of the young boys suggests that the webs of the past will trap all the
generations to come. Athos' legacy is ambivalent enough to blur
forever the boundaries between Fascism and antifascism, and make
black interchangeable with red.

By collapsing a claim of regional authenticity into a strategy of
deception, Bertolucci declares that the real of neorealism is as imaginary as the masks of the commedia dell'arte, and that the historical
referent is inaccessible. Bertolucci's view of history as story is as
totalizing as the ironic mode Hayden White associates with the
modern age. This is the time when illusion does not enrich, but
entraps, and when the boundless imagination of Giambattista Vico's child turns into the circular deception of Nietzsche's adult.[7] A
deep pessimism veins Bertolucci's modernism.

Film critics have often dwelt on the intense self-reflexivity of Bertolucci's work. A case in point is *The Conformist*, where the director turns the myth of Plato's cave into an allegory of Fascist Italy
and of Hollywood filmmaking, thus comparing the rhetoric of the
regime to that of narrative, commercial cinema. It is also true, how-

---

fied by the name Athos. On the vicissitudes of Athos and the death of his son,
see William A. McNair, *In Search of the Four Musketeers* (Sydney: Alpha Books,
1972).

[6] This sequence is reminiscent of Massimo Campigli's use of umbrellas and rows
of figures in his "archeological" paintings. On this Italian artist, see Massimo Carrà,
"Consapevolezza e nostalgie di Campigli," *Omaggio a Massimo Campigli* (Cortina
d'Ampezzo: Edizioni Galleria d'Arte Falsetti-Prato, 1973).

[7] Hayden White, "The Value of Narrativity in the Representation of Reality," in
*On Narrative*, ed. W. J. T. Mitchell (Chicago: University of Chicago Press, 1981), 1–
23.

ever, that Bertolucci's self-reflexivity rather than freeing the slaves makes their chains tighter.

The theme of inescapability from the cave emerges from the extensive use of "twilight" lighting as if *Spider* were taking place in the vicinity of René Magritte's house in *The Empire of Light* (fig. 47). In this painting, the daylight of the sky looks as absurd as when we step outside a movie theatre in the early afternoon. After the darkness enveloping the fiction, our eyes find reality to be hardly "real."

Vittorio Storaro's use of chiaroscuro and Bertolucci's sense that history amounts to moving shadows on celluloid complement each other. Bertolucci integrates iconographic elements with painterly allusions, on the one hand, and philosophical allusions with iconographic elements, on the other. Thus, the fire in Plato's cave from *The Conformist* (1970), the lighting of Magritte's house in *Spider* (1970), and Nietzsche's well-known remark on the "twilight" atmosphere of modernity manage to overlap: "Close to modern man's

**47.** René Magritte, *The Empire of Light*, 1950. Courtesy of The Museum of Modern Art, Collection. Gift of D. and J. de Menil.

pride there stands his irony about himself, his consciousness that he must live in a historical, or twilight, atmosphere, the fear that he can retain none of his youthful hopes and powers."[8] With Bertolucci, self-reflexivity is similar to a gesture that begins as a dancer's movement, folds back onto itself, and ends where it started, in the total stillness of a statue.

For Bertolucci, historiography is unreliable simply because history itself is unrepresentable, and this unrepresentability is the only form of knowledge possible about history. In a sense, Athos' discovery that historical knowledge is impossible is as painful as the unplotting of his father's plot.

After defiling his father's name carved on the tombstone, the son runs into the open countryside, stretching outside Tara's boundaries into the darkness. Young Athos and his father having the same name makes the son's attempt to erase the father's name ironically a gesture of self-effacement. Furthermore, the son's gesture expresses, with a painful degree of intensity, the director's anxiety about the past, for in making a film about his obsession with father figures, Bertolucci is perhaps pursuing the secret fantasy of a birth without origins. We see Athos crying, impotent and alone, as he stands under the open sky, surrounded by thick, high grass, while a fast train goes by. We look at Athos looking at the train. We only hear the noise of the train which we never see, because, like history, it is unrepresentable. The lamp Athos holds in his hand appears futile, for it cannot shed light on Tara's night and on the mysteries of its past. The lamp does not help us see the train and, at best, can only shine on the shadows of Plato's cave (fig. 48).

The placement of the train outside the spectator's visual field reasserts the artificiality of Tara's timeless, rural world. As documentary as they may look, *Spider's* neorealist images are deceiving. They repeat the compositional scheme of Giorgio De Chirico's paintings, where the silhouette of a black train often runs on the border of a stagy square.

Just as Mussolini never comes to inaugurate Tara's opera house, history and the train always remain outside of this town, which, thirty years later, still celebrates the antifascist struggle. Beccaccia, the local Fascist landowner Draifa blames for Athos' murder,

---

[8] Friedrich Nietzsche, *The Use and the Abuse of History*, trans. Adrian Collins, intro. Julius Kraft (New York: The Library of Liberal Arts Press of New York, 1957), 55.

**48.** The unrepresentability of history in Bernardo Bertolucci's *Spider's Stratagem* (1970). Courtesy of The Museum of Modern Art, Film Stills Archive.

"reigns" on his properties outside the borders of Tara. Beccaccia's nickname, the Tower, indicates that the power of Fascism is so totalizing that, in the end, it can only produce either conformity or marginalization, as if this second extreme were the hidden and disturbing flipside of the first. In De Chirico's paintings, lonely towers or tall chimneys casting ominous shadows on buildings and figures, stand near the side of a square, or on the line of the horizon. A comparable use of space informed the plan of modern Fascist cities. In Sabbaudia and in Littoria, the tower on one end echoes the Casa del Fascio on the other.[9]

De Chirico's towers are threatening emblems of patriarchal solipsism (fig. 49). Athos Magnani resembles one of De Chirico's towers when he stands on top of a belfry and asks his friends to kill

[9] Carlo Cresti, *Architettura e fascismo* (Florence: Vallecchi, 1986), 122.

**49.** Giorgio De Chirico, *The Red Tower*, 1913. Courtesy of Peggy Guggenheim Collection, Venice.

him, so that the execution of a traitor may look like the death of a hero. In *Spider*, sexual difference threatens to destabilize history, while iconography is consistently ambiguous. Signifiers such as the train of history and the tower of Fascism occupy symmetrical positions and are easily exchangeable.

There is no exit from the cave, only another cave; the outside coincides with the inside. When Athos visits Draifa, his father's mistress, he walks into a villa of optical illusions (fig. 50). There, the faint landscapes and blue-green flowery motifs of the wallpaper raise doubts that windows and doors open onto the garden, but lead, instead, to more walls picturing the outside inside.

By turning neorealism into opera and opera into neorealism, Bertolucci casts into relief the limit against which the neorealist project runs, while it mobilizes the Fascist statue. The injection of movement into the marble, the transformation of the statue into the dancer, does not challenge the ideological function fulfilled by the fascist body as a homogenizing term of identification for composite national audiences. On the contrary, in the molds left behind by the allegorical embodiments of Mussolini's cinema, neorealist

**50.** Alida Valli as Draifa in Bernardo Bertolucci's *Spider's Stratagem* (1970). Courtesy of The Museum of Modern Art, Film Stills Archive.

non-actors continue to function as mirror images of national stereotypes, whose function is to reconcile differences due to class, regional, and sexual identities.

With Bertolucci, neorealism departs from documentary and turns into surrealism. This radical transformation where supposedly "objective" images become highly "subjective" reminds us of André Bazin's insight that the cinema, born out of photography, produces an hallucination that is also a document. Bertolucci's use of neorealist casting and locations is comparable to André Breton's use of photographs in his two surrealist novels, *Nadja* and *L'Amour Fou*. As Sergio Bernardi explains, Breton's illustrations "rather than giving the stories which are told a realistic foundation, are meant, quite on the contrary, to give the real, the old Paris of Les Halles, with its streets, passers-by, women and statues by Giacometti, an imaginary foundation."[10] Like Breton's photographs, Bertolucci's ethnographic images do not point to the referent any longer. Rather

[10] Sergio Bernardi, "La serie infinita delle immagini," *Filmcritica* 37, no. 363 (March–April 1986): 135.

they document the transformation of neorealism into a mental state, into a subjective dimension[11] which parallels the collapsing of historical objectivity into storytelling.

Like Bertolucci, Pier Paolo Pasolini is also sensitive to the intersection of character and environment, of history and physiognomy. But, for Pasolini, the body of the non-professional actor is a marker for a process of defamiliarization so that something outside of logos, ancient and forgotten, stands against official history as a technology of writing, and as a practice of domination.

Bertolucci's men live in a heterosexual, patriarchal world which represses an undeniable homoeroticism. Pasolini's subproletarian "ragazzi di vita" belong to a culture where, in the peripheries of large cities, sexual promiscuity, poverty, crime, and prostitution *are* daily life. The bodies of Pasolini's actors scream their difference, release all their displacement, as if overly embarrassing and not fitting into national history and bourgeois society.[12] In Tara, instead, the integration of character and environment is as definitive and irreversible as the aging process, whose signs we detect on the withered faces of Bertolucci's antifascists.

To Athos' betrayal of antifascism corresponds Bertolucci's betrayal of neorealism. In *Spider*, the regional documents of the commedia age into the monuments of a national opera. The inhabitants of Tara appear unexpectedly in a deserted square. Under a dark arcade, they wait for the right moment to attack Athos. These old men look like an avenging chorus.

Especially when they listen to the music of Giuseppe Verdi's *Rigoletto*, streaming all over the town, the men and the women of Tara look like statues. Bertolucci makes the monumentalization of Tara's natives apparent with an ironic use of low angle. In 1933, during the making of *1860* Blasetti relied on a similar device, but with the intention of celebrating the heroic dimension of his peasant non-actors. In contrast to Blasetti's sociorealist approach à la Alexander Dovzhenko, Bertolucci's peasants are no innocent statues, but fit within the ironic perspective of recent Italian cinema. For this reason, the men of Tara are closer to Lina Wertmuller's baroque exaggerations or to Federico Fellini's carnivalesque types than

[11] André Bazin, *What Is Cinema?*, vol. 1, trans. Hugh Gray (Berkeley: University of California Press, 1967), 16.

[12] On Pasolini's use of the body and real locations, see the amazing photographs and insightful commentary of Michele Mancini and Giuseppe Perella, eds., *Pier Paolo Pasolini: Corpi e luoghi* (Rome: Theorema edizioni, 1981).

to Blasetti's naive populist emblems. For Bazin, the baroque is the mode of "tortured immobility."[13] Indeed, it appears that the repetitive routines of regional life keep the energetic movements of the commedia dell'arte trapped inside not just Bertolucci's characters, but also Wertmuller's and Fellini's. Unlike Wertmuller and Fellini, however, Bertolucci does not quite rely on the mode of the baroque-carnivalesque, because his irony is more paralyzing than irreverent. In comparison to Wertmuller's and Fellini's, Bertolucci's baroque is "tortured" from within rather than excessive and overpouring.

Opera casts on the natives of Tara a spell as strong as the one exercised by architecture on the peasant Tunin in Wertmuller's *Love and Anarchy* (1973). During an outing in the Roman countryside, on a summer afternoon, Tunin wanders amidst the buildings of Sabbaudia, a town built by the regime as a model of urbanization. Tunin is an anarchist and, like the antifascist Athos Magnani, plans to kill Mussolini. Sabbaudia and Tara, one a dream for the future, the other a dream in the past, are cities of the mind, perfect examples of modern, rationalist urban planning and of Renaissance perspectival architecture.

Like Bertolucci, Wertmuller uses the low angle to frame Tunin's body, who is literally encased within straight lines and contained volumes. In showing how Tunin's self-image fits a landscape of conformity, stemming from an ideal of self-effacement within a community, Wertmuller suggests that anarchy and Fascism share equal amounts of idealism, even though they belong to the opposite ends of the political spectrum. Fascism envisions complete state control, whereas anarchy rejects control imposed from above. Neither ideology accepts that society may outgrow either too much control or not enough control.

With *Spider*, Bertolucci relies on architecture to propose an equivalence as disturbing as Wertmuller's parallel between anarchy and Fascism. The director compares the ideals of Fascism to those of the Resistance. Again, this comparison depends on the thematic isomorphism of two different historiographical legacies, one emphasizing nation, the other class. In Tara, a town De Chirico must have dreamt of, stagy squares and arcades stretch toward the vanishing point; spaces are deep, but enclosed; façades promise the presence of full volumes, but with the void behind them. In such a

[13] Bazin, *What Is Cinema?*, 1:11.

landscape, historiography cannot offer a reliable perspective on the past and, therefore, flattens into story.

### THE STATUE AND THE DANCER, FATHER AND SON, BODY AS MONUMENT, AND BODY AS DOCUMENT

Before his death, Athos Magnani is not a statue but a dancer. In a *balera*, Athos leads a young woman in the stiff, puppet-like motions of the dance (fig. 51). The Black Shirts angrily look on, while Athos' dance makes a mockery of *Giovinezza*, a popular Fascist song that celebrates youth. Athos' performance as a dancer, however, casts a shadow on his antifascist stance. With his rigid whirling, the father seems to go through the motions of a military drill. The dance reveals that Athos' self-image, as an antifascist, shares the statuesque features of the ideal male ego cherished in the heterosexual, patriarchal culture of Mussolini's Italy.

51. Dance in Bernardo Bertolucci's *Spider's Stratagem* (1970). Courtesy of The Museum of Modern Art, Film Stills Archive.

The father is a hero for Tara, but his role as an object of desire for the community feminizes him. After all, with his penchant for colonial outfits and a red scarf around his neck, he becomes the most fashionable man in town, while staging a fantasy of escape into an exotic land for a provincial world. In Tara, heroism is a synonym for male heterosexuality. In the *balera*, and in daily life, Athos is not just an exuberant antifascist, but Tara's Don Giovanni. The father's heterosexual masculinity appears to be indisputable, since the whole town approves of his affair with Draifa.

Halfway through the film, we learn that a young lion, called Sultan, has run away from a German circus stationed in town. The lion's name reminds us that Athos is a Don Giovanni, a man with a harem. Yet a shadow looms over this virile onomastic. The wild beast, we are told, once captured, died of emotion. The lion is the only element of animal imagery Athos' friends discuss during a dinner held at Draifa's villa. Always anxious to model themselves on the hero's fame, Gaibazzi, Costa, and Rasori call themselves lions and mock Agenore Beccaccia. The local Fascist, they say, wanted to be called the bull, perhaps in defiance of rumors about his wife's adultery.

The lion and the bull—animals from the forest and from the countryside—are also embodiments of masculinity. The shared anxiety about self-imaging and womanizing blurs the distinctions between Fascism and antifascism, masculinity and femininity.

Athos' legacy as a Don Giovanni lives on in the words of an old man the son meets at a local *osteria*. The peasant's wrinkled face glows with pride, as he boasts to young Athos: "I am seventy-five and I still have a girlfriend." Such a statement of sexual prowess sounds enigmatic in a town like Tara, where T. Jefferson Kline remarks: "The only other time that women are glimpsed, they have been carted into town as if they were livestock on a trailer and sit outside the theatre during the performance of *Rigoletto*."[14] In Tara, old men womanize. More specifically, when young Athos first arrives in town, an old peasant man sings words that associate the theme of gender confusion with that of age difference: "When I was a little girl, my father. . . ." It is puzzling to hear the old man impersonating the role of the little girl in a song about the father.

[14] T. Jefferson Kline, *Bertolucci's Dream Loom: A Psychoanalytic Study of Cinema* (Amherst: The University of Massachusetts Press, 1987), 74.

The lack of young women in Tara and the stunning homogeneity of its population—old and male—finds an echo in the etymology of the hero's name. According to T. Jefferson Kline, Athos "evokes the most famous monastery in Greece, from whose territory all females, animal and human, are excluded."[15] What, then, is Tara? A town where women hardly appear and where only a handful of children live? Indeed Tara looks like the town Nietzsche had in mind when he wrote *The Use and the Abuse of History* (1874).

In his famous essay, the philosopher describes three different kinds of history: monumental, antiquarian, and critical. All these histories exist in Tara. The collective memory of the town amounts to a monument. Its regional atmosphere, geographical isolation, and the mapping of the hero's name on the walls constitute the "limited field"[16] Nietzsche ascribes to antiquarian history: "The history of his town becomes the history of himself: he looks on the walls, the turreted gate, the town council, the fair, as an illustrated diary of his youth, and sees himself in it all."[17]

Nietzsche's views on monumental and antiquarian history apply to the cult of antifascism practiced in Tara, while his description of critical history fits the son's decision to remain silent about his father's betrayal. This silence reasserts the deep disillusionment and ironic immobility constitutive of Bertolucci's modernism: "Lastly, an age reaches a dangerous condition of irony with regard to itself, and the still more dangerous state of cynicism, when a cunning egoistic theory of action is matured that maims and at last destroys the vital strengths."[18]

Nietzsche's three kinds of histories are comparable: monumental history is irreproducible; antiquarian history is sterile; and critical history destroys vital strengths. For Nietzsche, history for history's sake works against life. The fact that three types of death-giving histories thrive in Tara explains the widespread need to celebrate the flourishing of male heterosexuality, the continuity of the past, and the pleasures of the body through local gastronomy.

Young Athos constantly eats, with Draifa and with his father's friends, as if they are eager to nurture their "vital strengths" in a town of death. The guests recall that a former banquet presented

[15] Ibid.
[16] Nietzsche, *The Use and Abuse*, 19.
[17] Ibid., 18.
[18] Ibid., 28.

Sultan, the dead lion, as the main dish, Athos' alter ego as Don Giovanni. It is as if a strange Eucharist were necessary for the three friends so that they may regenerate the past by feasting on the lion. The animal is a surrogate of the hero's body around which the community regularly gathers and upon which it depends for its identity. In the shift from one generation to the next, this Eucharist degenerates into a desecration of the past. Instead of receiving strength from the lion, the son eats pork.

Tara, a living museum of old Don Giovannis, confronts an exquisitely Nietzschean dilemma: how to remain in the past without inhibiting life to the point that the statue cannot reproduce itself, or how to live in the past while passing on the legacy of antifascism to the future.

The solution to the Nietzschean dilemma is the gradual transformation of the son into the father, of the dancer into the statue. This transformation also emerges from the draining of movement from the comedic non-actors of neorealism who achieve the stillness of statues as they listen to Verdi's music. By the end of the film, the son occupies the place that previously belonged to the father in the community, and becomes a statue like him. "Identical, identical" is the comment that haunts Athos everywhere he goes. Bertolucci achieves this perfect physical resemblance by having the same actor, Giulio Brogi, play both roles. The fact that the son's body looks identical to the father's does not prove that the real is reproducible, but only that its simulation is possible.

The father is the past, the origin, the historical referent that is forever lost but endlessly referred to. Within this postmodern economy of simulation and effacement, the son represents the complementary opposite of the inhabitants of Tara, the individual reflection of its unified body politic.

Young Athos is a living simulacrum, a moving statue. His body does not point to an extra-textual reality. The referent does not exist any longer outside of him, but it has slipped inside his own body. Instead of an allegorical embodiment, the son's body is an imploding agent which incorporates its referent, the father, the past.

The son-as-the-father signals that the relation of the *body in history* posited by the documentary image of neorealism has come full circle and reappears in *Spider* with its terms reversed, as one of *history in the body*, namely as one of time caught inside a statue. For Bazin, photography satisfies the psychological necessity of embalming the past, but this insight also applies to the monuments of *Spi-*

*der*, for they truly store history. From neorealism to Bertolucci's film, the reversal of history and body rhymes with sets of complementary opposites such as photography and sculpture, document and monument.

At the beginning of the film, the art form associated with the son is photography. Draifa identifies young Athos while reading the newspaper. Traditionally, photography lends support to written historical documentation. By the end of the film, the son follows the fate of the neorealist non-actors of Tara. None of them is a document any longer; they are now monuments.

## THE BATTLE OF THE SEXES

As the credits roll, we see paintings by the naïf artist Antonio Ligabue (1899–1965). Ligabue depicts two animals fighting in a landscape where nature is untamed and threatens to take over buildings and farms. His work ties in well with the animal imagery used by Athos' friends to describe themselves and their enemies. As the critic Sergio Saviane explains, the struggle of Ligabue's animals is as eternal as the battle of the sexes: "These landscapes take us into a fantasy world where time has never elapsed. Ligabue is unaware of dates and does not know the value of time."[19] To stabilize the threat of sexual difference, the identification between father and son acquires the authority of a law as inevitable as that which, in Ligabue's paintings, witnesses a strong animal prevail over a weak one.

The scenario of the battle of the sexes is crucial to the logic of *Spider* because it locks the sexual with the political stratagem. This scenario does not just appear, however, in Bertolucci's appropriation of Ligabue's paintings. Rather, it has a long history in Italian cinema, from the melodramas of the silent period to the black telephone films of Raffaello Matarazzo during the involution of neorealism.[20]

At first it would seem that Bertolucci's *Spider's Stratagem* and

[19] Sergio Saviane, "Una Donna e Una Motocicletta," *L'Espresso*, February 12, 1961, 11. Also on Antonio Ligabue, see Cesare Zavattini, *Ligabue* (Parma: Franco Maria Ricci, 1967); Cesare Zavattini, *Toni Ligabue* (Milan: All' Insegna del Pesce d'Oro, 1974).

[20] On Raffaello Matarazzo, see Mira Liehm, *Passion and Defiance: Film in Italy from 1942 to the Present* (Berkeley: University of California Press, 1984), 145–46; Teo Mora, "Il melodramma di Matarazzo," *Filmcritica* 312 (February 1981): 71–76; Jean A. Gili, "Avignon 1974: Raffaello Matarazzo," *Écran* 30 (November 1974): 16.

Raffaello Matarazzo's *White Angel* (1954), a black telephone film, have nothing in common. At a closer look, however, it becomes apparent that these two texts are comparable not only in terms of sexual politics, but because they combine opera with neorealism. *Spider's Stratagem* and *White Angel* rely on a common iconography and conceptualize history by taking to an extreme the Hegelian version of Vico's law of the *ricorso* and flattening it from cycle to repetition.

In the melodramas of the silent film period the protagonists of the battle of the sexes are the diva and her lover, usually an aristocrat or an artist. According to Mary Ann Doane, the diva "is a woman of exceptional beauty who incites catastrophe, not by means of any conscious scheming but through her sheer presence. She is also a figure of the silent cinema who is defined by her exaggerated gestures and incessant miming."[21] The diva's ability to destroy a man presupposes "a certain conceptualization of history, of temporal determination blocked and frozen. . . . It is a history that is, of course, displaced, reworked, privatized, and sexualized. . . . History, from this point of view, is pure repetition."[22] The representation of history in melodrama is a sexual psychology, or the private side of the costume dramas and historical epics that were so popular in the silent film period.

This conceptualization of history as a repetition of holocausts unleashed by the sexuality of the woman belongs to the space of the boudoir and not of the square. The aura of despair surrounding the diva's body would be irreconcilable with the optimism sought by films about national history such as *Cabiria*, *Scipio Africanus*, or *1860*. This kind of historical film belongs to the public sphere, where an abstract national identity becomes human through a positive and self-assured view of heterosexual masculinity. In silent melodrama, the negativity of the diva's body seems to overwhelm her lovers. As womanizers, these idle aristocrats and conceited artists are weaker men than populist heroes such as Pastrone's Maciste.

In tracing the representation of sexual difference in the melodramatic genre, from the silent film period to the aftermath of neoreal-

---

[21] Mary Ann Doane, "The Abstraction of a Lady: *La Signora di Tutti*," *Cinema Journal* 28, no. 1 (Fall 1988): 70.
[22] Ibid., 71.

ism, all the terms Doane employs to describe the implosion of history into the body of the diva apply just as well to the male protagonist of Raffaello Matarazzo's *White Angel*.

In this film, the tall, broad-shouldered Amedeo Nazzari plays the role of Count Guido Carani who loves many women. One of them, Lina, is played by an actress of Greek origin, Yvonne Sanson, a Mediterranean beauty oscillating between the slightly overripe sex-symbol and the worn-out homemaker. In the company of Amedeo Nazzari, a well-established star since the 1930s, Yvonne Sanson becomes the major female lead of the black telephone film.

In the aftermath of the neorealist concern for social problems, the black telephone film takes place in lower-class milieux and often deals with archaic Italian problems such as emigration, crimes of honor, and the Mafia. Unless she is a mother or a nun, the sexuality of the woman is the distant origin inciting privatized forms of public onslaught the man must struggle against. The aura of negativity that once surrounded the body of the diva turns to this perverse form of social commentary.

In contrast to the neorealist films at the end of World War II, shot on location with natural lighting, the atmosphere of a black telephone film repeats the haunting and claustrophobic features of a history constricted to the female body, to biology, and alien to change. Mostly shot in studios, black telephone films rely on expressionistic lighting and use of shadows. The theatricality of the genre is further accentuated by the fact that the characters seem to chant their lines, as if they were performing on a closed, airless operatic stage, acting out the timeless struggle of good against evil.

In opera, the libretto is subordinate to the music, the word to the singing. In a black telephone film, the causal chain of events is weakened by the proliferation of random circumstances. Unexpected but fatal encounters, mistaken identities and formidable reversals are typical of melodrama. In conjunction with a predictable dialogue, the clearing house of such a thin plot is, of course, the black telephone. This is the major piece of technology channelling actions concerned with emotions. The dark side of these emotions justified the color switch in the generic label from "white" to "black," or better the contrast between black telephone films and the light-hearted, escapist melodramas or comedies of the 1930s, the so-called white telephone films.

In *White Angel*, the count's women do not weaken him into the womanizer of silent melodramas. Rather, these relationships reinforce the count's heterosexual reputation. Carani has the statuesque, bigger-than-life features of a Maciste. Carani is an aristocrat, but, like Maciste, he, too, belongs to the national *corpus mysticum*, while, like Scipio, he is the head of it all. The count, for example, acts like a father toward his employees. The model of the Church as extended family contains the divisions of society.

Carani's monumental figure is commensurate with his inconsolable pain at having lost his child Bruno during an explosion in the marble quarry he owns. Marble, indeed, ties the son to the father, who spends hours in the cemetery in front of a cold monument. Marble is a signifier of how the past is "blocked," "frozen," therefore indelible and prone to repeat itself, without changes, through the memory of the present. In this narrative universe of stones, heterosexual masculinity is not destructive as long as it is the origin of a homosocial genealogy, of a legacy from father to son.

In keeping with Doane's description of a diva, Count Guido Carani, too, has a sexuality without consciousness. In fact, nobody ever seems to hold him responsible for the deaths of his wife Elena, their daughter Anna, and his two lovers, Luisa and Lina. Luisa dies metaphorically by becoming a nun after the death of the illegitimate child, Bruno, she conceived with the count. Lina actually dies, giving birth to the count's second son, named Bruno in memory of the first. Unlike a diva who destroys herself by destroying others, Count Carani manages to survive every woman he encounters and his name lives on in the newly born son.

In Matarazzo's black telephone, the sexual politics of the two most important genres of the silent film period, the historical film and melodrama, cross paths. The father allows the axiom of history as repetition to turn from negative and haunting to positive and reassuring, while the passing on of his name to his son becomes an antidote against the disruptive sexuality of the diva.

Like *White Angel*, *Spider's Stratagem* is a reworking of the domains of Maciste and the diva. These two types are comparable and symmetrical, because their bodies, one in the square, the other in the boudoir, cut across sexuality and history. Like generic matrices or family statuettes sitting on the mantelpiece of Italian cinema, Maciste and the diva preside over the weaving of the private with the public sphere, of the sexual with the political stratagem, and of opera with neorealism. As her name indicates, the diva is a goddess of opera, while Maciste is a non-professional who becomes a star by virtue of his physical appearance. He follows the example of the athletic actors of the commedia dell'arte. Matarazzo transfigures the diva of silent melodrama into a cruel world of adverse fate. Consequently, only when the diva becomes a nun, can the man feel safe. This interdependence of excessive eros and social disaster underpins the casting of Francesca Bertini as a nun in Bertolucci's *1900* (1975–1976). In this truly monumental film, Italian political history degenerates into Fascism and Bertolucci's operatic style turns to *grand guignol*. In *1900*, the famous diva makes only one cameo appearance, but her role as nun is an effective reminder that the origin of social disasters lies in the excessive sexuality of the diva. Furthermore, Bertolucci makes explicit the interdependence of body erotic and body politic by having the takeover of Fascism follow the loss of female virginity. In the very same stable where his wealthy father died in a bed of manure, Alfredo deflowers Ada, while the Black Shirts begin to burn and vandalize outside.

In Matarazzo's *White Angel* and in Bertolucci's *Spider's Stratagem*, the alignment of history with biology, for the sake of continuity from male to male, requires different levels of gender confusion and role contamination. From the popular melodramas of the 1950s to the cerebral modernism of the 1970s, the signifiers of heterosexual masculinity have become less stable. In comparison to the pathological world of Matarazzo, with clear-cut Manicheistic emotions, in Bertolucci's film, the level of ambiguity is stronger and the drawing of distinctions more difficult. This is because, in *Spider*, all is made to depend on a gamble on sexual difference, combined with the intellectual challenge of the art film.

To move from silent melodrama to *Spider's Stratagem*, it is clear that Doane's description of time "blocked" and "frozen," applies to the statue of Athos Magnani. And the ending of Bertolucci's film is endowed with a compulsive quality, Vico's law of the *corsi* and *ricorsi*. For Vico, repetition is meaningful, but Bertolucci drains movement out of the body and meaning out of repetition. History, thus, becomes the recitation of a fixed text, or "pure, hollow repetition." Furthermore, Athos is both a Maciste and a diva, a statue and a womanizer. As a Don Giovanni dancing to "Giovinezza" and as an antifascist dying in the role of the Duce, his gestures are exaggerated. The behavior of "incessant miming," typical of the diva, applies to Athos who performs around the clock. In imitating the crow of a rooster in the middle of the night, Athos wakes the whole countryside.

The casting of Alida Valli,[23] a star since the 1930s, to play the role of Draifa, and the diva-like features of her acting style, confirm that Athos, too, is a diva. Within the symmetry of the battle of the sexes, Draifa's name indicates that she is the female alter ego of a character with the double identity of hero and traitor.

Draifa's fainting echoes the "exaggerated gestures" of the diva, and her walk among huge columns, now fast, now slow, evokes the discontinuous rhythm of Gabriele D'Annunzio's erotic language. D'Annunzio is one of the cultural sources used for the construction of the diva in silent cinema. In *Forse che si' forse che no* (1910), D'Annunzio's heroine resembles Lyda Borelli, a diva always torn between uncertain and feline movements, feverish and youthful looks:

> Even her body was mysterious, nearly gifted with duplicity, as if it were hidden and revealed in an endless story. Here she was going up step by step, with a plasticity that seemed to lengthen her legs even more, slim her hips, and thin her waist: she was light, slender, as fast as a young boy trained to race. Here, she dwelt on the landing, drawing a great sigh. She stopped; then she moved a few steps toward the first hall. The play of the knees created, like an interior elegance in her skirt, another kind of grace which from within animated every fold.[24]

D'Annunzio's language oscillates between pauses and leaps. Discontinuity of movement props Draifa's duplicity of sexual identity. D'Annunzio combines "a young boy trained to race," with "an interior elegance in her skirt." Together these two images release out

---

[23] On Alida Valli, see Ernesto G. Laura, *Alida Valli* (Rome: Gremese Editore, 1979).

[24] Fausto Montesanti, "La parabola della diva," *Bianco e Nero* 13, nos. 7–8 (July–August 1952): 63–64, n. 3. "Anche il corpo di lei era ingannevole, quasi duplice, come dissimulato e rivelato in una perpetua vicenda. Ecco, ella saliva di grado in grado con una pieghevolezza che pareva allungarle ancor più le gambe, attenuarle i fianchi, assottigliarle la cintura; era magra, snella, veloce come un giovinetto allenato alla corsa. Ecco, ella si soffermava sul ripiano traendo un gran respiro. . . . Si soffermò ella; poi fece qualche passo verso la prima sala. Il gioco dei suoi ginocchi creava nella sua gonna una specie di eleganza interiore, una grazia alterna che di dentro animava ogni piega."

in the open the latent, unconscious homoerotic component of Tara's heterosexual, patriarchal, homosocial life style.

## MOTHER OR MISTRESS

At the center of Tara's square the body of the son simulates its referent, the father. Within this view of history as a genealogy from father to son, women are confined to the role of either anonymous mother or official mistress. In both cases they are instrumental to the exchange of identities from an older male to a younger one, that is, to the repetition of the past in the present.

Athos' biological mother functions as an agent of continuity. As the bearer of life, she allows Tara to circumvent Nietzsche's warning that an abuse of history leads to death. Whereas Draifa's role as adoring mistress, deflects the attention away from the homoerotic subtext of the political stratagem.

Athos' biological mother and Draifa, the childless mistress, are comparable in more than one way. On the night of the murder in the opera house, both women are out of town. This absence calls attention to their marginalization from the historical process and from the key scene of the political stratagem men orchestrate by themselves.

Both Athos' biological mother and Draifa occupy the position of sphinx. Draifa is a verbal sphinx, because she poses to the son the riddle of the father's identity. Athos' biological mother, instead, is nameless and speechless. The son encounters for the very first time this silent sphinx in a barn, as dark as the mystery surrounding his father's death. There, she is no more than a half-glimpsed image. She appears in the guise of a painting by Antonello Da Messina entitled *L'Annunziata*, which Athos' lit match accidentally discovers (fig. 52).[25]

[25] There are two versions of Antonello Da Messina's *L'Annunziata*: one is at the Galleria Regionale of Palermo; the other is at the Galleria dell'Accademia of Venice. In the film, Bertolucci is probably using the Madonna of Palermo, which, in contrast to the one in Venice, has no halo around her head. Furthermore, in the Venetian version, the name of the artist is inscribed along one side of the wooden lectern. On the iconography, the dating, and the Flemish influence in Antonello's early work, see Penny Howell Jolly, "On the Meaning of the Virgin Mary Reading Attributed to Antonello da Messina," *The Journal of the Waters Art Gallery* 40 (1982): 25–35; Attilio Podestà, "Roma: Mostra di dipinti restaurati di Antonello da Messina," *Emporium* 97 (January 1943): 33–36; Anthony W. Robins, "The Paintings of Antonello

**52.** Antonello da Messina, *L'Annunziata*. Courtesy of Galleria Regionale della Sicilia, Palermo.

The title of Antonello's painting is a past participle that means "she who is told an announcement." The camera lingers only on the upper half of the painting. We recognize the blue cloth that traditionally covers the Madonna's head. We hardly have the time to catch the expression of her eyes. Halfway between inquisitive and tender, they barely suggest the enigmatic, timid beginning of a smile. For a moment, the sudden appearance of Antonello's Madonna challenges Athos with an enigma whose solution he will not speak aloud.

What we are not allowed to see is the lower half of the painting. Were we to look at the image as a whole, we would discover an open book in front of the Madonna, placed on a wooden lectern. The gesture of her hands, placed slightly above the book, sets in motion a dynamic of contradictory outward-bound and inward-bound directionality. With her right hand she holds together the two folds of her blue veil. Her left hand, instead, is oriented toward the viewer, but it is not clear whether this is a gesture meant to draw the viewer's eye in, or to ward off the angel announcing her pregnancy. The ambivalence of this second gesture is further reinforced by the book which is not only open, but also has its pages flying upward.

But what about the contradictory directionality of the Madonna's gestures? The right hand is inward bound and, to rephrase the riddle of the sphinx in Freudian terms, it posits the enigma of a feminine identity: "As your biological mother, who am I?" The left hand, instead, points outward, toward the metonymic chain: the angel-the-viewer-the-son-the-father, hence toward a masculine origin whose mystery must be solved outside the womb-like barn. The Freudian riddle of femininity conceived in biological terms and the one of masculine origin posited as an historical question only seem different, for their contradictory directionality outlines the two halves of a circle.

The circle summarizes the narrative movement of *Spider* and of the sphinx's riddle. As Teresa De Lauretis explains, "Oedipus is addressed, he solves the riddle, and his answer, the very meaning or

---

da Messina," *The Connoisseur* 188, no. 757 (March 1975): 186–93. In *Painting and Experience in Fifteenth-Century Italy* (London: Oxford University Press, 1976), Michael Baxandall writes: "Most fifteenth-century Annunciations are identifiably Annunciations of Disquiet, or of Submission, or—these being less clearly distinguished from each other—of Reflection and/or Inquiry" (p. 55).

content of the riddle, is—man, universal man, Oedipus therefore."[26] Circularity explains why the old men of Tara exchange left with right and right with left when they give directions to the son. One of Draifa's young maids looks like a boy until she removes her hat and long hair freely flows out. The gender of a rabbit is difficult to establish: it produces a disagreement between one of Draifa's servant boys and Athos. Circularity depends on confusion of gender, contamination of roles. This is why the Madonna is both "she who is told an announcement," and an *Annunciatrix*, a powerless sphinx, like Draifa.

The camera does not allow us to see the lower half of the painting because the positioning of the hands is the key we would need to unlock the meaning of the upper half of this icon of femininity. My reading goes against the behavior of the camera. As a female spectator, I choose to read the open book in front of the Madonna. Thus, I decipher the sexual stratagem behind the political one and expose Bertolucci's representation of history as a narrative of male identity.

After her appearance inside the dark barn, in the guise of Antonello's Madonna, Athos biological mother becomes visible again. She is the young woman who rescues her child from the arrival of Sultan, the lion. In this instance, she is not just nameless and speechless, but is also shown from behind, hence faceless. Athos' biological mother does not need to become a character, because it is the father who mothers young Athos.

The fear of castration, onto which Bertolucci's representation of sexual difference depends, spells the name of the town. In Italian, *tara* means an indelible physical weakness, or lack. "Tara" is also the first word young Athos says walking out of the railway station, as if he were an infant emerging into the world with the name of the mother on his lips.[27] If young Athos enters language by saying the name of the mother, this call is soon rerouted toward the authority his father's name exercises on his perception of selfhood. For this reason, Draifa's language does not belong to her, but to Athos.

Masculinity is the term of reference of female speech throughout the film. Draifa compares herself to a jealous Othello. When she is rejected by her lover, she compares her pain to a mutilation, one more metaphor of castration. And the clues about the father's death

<hr />

[26] Teresa De Lauretis, *Alice Doesn't: Feminism, Semiotics, Cinema* (Bloomington: Indiana University Press, 1984), 111.

[27] On Tara as *tarantula*, see Kline, *Bertolucci's Dream Loom*, 66.

she furnishes to Athos echo the details the old women of Tara offer to the son before he discovers the truth. Draifa and the old women are information givers who recite over and over again the fixed script of history men write by themselves.

With *Spider's Stratagem* we reach the end station, so to speak, of Italian cinema. This extreme point in space and time marks Athos' inability to leave Tara by train. It also constitutes an irreversible, modernist critique of the neorealist project and an exasperation of the historiographical theme of continuity. This theme informs the popular historical perception of the so-called "antifascist unity," a unity which, in the postwar period, the Catholics linked to nation in the footsteps of Croce and Alcide De Gasperi, and the communists to class after Antonio Gramsci and Togliatti.

With Bertolucci, the themes of unity and continuity enable the national body politic to be a container of difference and carry out the sexual politics of a homosocial stratagem. Standing like signposts at the end station of Italian cinema, unity and continuity reverberate obsessively to the point of acquiring the added semantic force of two synonyms: homogeneity and genealogy. In partaking of the same Latin root, *genus/generis*, homogeneity and genealogy result from a closed, circular movement where every image, every word, does not invoke its referent but refers to another image, to another word.

The common etymology of homogeneity and genealogy also points to the fact that *gender* is where the private politics of *genre* play themselves out, just as the black telephone film, the ultimate melodrama of the 1950s, explores the sexual side of the historical film in the silent-fascist period. It is on this private side, that is on the sexual stratagem, that Bertolucci does not cast a critical light, for the political stratagem and the representation of history in *Spider* are built on the Freudian assumption that femininity is threatening.

In mirroring each other, (homo)*gene*ity and *genea*(logy) establish that the logos, or the language of the film, falls under the rubric of *homo, hominis*. While fathers become monuments, standing at the center of the town square, under a scorching sun, mothers are no more than half-glimpsed images in the darkness, or faceless and speechless characters, seen for a span of time as brief as a snapshot.

With their well-known iconography of monuments, trains, towers, squares, and arcades, I think De Chirico's paintings can help us explicate the representation of history and the handling of sexual difference in *Spider*. In *The Melancholy and Mystery of a Street* (1914), for example, the silhouette of a young girl running after a hoop introduces movement in a static composition (fig. 53). Remarkably, she is the only element alive in a world of shadows, statues, and death. The brown, black and yellow color scheme of the painting matches the distribution of dark and light areas we are

**53.** Giorgio De Chirico, *The Mystery and Melancholy of a Street*, 1914. Private Collection.

likely to find in an undeveloped photograph. Photography and biology are the simulacra of truth and sameness in *Spider's Stratagem* and in postmodern culture. It is as if in this work by De Chirico, photography had become the flip side of painting, and surrealism of Renaissance perspective, while a crisis of male identity subtends the exclusion of women from history.

In contrast to Oedipus, whose movement across the land and in historical time follows the paths of duty and law, the girl moves while playing. And yet, despite her motion for the sake of pleasure, the girl's body in dark associates her with an ominous shadow in the upper half of the painting. The origin of this second shadow may be a monument we cannot see standing in the square, stretching out beyond the arcade. Unlike the still male statue of history, by virtue of her motion the girl belongs to utopia. So did Federico Fellini's Gelsomina (Giulietta Masina) dancing in *La Strada* (1954). The director highlights the utopian potential of Gelsomina by turning her into a visionary tramp, a wise fool. In *La Strada*, the man is the brute Zampanò played by Anthony Quinn. A visionary tramp in touch with the magic edge of daily life, Gelsomina humanizes the beastly Zampanò. Gelsomina, however, remains a child-like creature and never counts as an adult woman in Zampanò's life. Gelsomina's redeeming role in relation to the male depends on her infantilization. It would seem that utopia applies only to little girls and not to adult women. Both Fellini and De Chirico can be said to be referring to Vico's link between childhood and utopia, the age of gods and fantasy, but they do so in order to exclude adult women from history.

De Chirico's girl can move because she has not yet entered adult sexuality, or history, but I suspect that, like Bertolucci's Madonna in the barn, her figure would like to leave once and for all the dark shadow De Chirico paints over her. De Chirico's girl is also reminiscent of the Tavianis' child, Cecilia, in *Night of the Shooting Stars*. A German airplane called "the stork" flies over the woods where the villagers work. In order not to be seen by the enemy, men and women stop moving, except for young Cecilia. Standing only on one leg, she mimicks the stork, thus prefiguring her maternal role as an adult. Yet Cecilia is unable to keep still in this difficult posture, and slightly wavers, even though all the adults expect the child to balance herself just on one leg. The effect of the German plane on the motionless villagers recalls the interpellation fascist ideology exercises on individuals who model themselves on a lifeless, corporate ideal. Cecilia is the only one unable to conform and stand still like a statue. By virtue of her age, like De Chirico's girl, she upsets the heterosexual equilibrium of a homosocial history. De Chirico's girl and the Tavianis' Cecilia are only two examples of many other female figures who, because of their young age, do not appear as threatening as adult women. With De Chirico, Fellini, and the Tavianis, the association of femininity with play, utopia, and movement, travels from painting to film, from the modern to the postmodern, and begins to show the way out of the immobilizing scenario of the battle of the sexes in Bertolucci's *Spider's Stratagem*.

# CONCLUSION

## Nouvelle Histoire, Italian Style

Although some paths have been opened by literature and the occupation, the phenomenon [neorealism] cannot be explained on this level alone. . . . The body of references I have adopted has excluded similarities even less disputable, for example, the Italian "tale," the *commedia dell'arte* and *the technique of the fresco.*

—André Bazin, *What Is Cinema?*

THE CASTING of non-professional actors in neorealist cinema opened up a new way of thinking about the representation of history. Reflecting on the non-professional actors cast by Rossellini in *Paisà* (1946) for the episode set in the Po Valley, Gian Piero Brunetta writes:

History passes over the body of these characters and even today . . . we are struck by the perfect congruence of all elements and by the perception of a profound change in an apparently *immobile* landscape and *body politic* . . . with one blow, Italian cinema *shakes off* a whole literary and theatrical tradition and, bringing popular characters back to center-stage, it *upsets* [sconvolge] a static system of representation thus narrating the breakthrough of a *new history* in the Venetian peasant world.[1]

How useful are Brunetta's insights on the body politic as an historical variable and on the challenge neorealist non-actors put to the statues of Fascism? Can these insights lead to a better understanding of the dialogue between French history and Italian cinema, French cinema and Italian history, that I see staged through the actors' bodies in Ettore Scola's *Le Bal* (1983)?

[1] Gian Piero Brunetta, "Il cinema come storia," in *La cinepresa e la storia, fascismo, antifascismo, guerra e resistenza nel cinema italiano* (Milan: Bruno Mondadori, 1985): "La storia passa sul corpo di questi personaggi e ancora oggi . . . siamo colpiti da questa perfetta congruenza di tutti gli elementi e dalla percezione di un mutamento profondo in un paesaggio e in un corpo sociale in apparenza immobile. . . . il cinema italiano *si scrolla di dosso*, con un solo colpo, tutta la tradizione letteraria e teatrale e riportando il personaggio popolare al centro della scena *sconvolge* un sistema di rappresentazione statico raccontando l'irruzione nel mondo contadino veneto di una nuova storia" (p. 50). Emphasis is mine.

## FROM THE COMMEDIA DELL'ARTE TO LATE NEOREALISM

In light of Brunetta's remarks, one could argue that neorealist cinema consists of a move away from academic literature and toward the body. Working with non-professional actors becomes much more important than carefully revising the cinematic treatment of a novel or the details of a traditional script.[2] This emphasis on the corporeal over the verbal is a reaction against an anemic Italian literary scene. It is also a reaction against the films of the regime, whose actors Luchino Visconti compared to "corpses."[3]

In an attack against productions glorifying high culture, such as Carmine Gallone's *Scipio Africanus* (1937), Visconti hypothesized the birth of an "anthropomorphic" cinema:

> Among all my activities in the cinema, my favourite is working with actors; with the human material from which we build those living men who give birth to a new reality, the reality of art. The actor is above all a man possessing key human qualities. . . . My experience has taught me that the heft of a human being, his presence, is the only thing which really fills the frame; that *he* creates the atmosphere with his living presence.[4]

Here Visconti replaces the Fascist statue with a live human being. Furthermore, with the image of a man standing against a bare wall, he summons the humble stage of the commedia: "I could make a film in front of a wall if I knew how to find the data of man's true humanity and how to express it."[5]

---

[2] On the status of literary and traditional scripts in neorealist cinema, Cesare Zavattini, De Sica's screen writer, argues: "The term neo-realism, in its larger sense, implies the elimination of technical-professional collaboration, including that of the screen writer. Manuals, grammar, syntax no longer have any meaning, . . . In neo-realism, the screen writer and the writer of dialogue disappear; there will be no scenario written beforehand, and no dialogue to adapt." David Overbey, ed., *Springtime in Italy: A Reader on Neo-Realism* (Hamden, Conn.: Archon Books, 1979), 76.

[3] Luchino Visconti, "Anthropomorphic Cinema" in Overbey, *Springtime in Italy*, 84. This piece first appeared in *Cinema* 173–74 (September 25–October 25, 1943): 108–9.

[4] In *Passion and Defiance: Film in Italy from 1942 to the Present* (Berkeley: University of California Press, 1984), Mira Liehm cites Visconti's appeal that first appeared in *Cinema* 119 (June 10, 1941): 386: "But the day will come of which we dream. Then the young forces in our film will be allowed to state clearly and loudly: 'The corpses to the cemetery!' " (p. 52).

[5] Luchino Visconti, "Anthropomorphic Cinema" in Overbey, *Springtime in Italy*, 85.

Following Visconti's rejection of corpses and his turn to an "anthropomorphic" cinema in 1954, *Senso* is no celebratory return to the stale operas of Fascism but an ironic glance at nineteenth-century melodrama, after a revitalizing detour through the commedia dell'arte in neorealist cinema.

In 1942, shortly after writing his comments on actors, Visconti shot *Ossessione*, a frank portrayal of adultery and provincial squalor based on James Cain's novel *The Postman Always Rings Twice* (1934), first published in Italy in 1945. By then, Italian film culture had outgrown the literary proprieties of the calligraphic genre[6] and the redundant echoes of D'Annunzio's imitators. Arriving on this anemic scene, American literature revitalized Italian writers and filmmakers like a powerful blood transfusion. The language of Dos Passos, Hemingway, Sherwood Anderson, and Sinclair Lewis spoke to Cesare Pavese and Elio Vittorini, to Rossellini and Visconti, because it was less literary and flowery, and closer to daily speech and lived experience.[7]

In an attempt to explain the shift called for by Visconti, from an anemic to an "anthropomorphic" cinema, from literature to the body, historians and critics discuss at length the impact of foreign influences on Italian cinema, such as American literature, the British documentary school, French poetic realism, and sociorealist Soviet films. Undoubtedly, in the late 1930s all these elements converged on the future protagonists of the neorealist scene.[8] Historians and critics, however, have given little attention to the role played in the development of the neorealist style by the national anti-literary art, the commedia dell'arte.

Did the privileging of foreign sources, a tendency that is still detectable in recent work on the origins of neorealism, stem from the desire of postwar historians to de-nationalize and de-provincialize the history of Italian cinema in reaction to decades of Fascist autar-

[6] The calligraphic genre is the genre of literary adaptations. Its major representatives are Mario Soldati, Luigi Chiarini, and Alberto Lattuada. See Gian Piero Brunetta, *Storia del cinema italiano 1895–1945* (Rome: Editori Riuniti, 1979), 427–39.

[7] On the impact of American colloquial speech on Italian writers, see James D. Wilkinson, *The Intellectual Resistance in Europe* (Cambridge, Mass.: Harvard University Press, 1983).

[8] On the sources of neorealism, see Millicent Marcus, "Introduction," *Italian Film in the Light of Neorealism* (Princeton, N.J.: Princeton University Press, 1986), 3–29. Also see, Franco Venturini, "Origins of Neo-Realism," in Overbey, ed., *Springtime in Italy*, 169–97.

chy? The foreign sources of Alessandro Blasetti's *1860* prove that Mussolini's censorship did not succeed in sealing Italy off from the rest of the world. Yet, it is also true that, since its early days, Italian cinema depended on national culture for its stylistic and generic development.[9] Just as opera is a crucial term of reference for the silent film and fascist film periods, so the commedia dell'arte is one of the salient sources for neorealism.

Anticipating by four centuries the neorealist dictum of casting non-professionals, the actors of the commedia are effective on stage more by virtue of their physical appearance and stereotypical behavior, than by their skills as professional interpreters of a literary text. These mountebanks look correct and know how to use their bodies in an expressive fashion. They do not work with an ironclad script rich in literary nuances. In the commedia, the literary text becomes a mere *canovaccio*: a brief, rough plot outline, with plenty of room for improvisation and pantomime, acrobatics and slapstick.

Critics have downplayed the link between the commedia dell'arte and neorealist cinema in favor of a horizon of international literary and cinematic influences. I would attribute this to an oversight in the history of the representation of the body in Italian culture.[10] More specifically, it points to a lack of awareness that the body on screen serves as the reflection of a fictional, national self. Were we to connect neorealist casting and the masks of the commedia, we could more easily contrast Fellini's carnivalesque construction of character[11] with Pasolini's unsettling depiction of marginality. We could also contrast Pasolini's irreverent bodies with the predictable exploitation of national types in the star system of the New Italian Comedy. The asymmetrical physiognomy of the Neapolitan comedian Totò acquires a subversive edge in Pier Paolo Pasolini's *Hawks and Sparrows* (1966), while his irregular face reinforces national stereotypes of criminal ingenuity in the New Italian Comedy.

[9] Gian Piero Brunetta, "La migrazione dei generi dalla biblioteca alla filmoteca dell'italiano." *Italian Quarterly* 21, no. 81 (Summer 1980): 83–90.

[10] In 1981, the University of Aix-en-Provence sponsored a colloquium devoted to the representation of the body in Italian literature. Also see, Virgilio Melchiorre and Annamaria Cascetta, eds., *Il corpo in scena: La rappresentazione del corpo nella filosofia e nelle arti* (Milan: Vita e Pensiero, 1983).

[11] On the influence of the commedia dell'arte on Fellini's style, see Marcus, "Fellini's *La Strada*: Transcending Neorealism," *Italian Film in the Light of Neorealism*, 144–63.

Linking neorealism to the commedia dell'arte yields more than just an understanding of a network of stylistic influences. This turn away from opera, monuments, and literature, toward the humbler scale and movement of the commedia, breathes fresh air into Visconti's world of "corpses." With neorealism, an "apparently immobile landscape and body politic" begins to move, in contrast to the motionless statues of Fascism.

The revolutionary charge of this new orientation, however, lasts little longer than the span of a breath. I suspect this is so because, although neorealism is better suited to the representation of daily life among average Italians, this shift in scale and rate of movement lends itself to cooptability by Italian cinema as easily as does the previous operatic orientation. For me, Italian cinema is a social technology[12] presiding over the production of national stereotypes, reflections of different facets of an imaginary, national self. Cooptability is operative in Rossellini's and De Sica's neorealist construction of character. In contrast to the Marxist Visconti who, through Antonio Gramsci, addresses head-on differences due to class, regional, and sexual identities, Rossellini and De Sica stress the need for civic cooperation among different classes or denounce the disastrous effects of social injustice on individual lives.

Most film historians associate the spectacular-allegorical style of Italian cinema with opera, without acknowledging that spectacle and allegory also belong to the stage of the commedia. The connection with opera is a crucial, but partial one. It only illuminates how, in representing the past, Italian cinema follows the tracks of a dominant historiography of Rankean descent: a history made of great men, crucial battles, and memorable events. I have argued instead that, in appropriating the scale of the commedia dell'arte, Italian cinema represents "another" type of history.

While the operatic scale historicizes the deeds of the rich and famous, the comedic enables the exploration of the interface between anonymous individuals and history, daily life and public events. As soon as the uneventful lives and idiosyncratic manners of supposedly "typical" Italians appear on screen, their faces and bodies, just

---

[12] In *Alice Doesn't*, De Lauretis explains: "The fact that films, as the saying goes, speak to each and all, that they address spectators both individually and as members of a social group, a given culture, age, or *country* [emphasis mine], implies that certain patterns or possibilities of identification for each and for all spectators must be built into the film" (p. 136).

like the masks and the costumes of the commedia, allegorize an imaginary nation called "Italy." Thus Italy becomes the ultimate referent of a national cinema, one cultural function of which I can at last summarize: the construction of an all-encompassing, but multifaceted historical identity grafted onto stereotypes of difference which, in turn, are linked to class, region, and gender.

I see the coexistence of these two scales—one based on opera, the other on the commedia dell'arte—as echoing the opposition between written and oral histories, between textbook history written by institutions and the non-histories of marginal areas of society. These two types of histories are forms of narrative. Yet operatic macrohistory leans toward myth, while comedic microhistory veers toward the documentary. Until recently, the so-called "non-histories" have survived in popular memory and regional folklore. These "non-histories" have now become a fashionable subject of study in academia. The increased popularity of the "new" history is due, in part, to the work of Carlo Ginzburg and Michel Foucault, who have researched peripheral histories and unearthed "suppressed knowledges."[13] Whether or not the deployment of these two scales for representing national life dates back to the silent film period—a period in which some film historians locate the origins of neorealism[14]— the direction of non-professional actors and casting based on physical appearance highlight a shift away from an operatic mode toward a comedic way of historicizing the Italian identity.

It is possible that my metaphor of neorealism as a shift of gears may seem too reductive to those film historians who place great significance on the ethical tension emanating from this period of Italian cinema. Nevertheless, I would argue that the fervor of intent and the social commitment that marked the neorealist generation, appear, retrospectively, as symptoms tied to an historical momentum rather than to a well thought out and viable program of social reform. Both experimentation and improvisation animate the neorealist season. I am here self-consciously borrowing the term impro-

[13] On the application of Foucault to film history, see Giuliana Bruno, "Towards a Theorization of Film History," *Iris* 2, no. 2 (1984): 41–55.

[14] The critic Umberto Barbaro argued that the roots of neorealism were to be found in the Neapolitan silent film school that produced Nino Martoglio's (1870–1921) realist melodrama *Sperduti nel Buio* (Lost in Darkness, 1914). See Liehm, *Passion*, 13. On the use of non-actors in the silent film period, see Claudio Camerini, "La formazione artistica degli attori del cinema muto italiano," *Bianco e Nero* 44, no. 1 (January–March 1983): 7–43.

visation from the vocabulary of the commedia. Both these features—experimentation and improvisation—might help us explain how it is that neorealism continues to affect international filmmaking, even though its own moment in the sun was so brief.

Neorealism constitutes one of those cinematic phenomena that elude definition in a single sentence. At the heart of neorealism lies an unresolved contradiction between *continuity with* and *break from* the past. To better analyze Scola's interpretation of the neorealist legacy and the history of its reception in French film culture, I would like to clarify the terms of the neorealist contradiction: on the one hand, neorealist cinema continued to operate within an ideology of national culture. It produced a position for viewing subjects whose class, regional, and sexual differences are a real and pressing issue, but one eventually superseded by an abstract, imaginary, national identity. According to this first description, neorealism does not seem to have broken away from Fascist cinema. Before and after World War II, Italian cinema operates as a social technology. The assumption that individuals draw their identity from the national self persists, but, through a change in scale and rate of movement, the Italian body adjusts to a new historical junction: the experience of the Resistance.

On the other hand, the novelty of neorealism lies in its ability to thaw a frozen equation, one inherited from the operatic practice of fascist cinema, and one conflating the individual with the national, the daily with the historical. As naive as Cesare Zavattini's emphasis on documentary authenticity may sound today, if reread against the background of silent and fascist historical films, Zavattini's statements describe the most original aspects of the neorealist project: to shoot in the present tense in order to explore the impact of history on daily life; to rely on an episodic narrative in order to historicize the role played by chance encounters; to use the bodies of non-professional actors in order to show that the flow of public history and the rhythm of private behavior are neither neatly joined nor totally unrelated but, most of the time, at odds, while their effects overlap and intersect with each other.

The neorealist contradiction can be quickly summarized: neorealism relies on a comedic scale to disengage itself from a previous representational formula of operatic proportions. In this way, neorealism produces a different, *but not disruptive* way of historicizing the national identity. Although this comedic microhistory of daily

life counteracts operatic macrohistory, it does not necessarily undermine the ideology of a national cinema presiding over the construction of spectators as national subjects, regardless of their class,
regional, or sexual differences.

From the Roman epics of the 1930s to the late neorealist *bozzetti*
of the 1950s, the quick hand of the caricaturist takes over the cosmetic stylings of fascist kitsch. The key terms of the encounter between cinema and history are no longer popular icons drawn from
high culture or official history. In this new kind of microhistory for
the screen, the bodies of the performers are non-documents that rise
to the status of national types. In late neorealism, the actors' bodies,
their movements, and their behavior all point to an historical referent, convey a regional identity, cement traditional sexual roles,
and display class affiliations. In so doing, these non-documents coexist next to, or even replace, the written records of official institutions. These bodily non-documents tell a history that has been
considered unworthy of literature, but more appropriate for filmmaking, for *photoromans*, and for comic strips. These non-documents record what two major founders of the "new" history, Lucien
Febvre and Fernand Braudel, call the long duration[15] of deeply in-
grained national attitudes. The concept of long duration is helpful
in an Italian context for understanding the distrust felt by people in
general toward institutions; the petty corruption lurking under the
narrow boundaries of provincial life; the machismo of the heroes of
the New Italian Comedy and the criminal ingenuity of Lina Wertmuller's oppressors and oppressed.[16]

The connection between the "new" history and Italian cinema is
apparent in a filmic text I will consider in some detail. In Ettore
Scola's *Le Bal* (1983), operatic macrohistory and comedic microhistory constantly cross paths in the ballroom of French history.
Allegorical embodiments from each camp may dance together, or
may drift apart. The trajectory of Scola's career, from his early work
in the New Italian Comedy to his later, sophisticated historical
films, rewrites in reverse the table of contents of the history of Ital-

[15] See the chapter devoted to the *École des Annales* in George G. Iggers, *New Directions in European Historiography* (Middletown, Conn.: Wesleyan University Press,
1975), 43–79.

[16] On the commedia dell'arte in Wertmuller's films, see William Magretta and Joan
Magretta, "Lina Wertmuller and the Tradition of Italian Carnivalesque Comedy."
*Genre* 12 (Spring 1979): 25–43.

ian film genres. During the silent film period, the historical film and melodrama were stronger genres than comedy. Opera, thus, weighed over the commedia dell'arte. In the 1970s, however, the New Italian Comedy flourished, thus demonstrating, on the one hand, the shift from macrohistory to microhistory, and, on the other, the endurance of spectacle, allegory, and body as parametric forms. Thus, Scola's turn from comedy to history becomes more understandable as soon as we remind ourselves of the dialectic between opera and the commedia that characterizes Italian cinema throughout its history.

In Scola's *Le Bal*, several lines of inquiry intersect: the representation of the past in recent Italian films; the history of France before and after World War II; the history of the influence of Italian neorealism on the French nouvelle vague; the formulation of a new way of conceiving the historical process that originates among the historians of the *Ecole des Annales*. And, finally, *Le Bal* sheds light on the historicization of national life in Italian cinema.

*Le Bal* is a useful (pre)text to play all these lines of inquiry against each other, to trace the stylistic history and theoretical significance of "a certain tendency" toward the bodily, travelling first from Italy to France, and then returning.

### FRENCH INSIGHTS ON POSTWAR AND RECENT ITALIAN CINEMA

In contrast to the neglect of the commedia in Italian neorealist historiography, the French critic Jean Gili, following André Bazin's insight, traces the influence of this popular theatrical form in the context of the New Italian Comedy.[17] In this genre, Alberto Sordi, Nino Manfredi, Vittorio Gassman, and Ugo Tognazzi embody national vices and virtues much as the somatic features of Arlecchino, Colombina, and Pulcinella are eternally impregnated with a moral and

---

[17] On the relation between the new Italian comedy and the commedia dell'arte, see Jean-A. Gili, *Arrivano i mostri: I volti della commedia italiana* (Bologna: Cappelli, 1980): "This mixture of clownishness and desperation—states Monicelli—truly belongs to the Italian tradition, it is something which comes from the commedia dell'arte. The heroes of the commedia dell'arte are always desperate, poor devils, who fight with life, the world, hunger, poverty, illness, violence" (p. 181). Also, on the relation between the commedia dell'arte and film style, see Martin Green and John Swan, *The Triumph of Pierrot* (New York: Macmillan Publishing Company, 1986).

social commentary that transcends their immediate associations with class, regional, and sexual stereotypes.

How significant is it that remarks on the relationship between the commedia dell'arte and Italian cinema appear in the work of a French film historian? From André Bazin and the circle of young critics at *Cahiers du cinéma*, to Jean Gili, evidence of this French connection accumulates. Why is it that French film culture is sensitive to the way in which neorealist and recent Italian cinema utilize the actor's body on the screen at the expense of dialogue and narrative development?

In the late 1940s, André Bazin and the *Cahiers du cinéma* circle were the first critics to acknowledge Rossellini's achievement in *Open City* and in *Paisà*.[18] By contrast, most Italian critics found these two films "choppy" and "hard to follow."[19] In the mid-1950s Bazin again defended Fellini's right to allegorize a private rather than a public self in *La Strada*.[20] The Italian Left, headed by Guido Aristarco, rallied against Fellini, lamenting his betrayal of the neorealist commitment to social change.[21] The heavily politicized debate surrounding the juxtaposition of Visconti's Lukácsian realism in *Senso* and Fellini's interest in the life of the inner self, marked a struggle to reassess the extent to which the personal depends on the political, the individual on the national.

The impact of Italian neorealism on French critics and filmmakers becomes all the more evident through an analysis of the stylistic innovations introduced by les enfants terribles of the early nouvelle vague. Their war against the literary adaptations of Jean Aurenche and Pierre Bost for a "Tradition of Quality" is not indifferent to Roberto Rossellini's direction of actors, Vittorio De Sica's use of real time, and Cesare Zavattini's rejection of an Aristotelian plot. By "Tradition of Quality" I mean a branch of the French film industry that specialized in bringing to the screen the great books of the national tradition. From the 1940s to the 1950s, neorealism offered

[18] André Bazin, "An Aesthetic of Reality: Cinematic Realism and the Italian School of Liberation," *What Is Cinema?*, vol. 2, 16–40.

[19] Marcello Vazio, "Venezia ogni giorno," *La Rivista del Cinematografo* 29, no. 3 (June 1946), as cited in Gian Piero Brunetta, *Storia del cinema italiano dal 1945 agli anni ottanta* (Rome: Editori Riuniti, 1982), 113.

[20] André Bazin, "Cabiria: The Voyage to the End of Neorealism," *What is Cinema?*, 2:83–92; "In Defense of Rossellini, A Letter to Guido Aristarco, editor-in-chief of *Cinema Nuovo*," *What Is Cinema?*, 2:93–101.

[21] Guido Aristarco, "La Strada," *Cinema Nuovo* 3, no. 46 (November 1954): 312.

to Italian and French cinema a standpoint from which to challenge Fascist historical epics and the literary adaptations so frequent in the "Tradition of Quality" in French postwar cinema. A major feature of this French-Italian connection is its rejection of a literary script in favor of gestures, facial expressions, and behavior as a way to construct characters, to explore an existential dimension, and to tell a story. This rediscovery of the signifying power of the body on the screen leads to a downplaying of literary sources.

Bazin's and Gili's observations, as well as the influence exercised on Jean-Luc Godard and on François Truffaut by neorealist casting and direction of actors, demonstrate that the commedia dell'arte is a hidden dimension. The commedia intertwined with the history of both Italian cinema and the nouvelle vague, and not just as a representational formula limited to the comedic genre. Furthermore, the ties between neorealism and the nouvelle vague explain why French film culture so promptly appreciated the work of Ettore Scola, a major proponent of this comedic legacy. Indeed, *Le Bal* exemplifies the use of the commedia dell'arte, in conjunction, however, with an operatic scale. Scola's allegory lends an emblematic edge to the behavior of anonymous individuals whose lives unfold in the shadow of prominent historical figures and events.

In *Le Bal*, a group of dancers tell the history of the French national body politic. Scola recounts fifty years of French history, from the Popular Front to today, using dance, music, and lighting but no spoken dialogue. As a non-verbal film, *Le Bal* is an anachronism that defies the course of international film history since the advent of sound in the late 1920s. This unorthodox film, in which movements and glances replace words, is not Scola's first successful attempt to work within a French-Italian cultural milieu. Other of his recent films have been marketed to international audiences under French titles: *Une journée particulière* (1977) and *La Nuit de Varennes* (1982), for example, as if Scola were a French, instead of an Italian, director. Scola emigrated officially to France shortly after *We All Loved Each Other So Much* (1974),[22] a film that reviews the

---

[22] Scola's previous box-office success in France was *Dramma della gelosia, tutti i particolari in cronaca* (1970), *Drame de la jalousie*. Scola's career developed out of many influences and interests: neorealism, comedy, history and caricatures. He drew for *Marc'Aurelio*, a satirical magazine on which Fellini also collaborated. Before turning to the historical film, Scola contributed to Comedy Italian Style. See for example: *Will Our Heroes Succeed in Locating Their Friend Mysteriously Disappeared in Africa?* (1968) and *Dirty, Mean and Nasty* (1976). On Scola's drawings, see Pier Marco

changes and disillusionments in post–World War II Italian society and the eclipse of Rossellini's, Zavattini's, and De Sica's neorealism.[23]

Dating Scola's emigration to France with a reference to *We All Loved Each Other So Much* may not be entirely accurate. Nevertheless, it is a convenient mark in time to stress the vitality of Scola's relationship with Italian neorealism. The tone of this film oscillates between nostalgia and disillusionment. This ambivalence hints at Scola's difficulty in carrying out the neorealist project begun in the 1940s within the Italian film industry of today, where either old auteurs dominate or cheaply made box-office successes proliferate. Scola's expatriation may also be due to the fact that his work, just like *Open City, Paisà,* and *Umberto D* thirty years ago, was acclaimed more promptly in France than in Italy. Although recent Italian directors, such as Liliana Cavani, Bernardo Bertolucci, the Tavianis and Ermanno Olmi, rely on RAI, the national television network, to sponsor their films (*Francesco D'Assisi* [1966], *The Spider's Stratagem* [1970], *Padre Padrone* [1976–1977], and *The Tree of the Wooden Clogs* [1978]), Scola has weathered the crisis of recent years thanks to French and international audiences.[24]

Such a sympathetic response is nothing new for French film culture, always alert and vibrating with initiatives in favor of Italian cinema. Cases in point are the retrospectives held at the Centre Georges Pompidou,[25] and two annual festivals at Annecy and Nice, devoted to recent Italian films.[26] The success of *Le Bal* in France may also be due to the way in which this film exemplifies, in Truffaut's words, "a certain tendency"[27] of Italian cinema, a cinema

De Santis, "Scola e Scarpelli dal disegno al film," *Bianco e Nero* 47 no. 1 (January–March 1986): 49–67. In any case, the connection between neorealism and comedy is not just in Scola. See, for example, Mario Bonnard's *Campo de' Fiori* (1943, Cines), starring the famous pair of Rossellini's *Open City,* Anna Magnani and Aldo Fabrizi.

[23] Both Scola's *We All Loved Each Other So Much* and *La Nuit de Varennes* deal with the aftermath of a revolutionary phase and its incorporation into private life and individual behavior.

[24] On Scola's popularity with French audiences, see Roberto Ellero, "Le fortune presunte del cinema italiano in Francia," *Bianco e Nero* 47, no. 1 (January–March 1986): 60–65.

[25] See the volume published in conjunction with a retrospective on Italian silent cinema, Aldo Bernardini and Jean A. Gili, eds., *Le Cinéma Italien: De la prise de Rome (1905) à Rome ville ouverte (1945)* (Paris: Centre Georges Pompidou, 1986).

[26] Recent Italian films are regularly screened at the "Rencontres avec le cinéma meditérranéen," sponsored by the cinéclub Jean Vigo and the city of Montpellier.

[27] François Truffaut, "A Certain Tendency in French Cinema," in Bill Nichols,

that survived the end of neorealism with the Giulio Andreotti Studio Law (1949), by emigrating to France.

After inspiring nouvelle vague filmmakers in the 1950s and the 1960s, this tendency toward the bodily reappears with new energy in the Italian cinema of the 1970s and 1980s. In the recent cinema of Scola, Olmi, the Taviani brothers, and Francesco Rosi, a fascination with great spectacles coexists with the close observation of daily life and behavior. Scola's early comedies and recent historical films are rich in neorealist influences with regard to casting and direction of actors, and their spectacular-allegorical mise-en-scènes stand comparison with the huge frescoes of the silent film period, the stagy dreams of Fellini, and Bertolucci's psycho-political melodramas.

Neorealist preoccupations with an overall national identity lost their vigour by the time they reached France. In this new cultural context, the *Cahiers* circle disregarded the address to an Italian national subject in favour of a more location-bound approach, such as shooting in the countryside or in the streets of Paris. The films of these young directors are much more tied to a specific region or city than to the French nation as a whole.

Weary of the provincialism that has always loomed over the history of Italian cinema, neorealism included, the nouvelle vague flourished in international film history, in contrast to the narrow, domestic focus of high-budget screen adaptations based on the great masterpieces of French literature. The *Cahiers* directors rejected the work of their immediate fathers (Henri-Georges Clouzot, Claude Autant-Lara, André Cayatte, Marc Allégret, and Jean Delannoy), whose authority they replaced with a little pantheon of foreign role models. Their films often include reverent allusions to Fritz Lang, Carl Dreyer, Samuel Fuller, Howard Hawks, and Alfred Hitchcock.

Despite Scola's expatriate identity, *Le Bal* is a nationally contained film, whose characters never venture beyond the boundaries of the ballroom, an allegory of the French national territory. As soon as songs, clothing, and fads from the outside break into this sealed space, foreign signs become emblems of a patriotic universe. In a similar way, recent Italian cinema, with its representations of

---

*Movies and Methods: An Anthology* (Berkeley: University of California Press, 1976), 224–36. Truffaut's famous manifesto of the nouvelle vague first appeared in *Cahiers du Cinéma*, no. 31 (1954).

the Fascist regime and of the postwar period, preserves the national address of neorealism. The persistence of this orientation suggests that at the heart of neorealism lies an unresolved contradiction between stylistic novelty and an ideological continuity of appeal to national audiences, whether they are those at the end of the war or those of the television age.

## GESTURES AND HISTORY IN NEOREALISM, TRADITION OF QUALITY, AND NOUVELLE VAGUE

A new awareness of the relation between physical being and theatrical persona marks the shift from the "Tradition of Quality" to the nouvelle vague, a shift to which neorealism contributes as one among many domestic and international influences. The nouvelle vague filmmaker delighted in allowing habitual gestures, tics, and behavioral patterns of a performer to take over the script, either through improvisation or by allowing the camera to linger on the actors as they step out of character, or on lapses of time, the "empty" pauses between more regimented involvements with the dramatic action.[28]

This interest in the body of the performer recalls the challenge posed by the commedia dell'arte on French baroque painting and theatre, which were heavily dependent on literary sources (fig. 54). In *Word and Image*, art historian Norman Bryson comments on the victory of Arlecchino's body over a carefully worked out French play for the *Académie*, where logos traditionally prevails over soma: "The Italian comedy breaks with this tradition. Its acting is less verbal and script-dominated and far more closely-bound to somatic character-typing, and to physical exertion; whoever plays Arlecchino needs the stamina of an acrobat. Each of the stock characters has its specialized physique. . . . Already these rules dislodge

---

[28] In comparison with other Italian directors, Antonioni's connections with neorealism are less obvious. Yet Antonioni's direction of acting falls within the neorealist tradition, when he says: "I thought, after all, that it was right not to abandon the characters in those moments in which, the analysis of the drama completed, or at least of what was interesting in the drama, its most intense climaxes completed, the character would remain alone with himself, with the consequences of those scenes or of the traumas or of those intense psychological moments which undoubtedly had a determining function and made him progress psychologically toward the subsequent moment." Giorgio Tinazzi, *Michelangelo Antonioni* (Florence: La Nuova Italia, 1985), 6–7.

**54.** The commedia dell'arte goes to France in Ettore Scola's *La Nuit de Varennes* (1982). Courtesy of The Museum of Modern Art, Film Stills Archive.

the supremacy of the script."[29] Bryson uses these associations of Italy with soma and France with logos to shed light on Jean Watteau's project of elevating the Italian theatre and its protagonists. The vulgar *lazzi* of the commedia are close to the body and the earth, thus infinitely removed from the dream-like concentration of Philippe Mercier's Pantalone performing a trivial act with metaphysical resonances: the capture of a fly (fig. 55). In a sense, Watteau's delicate Gilles is a spiritualization of the loud Pulcinella. Watteau's Gilles also is an eighteenth-century ancestor of the nineteenth-century mime Debureau played by the sensitive Jean-Louis Barrault in Marcel Carné's *Les Enfants du paradis* (1943–1945), a film that truly exemplifies the French reworking of the Italian commedia.

[29] Norman Bryson, *Word and Image: French Painting of the Ancien Régime* (Cambridge: Cambridge University Press, 1981), 114.

**55.** Philippe Mercier (attrib. to), *Pierrot Catching a Fly.* Courtesy of The Art Institute of Chicago, bequest of Mrs. Sterling Morton.

Bryson's equivalence of France with the verbal is perhaps overly definitive and forgetful of the challenge brought by François Rabelais' irreverent body to a refined literary tradition. Instead of juxtaposing countries, it might be more fruitful to situate the bodily at the center of a conflict between high and popular culture. In France, as in Italy, the effects of the corporeal-grotesque and of the acrobatic-comedic do not "upset" [sconvolgere] but set in motion what Brunetta calls "a static system of representation."

Brunetta's choice of the verb "upset" [sconvolgere] inadvertently risks positing that 1945 is a year zero, that neorealism breaks with fascist cinema. To be sure, neorealism is not the origin of the postwar composite style. The general histories and period studies devoted to Italian cinema have not completely understood neorealism, largely due to the fact that these studies place cinema into one of two periodizations: either from 1922 to 1943 or from 1943 to the 1980s. Consequently, their chronological orientation would block, for example, a redefinition of 1945. Attention to cultural sources demonstrates that, from the period of silent film to today, Italian cinema has been oscillating between two impulses: recording the daily and celebrating the historical; two styles: the documentary and the epic; two extreme ways of thinking about subjectivity: such as the anonymity of Rossellini's characters in *Paisà* compared to the pressure of an indelible identity in Bertolucci's *Spider's Stratagem*.

In neorealism, casting and direction of actors are the most important aspects of a director's job. This is also the case in the nouvelle vague. With *Une Femme est une femme* (1961), Jean-Luc Godard addresses the relation between Anna Karina, the woman, and Anna Karina, the actress. Likewise in *Stromboli, Terra di Dio* (1949–1950) and in *Voyage to Italy* (1953), two stories of cultural difference, Rossellini cast Ingrid Bergman. Like her filmic characters, the actress came to terms with her personal and professional lives in a Mediterranean environment. Working with Rossellini, Bergman also had to adjust to a style of filmmaking different from Hollywood. Rossellini understood that stories do not always need words to be told, but can grow out of the interaction between individual and environment, private identity and public role, performer and character.

In the "Tradition of Quality," facial expressions and body movements visually support the narrative and intensify the dialogue. By contrast, in the nouvelle vague, the use of onomatopoetic sounds as vocal gestures neither contribute to the dialogue nor advance the narrative. Jean Collet cites André S. Labarthe's remarks on Godard's direction of acting: "Words are not there to convey a message, but to signify the character. . . . They are reagents."[30] Godard empties words of their signifying power and turns them into *props* for the character. Thus, with Godard, environment and behavior replace words, while words become the locus of an identity, just as, with Rossellini, De Sica, and Visconti, the landscape and the gestures *are* the character.

In *Breathless* (1959), Michel Poiccard (Jean-Paul Belmondo) hums the first syllable of Patrizia's (Jean Seberg) name. In this way Belmondo conveys the nervous qualities of Michel's energy, his impa-

---

[30] In "L'acteur à son insu dans les films de la nouvelle vague," *Etudes Cinématographiques* 14–15 (Spring 1962), we can read that: "Les mots ne sont pas là pour exprimer quelque chose, mais pour exprimer les personnages. . . . Ce sont des réactifs" (p. 47).

tience and hystrionic inclination to play with sounds and facial expressions. Rather than using dialogue, Godard relies on the jazzy beat of Michel's humming to integrate his character into an unpredictable and jumpy narrative. Like Miles Davis' soundtrack for Godard's film, Poiccard's voice is an extension of the quick and erratic body movements he performs in front of a metro station. He energetically opens a newspaper; briefly stops with a jerky forward motion of the chest as he is struck by the headlines reporting that the police are pursuing him; he nervously folds the paper and uses it to shine his shoes before throwing it away. Like a prop for a dance, the paper becomes the pretext for the proliferation and displacement of Michel's movements.

Michel's transformation of the newspaper into a shoerag exemplifies his alienated, quasi-Chaplinesque relationship with objects. In a Hollywood film, Humphrey Bogart, Michel's role model, would have at least glanced through the newspaper article to decide his future course of action. Similarly, in the "Tradition of Quality," the use of objects reinforces the codes of verisimilitude. Michel misuses the paper as a shoe rag or, at the beginning of the film, as a screen behind which to hide.

The "Tradition of Quality" establishes a relationship between narrative and character at the expense of the actor. John Hess argues that in the nouvelle vague, "The actors must, through identification with the roles and through the gestures they develop to express both themselves and the character they represent, reveal their spiritual dimension."[31] In Hollywood acting, as in the "Tradition of Quality," a character's voice, physical appearance, movements, and posture are subordinate to narrative development. In classic American cinema, however, the relations among director, character, and star differ from those developed in French adaptations for the screen.

In the "Tradition of Quality," the director's construction of character sets the boundaries within which the star can operate. Maria Schell's escalation to stardom, for example, can never completely transcend her initial association with René Clément as the female lead of *Gervaise* (1956). Clément's choice of title for his adaptation of Émile Zola's *L'Assommoir* (1877)—scripted by Jean Aurenche and Pierre Bost—suggests that after the making of *Gervaise*, the

---

[31] John Hess, "La Politique des Auteurs," *Jump Cut* 1–2 (May–June 1974): 19.

popularity of Maria Schell as a star[32] born in the "Tradition of Quality" will be forever bound to nineteenth-century naturalistic fiction.

In contrast to the actor in the "Tradition of Quality," the Hollywood star enjoyed a higher degree of intertextual and intergeneric mobility. The literary sources of the "Tradition of Quality" dictated the range of roles available to the actor. The scripts of classic Hollywood cinema, instead, could be custom-made with one or more specific stars in mind. While the "Tradition of Quality" was a cinema where the literary masterpiece ruled the actor, Hollywood and nouvelle vague films were comparable to the extent that they both depended more on the appeal of their star's physical persona than on the authority of high art sources. They both relied on the formula of "the actor-living-beyond-the-roles."[33] The powerful presence of an American star in the construction of a nouvelle vague character is clearly exemplified by Godard's superimposition of Bogart's tic onto Jean-Paul Belmondo's face. Belmondo's mimicry of Bogart's gesture is an indicator of the character's self-image and of the actor's experience in the gangster's role.

In *Gervaise*, Schell's gestures firmly tie the protagonist's psychology to Zola's depiction of Parisian lower classes in the nineteenth century. Within this social milieu, the construction of character contributes to the representation of an historical universe and its effects on individuals as members of a social class. After a violent fight with her husband's lover, Virginie, Gervaise tidies her hair. This gesture defines her as a working-class woman whose daily

[32] For *Gervaise*, Maria Schell won Best Actress at the Venice Film Festival in 1956. She reached the height of her international reputation with an expensive color co-production by Alexandre Astruc, *Une Vie* (1958), based on the novel by Guy De Maupassant. Like Clément in *Gervaise*, Astruc carefully reproduced the period setting of his nineteenth-century literary source. *Une Vie* seems to be the French equivalent of an Italian calligraphic film, for example Mario Soldati's *Piccolo Mondo Antico* (1941). On Maria Schell's life and career, see Nancy Jane Richards, "Maria Schell," in *The International Dictionary of Films and Filmmakers: Actors and Actresses*, vol. 3 (Chicago: St. James Press, 1986), 558–59. On the popularity of Schell as a star in Italy, see Luigi Chiarini, "La difficile arte dell'attore: Tre domande a Maria Schell," in *Il mito dell'attore*, ed. Guido Aristarco (Bari: Edizioni Dedalo, 1983), 163–69.

[33] In "De l'acteur américain," *Etudes Cinématographiques* 14–15 (Spring 1962), Claude Beylie elucidates the model of the actor-living-beyond-the-roles: "The American actor is born to *exist* on the screen, to be one body with his character, and he achieves this so convincingly and with such a self-assuredness, that the image easily goes on living beyond the screen" (p. 72).

struggle, in the public laundry, leaves little room for feminine vanity. The hardship of Gervaise's existence restricts her womanhood to a behavior of conformity, of imitation of wealthier classes. A conflict emerges from this use of behavior; in Zola's narrative the exploration of an individual dimension is subordinate to the representation of class identity. Moreover, Gervaise's physical handicap is a metaphor for her inability to move and behave like an attractive female. Akin to her gestures, this handicap reverberates more with class than with sexual connotations. As a cripple, Gervaise is trapped in the lowest stratum of society.

The nearly unconscious movements of nouvelle vague actors—Jean-Paul Belmondo's lipstroke à la Humphrey Bogart in *Breathless*—do not have an explicit social referent. In *Gervaise*, instead, a pattern of choral gesturing defines the women in the laundry as members of the same social class. During the fight scene, their hands placed firmly on their hips characterize them as a collectivity, rather than as single individuals. The aggressive and masculine connotations of the hands-on-hips posture of the group are in opposition to Gervaise's individualized, feminine movement. Yet, the choral gesturing of the women discloses Gervaise's role as the protagonist of the fiction. This juxtaposition between a collective posture and an individual gesture of femininity echoes the tension between sexual and class identity.

Whereas in the "Tradition of Quality," gestures ground the character solely in historical context or social class, in the nouvelle vague, gestures highlight the situation of the actor who consciously experiences a role. The exploration of a role by an actor is comparable to the fitting of body and soul, behavior and morality. Thus, gestures become visual vehicles as they allow the spectator to enter an existential dimension, which a traditional construction of character would have downplayed to privilege codes of historical verisimilitude. Although many film historians[34] have argued that the nouvelle vague is the first French style to represent adequately its contemporary era, namely the new youth culture of Paris, gestures do proliferate independent of narrative or context. Gestures call at-

[34] In *French Cinema* (New York: Oxford University Press, 1985), Roy Armes explains that: "The New Wave . . . captures the surface texture of French life in a fresh way. . . . But this contemporary flavour was not accompanied by any real social or political concern on the part of the new film makers" (p. 169).

tention to themselves and undermine the dictum of acting-in-character.

Vincent Pinel's remarks on Robert Bresson's choice of actors confirm that, in addition to Italian neorealism, the nouvelle vague can learn from a French source to equate acting and being. In the "Tradition of Quality," instead, acting always means interpreting. According to Pinel,

> Bresson's system consists in looking for an interpreter whose moral universe resembles as much as possible the character's, in such a way to construct the latter starting from the real personality of the interpreter chosen. . . . The role of the director, then, is to reveal the deep personality of the interpreter, to integrate him in the general tone of the film and, thus, create the character.[35]

By emphasizing the gestures of his actors, Bresson suggests that filmmaking is comparable to a moral journey toward an unknown spiritual destination. The director confirms this comparison when he says "What I look for is a movement toward the unknown. It is necessary that the audience realizes that I go toward the unknown, that I do not know ahead of time what is about to happen."[36] Bresson's attitude toward filmmaking and direction of acting emerges from the relationship between narrative and movement in *Pickpocket* (1959). Michel's clever hands skillfully move in unfamiliar purses, bags, and pockets, without knowing the outcome of their search. The probing of the pickpocket's hands in the dark is comparable to the movement of Bresson's camera in metaphorical darkness at the beginning of a new film (fig. 56).

In the opening credits, a short paragraph establishes a parallel between pickpocketing and beginning a spiritual journey. Toward the end of the film, Michel acknowledges that the outcome of his journey is the discovery of love: "Oh, Jeanne, what a strange path I had to take to find you."[37] The movement of Michel's hands becomes a dynamic metaphor of his search for Jeanne's love.

[35] Vincent Pinel, "Le paradoxe du non-comédien," *Études Cinématographiques* 14–15 (Spring 1962): 81.

[36] Robert Bresson as cited in Vincent Pinel, "Le paradoxe du non-comédien," *Études Cinématographiques* 14–15 (Spring 1962): 82.

[37] Bresson's use of movement as a metaphor for a spiritual search justifies the parallel which Daniel Millar draws between *Le journal d'un curé de campagne* (1950) and *Pickpocket*: "Even so, the possibility that Michel functions as a sort of reversed mirror-image of the *curé de campagne* need not be dismissed out of hand—and is

**56.** Movement in Robert Bresson's *Pickpocket* (1959). Courtesy of The Museum of Modern Art, Film Stills Archive.

For the French nouvelle vague, Italian neorealism meant the development of a new acting style and casting criteria where the corporality of the actor had priority over the words of the script. In contrast to the chronic weakness of the word in Italian cinema, the literary has always been appealing to French filmmakers, with different results. Jacques Prévert's scripts, for example, enhance the visual dimension of Marcel Carné's poetic realist films. In this case we can truly speak of an erotics of word and image. On the contrary, the literariness of Aurenche's and Bost's adaptations weighs down the visual track in the films of the "Tradition of Quality."

Despite its rejection of academic literature, neorealist cinema did not make the nouvelle vague filmmakers dismiss the pull of language, or ignore the status of logos in French culture. The neorealist emphasis on anti-verbal forms of communication was only one of

even reinforced by Bresson's decision to invent a written text for Michel, since none already existed. Certainly, this *'journal d'un pickpocket de ville,'* of which we hear much more than we see, is nearer a spiritual confession than a legal statement, though naturally without the references to God and to movements of the soul which occupy much of the *curé*'s attention." *The Films of Robert Bresson*, ed. Ian Cameron (New York: Praeger, 1970), 85. Also on Bresson's direction of actors, see Robert Bresson, *Notes on Cinematography*, trans. J. Griffin (New York: Urizen Books, 1977).

the sources instrumental, in the postwar period, to restoring the balance between words and bodies, words and objects, words and images, which French poetic realist films already enjoyed in the 1930s, before surrendering to an excess of literariness in the stale "quality" adaptations of the 1950s.

In neorealist cinema, body tells more than language, to the point that characters with little speech become victims of society. This is the case with Maria, a servant girl in Vittorio De Sica's *Umberto D* (1951). She becomes pregnant and Umberto underscores how tragic her situation is by telling her that this has happened because she does not know her grammar. Umberto's remark is all the more ironic considering how inarticulate he is, how little he speaks, and how much he tells us with his movements: going to bed, getting up, walking, eating, counting money.

In the cruel society of *Umberto D*, language is power, and those who do not master it find themselves on the margins. To be sure, the dynamics of behavior and language interested the filmmakers of neorealism as well as those of the nouvelle vague. Umberto D's attitude toward Maria's pregnancy is a recognition of the power of language, even though, as a comedic character he himself does not master it. With Godard, language is not just social power, but an individual, powerful barrier. It fosters misunderstanding over communication. It is as if from *Umberto D* to *Vivre sa Vie* (1962), from Italy to France, language had become as important as the body, but all the more deceptive in the meantime. Thus, the denunciation of social evils, in neorealist cinema, led to existential anguish over the difficulties of interpersonal communication in the nouvelle vague and in the Italian art film.

In a Parisian café, Nana (Anna Karina), Godard's heroine, talks about language and identity with Brice Parain, a philosopher who plays himself in *Vivre sa Vie*. This is one of Nana's rare serene moments in the film and Godard's camera swiftly pans from Parain to her. In contrast to this scene, during the rest of the film Godard's camera avoids the shot-reverse-shot to underscore the isolation of the characters. Whenever the prostitute Nana is with a man, we see only the nape of her neck. Although one of her favorite topics of conversation is language, language hardly belongs to Nana. Without access to language, she remains an indecipherable image drifting among Parisian street signs. Abundance of speech and lack of communication is the paradox of Godard's cinema. Lack of speech and the socialization of the most private self is the achievement of De Sica's neorealism.

During a discussion of his casting techniques, Rossellini explained to *Cahiers* that he chose his non-actors "solely by the way they look."[38] In *Umberto D*, Carlo Battisti, a professor of linguistics from Florence, plays the main role. I cannot resist, here, the temptation of speculating on the possibility, in De Sica, of an involuntary foresight into Godard's use of Brice Parain. The neorealist director, after all, cast a scholar of language to play the role of an inarticulate man victimized by a landlady fond of opera, the art of anti-verbal pathos. De Sica's task does not consist in telling Battisti what to do, or how to act to become "Umberto D," but in observing the professor's daily gestures, while this non-actor discovers the dignity and the values of the "Umberto D" he already *is*. Acting in character is thus replaced by finding the character within the actor.

Both Rossellini and De Sica wanted to establish a new relationship between actor and character. Even if he works with professionals, Bresson's techniques are compatible with those of the neorealist directors, for he pays close attention to his actors' ordinary movements. Daniel Millar argues that the French director finds the character of the pickpocket in the behavior of Martin Lassalle: "Martin Lassalle's shifts, waverings, uncertainties, resorts to rhetoric, empty-eyed evasions, add up to a Michel who spends the whole film discovering his true self, who therefore exists only after the film."[39] Both De Sica and Bresson construct characters to explore the moral being of their actors. Yet Battisti, a non-actor, is "Umberto D" even before the film is shot. De Sica cast him with

---

[38] In *Springtime in Italy*, Overbey quotes Rossellini on casting and direction of acting: "It is too often believed that neo-realism consists in finding an unemployed person to play an unemployed person. I choose actors solely by the way they look. You can choose anyone in the street. I prefer non-professional actors because they have no preconceived ideas. I watch a man in life and fix him in my memory. When he finds himself before the camera, he is usually completely lost and tries to 'act,' which is exactly what must be avoided at all costs. There gestures which belong to this man, the ones he makes with the same muscles which become paralyzed before the lens. It is as if he forgets himself, as if he never knew himself. He believes he has become a very exceptional person because someone is going to film him. My task is to return him to his original nature, to reconstruct him, to *reteach* him his usual movements" (p. 98). More specifically, on Rossellini's choice of actors for *Paisà*, see the fascinating testimonies gathered by Franca Faldini and Goffredo Fofi, *L'avventurosa storia del cinema italiano raccontata dai suoi protagonisti 1935–1959* (Milan: Feltrinelli, 1979), 108–09.

[39] Millar, "Pickpocket," *The Films of Robert Bresson*, 88.

the implicit assumption that, as Fellini has argued, "all the faces are always right, life does not make mistakes."[40]

Martin Lassalle, on the contrary, a professional actor, can discover the "Michel" in him only after making the film. Through the character "Umberto D," Carlo Battisti learns about an inner self that the presence of the camera might have inhibited. Through "Michel," Lassalle discovers a new self that can only emerge as the result of an interaction with Bresson's camera. De Sica's casting takes place under the sign of a calculated guess, whereas Bresson's direction of acting takes place under that of an unforeseeable discovery.[41]

In De Sica's and in Bresson's direction of acting, the emphasis is on the actor experiencing the role. This process endows Lassalle— and Bresson's camera—with the knowledge of a new spiritual dimension. In De Sica's cinema, filmmaking is not a journey but a catalyst whose only purpose is to let the "Umberto D" in Battisti emerge.

In Scola's *Le Bal*, actors and actresses have no need to experience

[40] In an interview with Giovanni Grazzini, Fellini illustrates his casting criteria: "My casting of actors is also a little peculiar, in the sense that despite all the esteem, sympathy, complicity I have always felt for actors, when I am about to choose one of them for a character in one of my films I am not attracted by his talent, in the traditional sense of the word, or by his professional skills or training; likewise, when choosing a non-actor, I am not worried about his lack of experience. For me it is the character which must coincide with the actor. I look for faces that say everything about themselves as soon as they appear on the screen; I even like to underline the features of these faces, making them more apparent with make-up and costuming, just like it happens with the *maschere* [in the commedia dell'arte] where everything is instantly clear, behavior, fate, psychology. The choice of the actor for the character I have in mind depends on the face in front of me, from what it communicates to me and also from what it allows me to perceive by intuition, to recognize, to guess behind it. I do not oblige the interpreter to step into alien clothing, I prefer to make him express what he can. The result, for me, is always positive; everybody has the face he deserves, he cannot have a different one: and all the faces are always right, life does not make mistakes." See Giovanni Grazzini, *Federico Fellini: Intervista sul cinema* (Bari: Laterza, 1983), 80.

[41] In *Springtime in Italy*, Overbey quotes Zavattini's views on actors that are relevant to De Sica's films: "I have often had to explain that I do not wish to prohibit actors from playing in films. Of course actors have a place in films, it is simply that they have very little to do with neo-realistic cinema. The neo-realistic cinema does not ask those men in whom it is interested to have the talent of actors; their professional aptitudes have to do with the profession of being men. They need to be made aware of this, of course, which is the responsibility of the cinema. It is evident that this awareness can only be created or reinforced through the knowledge which we give them of themselves, knowledge which we will attain through neo-realistic cinema" (p. 75).

a role. In fact, they are there, on the screen, as living stereotypes, whose selves are forever imprisoned within their own physical appearances. The distance between acting and being is collapsed into *being* as such. Without any inhibition, but with the self-confidence of the obvious, the unmistakable, the easily recognizable, they enter the ballroom and stare at themselves in the mirror. They unashamedly offer themselves to the inquisitive gaze of the camera which coincides with that of the audience meeting the characters for the first time, one after another, as in a silent film. This direct exchange of looks between characters and audience suggests that narrative pleasure is dependent on an identification with these characters' bodies. They are reflections of an imaginary, national self, grafted on to stereotypes of class, regional, and sexual identity.

## NOUVELLE HISTOIRE, ITALIAN STYLE

Unlike Rossellini and De Sica, Scola in *Le Bal* does not work with non-professional actors, but undertakes an equally radical project in the anti-literary vein of neorealism. He casts the twenty-four members of the professional troupe of *Le Théâtre du Campagnol*, which had already performed on stage the one hundred and forty roles of *Le Bal*, a piece originally conceived with music, dance, and pantomime by Jean-Claude Penchenat.[42] In keeping with Penchenat's idea, Scola rejected verbal dialogue in the cinematic version. He deprives the actors of the privileged signifier of the stage, the performance of the written word, thus focusing on movement and enhancing the cinematic potential of Penchenat's text (fig. 57). Without speech, Scola's actors cannot rely on their talent as interpreters of a traditional script in order to act-in-character.

The men and the women of *Le Théâtre du Campagnol* seem to be in Scola's *Le Bal* for two major reasons. First, they have been cast on the basis of physical appearance. By the way they look, they can tell a story without words. They are not novelistic, well-rounded, nuanced characters, but male and female bodies of one hundred and forty recognizable French stereotypes. Scola's project, therefore, is to observe the extent to which their behavior in the ballroom slowly changes over a span of fifty years, punctuated by fast political transformations.

---

[42] On the production of *Le Bal* for the stage and for the screen, see the "Special Dossier on Ettore Scola," in *Revue du Cinéma* 391 (February 1984): 49–60.

**57.** Dance in Ettore Scola's *Le Bal* (1983). Courtesy of The Museum of Modern Art, Film Stills Archive.

In *Le Bal*, French audiences have not simply found a contemporary version of the neorealist canon of typecasting. In contrast to Rossellini's and De Sica's early films shot outdoors, in a documentary vein, with non-actors, Scola's film proposes a theatrical and allegorical view of history. Spectacle and allegory fit within a tradition of Italian culture that neorealism rejected in reaction to the bombastic and nationalist films produced in the 1930s by the Fascist regime. The aftermath of neorealism, with its involution, demonstrates that this rejection is more a change in scale and rate of movement than a radical turning over a new leaf, more a sliding from the operatic to the comedic.

The theatrical mise-en-scène of *Le Bal* turns the dance floor into a sort of laboratory space where Scola can observe the ways in which public history shapes individual behavior. The representation of behavior on the screen is comparable to a set of instructions that provide the viewers with a term of identification, an image of how they need to see themselves, in order to have access to a national identity and imagine their roles in the historical process.

Texts inserted in the signifying system we call "national cinema" ask viewers to pay a price for the pleasure provided by identification, namely a subject-positioning aligned with the homogenizing discourse of this social technology on class, regional, and sexual differences.

Scola's interest in recording the spectacle of the past exemplifies an attitude shared by other Italian filmmakers in the 1970s. Like Scola in *Le Bal*, Federico Fellini, Franco Zeffirelli, Lina Wertmuller, and Bernardo Bertolucci rely on choreographed screen directions, theatrical lighting, and vivid costuming (fig. 58). But with Scola, the operatic impulse intersects with the legacy of the commedia dell'arte, thus leading to a magnification of small gestures. Scola's integration of these two traditions confirms that the neorealist experience, as well as silent and fascist historical films, contribute to the style of recent Italian cinema.

In looking at the past, recent Italian cinema oscillates between the noisiness of a circus barker and the silent gaze of a voyeur. In his essay on "Theatre and Cinema," Bazin compares the impulse of

**58.** Dance in Federico Fellini's *Amarcord* (1974). Courtesy of The Museum of Modern Art, Film Stills Archive.

cinema toward spectacle to a crystal chandelier, and its inquiring nature to a flashlight. The French critic borrows the metaphor of the chandelier from Charles Baudelaire:

> If one were called upon to offer in comparison a symbol other than this artificial crystal-like object, brilliant, intricate, and circular, which refracts the light which plays around its center and holds us prisoners of its aureole, we might say of the cinema that it is the little flashlight of the usher, moving like an uncertain comet across the night of our waking dream, the diffuse space without shape or frontiers that surrounds the screen.[43]

Like the headwaiter, who appears at the beginning of *Le Bal*, to light up the dance floor and restore to life a space of illusion, Scola plays with two kinds of lighting: Baudelaire's chandelier for staging a collective spectacle and Bazin's flashlight for illuminating the details of private behavior.

Bazin's juxtaposition of the crystal chandelier and the usher's flashlight can be applied to the whole history of Italian cinema. Cinema, as a crystal chandelier, shed a glorifying halo on the regime. This cinema of spectacle obliged disturbing images to remain latent until the advent of neorealism, which, like a flashlight, illuminated a reality of desolation. Recent Italian cinema avails itself of both an operatic and a comedic scale of representation. Its historical imagination relies on the chandelier to look back at the Fascist regime with mixed feelings. Think, for example, of the controversial *Claretta* (1984) by Pasquale Squittieri and of *La Storia* (1985) by Luigi Comencini, or of Bertolucci's *The Conformist* (1970) and Cavani's *The Night Porter* (1974). These directors spotlight the outline of those repressed images that inhabit the subconscious regions of an individual's subjectivity and the psyche of a whole culture. In Bertolucci's *The Conformist*, the microscopic is extremely private, hence psychoanalytic; whereas in Scola's *Le Bal*, the microscopic is utterly public, hence comedic.

Bazin's juxtaposition of the crystal chandelier and of the flashlight also comments on the experience of going to the cinema. In the darkness of the movie theatre, the spectators' pleasure is private and solitary, rather than public and participatory. Their behavior is voyeuristic and secret, in contrast to the exhibitionistic attitude of

---

[43] André Bazin, "Theatre and Cinema," *What Is Cinema?*, 1:107.

Scola's characters. The encounter between Italian cinema and history is public and spectacular, for it depends on the legacies of opera and commedia dell'arte. Anything that appears on the screen is bound to be on display. More forcefully than any other kind of narrative, a film set in the past reminds the spectator that his or her historical identity does not exist in a vacuum. Even in Rossellini's present-tense cinema, where non-actors replace the stars of Fascist epics, the positioning of the spectator in relation to the historical process depends on how a contemporary reality is allegorized and on the roles the characters perform.

From the silent film period to today, Italian cinema has been representing men as the active makers of history and culture, and women as the passive agents of biological continuity. In contrast to class and region, sexual difference, then, is the deepest layer examined in this study. Popular perceptions of history linked to the historiographical revisions culminating in May 1968 inform the films of Bertolucci and the Taviani brothers. These directors, however, do not put the sexual facet of spectatorship under scrutiny, because their splintering of class and regional identity, as well as their replacement of continuity with discontinuity, continue to feed an Oedipal pattern split between a rejection of the past and a longing for the father.

The "Tradition of Quality," too, was a fathering principle to rebel against for young French filmmakers in the 1950s. The Oedipal pattern switched from hate to love, as soon as the young turks of postwar French cinema looked across the ocean. The nouvelle vague reread American film genres against the corporate authority of the studios, while glorifying the individual auteurs of Hollywood.

The impulse at work in Le Bal feeds on an equally powerful Oedipal tension. In bringing together the immediacy of the actors' corporality and an extremely artificial mise-en-scène, Le Bal fulfills the ambition of Scola's career in comedy and history: to tap and weave together two competing strains in the history of Italian cinema, the operatic and the comedic. Eventually the anonymous, stereotypical, neorealist characters (the mother and the Resistance fighters of Open City, the workers of Vergano's The Sun Rises Again, the prostitute and the nurse of Paisà) become molds for accommodating allegorical embodiments of French political, cultural, and cinematic history: from Philippe Petain to Jean Gabin; from Juliette Greco to the students of May 1968; from the red flags of the Popular Front to the spaghetti of the Italian immigrant couple; from the fishnet panty hose in the 1950s to "Michelle" by the Beatles in the 1960s.

*Le Bal* differs, however, from the historical Hollywood film in its use of cultural clichés. There the commonplaces of the past do not draw attention to themselves, but function only to authorize the fiction and guarantee its historical verisimilitude. By contrast, Scola's blatant use of clichés in *Le Bal* adds a self-reflexive edge to this film, which ultimately tries to redefine the boundaries between cinematic and historical representation.

All the clichés of *Le Bal* suggest that in representing the past, cinema becomes a collector of images it raids from disparate areas of culture: literature, history, pop music, painting, and advertisement. This omnivorous nature leads cinema to disregard historical documents—in the most narrow, traditional sense of the term—in favor of any element of popular historical knowledge. In commercial narrative cinema, history can only be a representation that homogenizes the documentary with the fictional to feed the historical imagination of its audiences. *Le Bal* defies Hollywood's representation of the past on the screen. In Scola's allegorical mise-en-scène, every element calls attention to its emblematic nature, and, from Pétain to the panty hose, all these elements acquire the same degree of importance.

For Scola there are no clichés that are less artificial, and therefore more truthful, than others. Images, sounds, gestures, and lights from the past, as clichés, enjoy comparable status on Scola's screen, even though they have been produced under different historical circumstances and have circulated in culture in different ways. Yet, *Le Bal* is not just a film about clichés from the past. Scola's film is also about the plurality of dimensions that constitute the history of national culture. Scola weaves together the strands of different types of histories, ranging from political to musical, from fashion to film, and, in so doing, also recounts the history of the relations among the sexes. All these histories do not move at the same speed. World War II breaks out, Nazism invades France, rock and roll arrives, the slogans of May 1968 rise in the boulevards. But, in the midst of all this, the conventions of behavior between men and women—the approach, the chase, the flirt, the rejection—either evolve too slowly or, unfortunately, change in a superficial manner.

As Michel Foucault explains in *The Archaeology of Knowledge*, history is not a single-layered process, but the result of an accumulation of sedimentary strata, or, in Fernand Braudel's words, of processes of long duration: "Beneath the rapidly changing history of governments, wars and famines, there emerge other, apparently unmoving histories."[44] Foucault's "apparently unmoving histories," take us back to where we started, to the intersection of cinema and history in the bodies of neorealist non-actors, to Brunetta's description of an "apparently immobile landscape and body politic."

The traditional document belongs to the realm of fast-moving surface events. Ironically, it is the movement of the dancers themselves that, according to an Annaliste and Foucauldian perspective, inhabits the level of the "apparently immobile." It is in this latter level, that Scola, the historian-filmmaker, is interested. Scola's ambition in *Le Bal* is to show that the filmmaker, better than the traditional historian, can represent layers that move slowly and thus tell a history of looks, gestures, and movements, as if these last three elements existed at the intersection of nature with culture, on the edge between truth and fiction, writing and living, acting and being.

The old-fashioned expression, "motion pictures," underlines the two major components of cinema: audiovisual narrative and movement. A written narrative can acquire the authority of a truthful version of the past; for an audiovisual one, this is already a more difficult task to achieve. But, without a doubt, historians do not view movement as an acceptable document. Until recently, history has been unable to deal with those aspects of human existence that do not fall neatly either under the rubric of culture or nature, or in the domain of abstract, intellectual thought, or in that of concrete, physical limitations.

---

[44] Michel Foucault, *The Archaeology of Knowledge and the Discourse on Language*, trans. A. M. Sheridan Smith (New York: Pantheon Books, 1972), 3. In his latest film, *La Famiglia* (1987), Scola continues to underline the historical dimension, the long duration of sounds, movements, and objects in private life. On the representation of history in Scola's *La Famiglia*, see "Ecco la famiglia secondo Scola," *La Repubblica*, January 21, 1987, where Maria Pia Fusco writes: "The outside, the street, and, therefore, history are not there, one hears them not only through noises, the radio and the television, not only in the objects and household items that time alters, but above all in the behavior of the characters, in the language which public events affect" (p. 20).

It is possible that the problems encountered by film and by cultural historians will promote the diffusion of the "new" history and redefine the boundaries of what conservative historians up to now have considered to be their object of study. At the turn of the century, the advent of cinema rearranged the relations among the arts. Now that we live in a society of spectacle, in the age of the image, and that the study of cinema is becoming a legitimate academic enterprise, perhaps the new task of film is to push older disciplines to rethink their methodological premises, while learning from them at the same time.

The encounter of cinema and history is characterized by a mixture of tension and attraction. Scola's juxtaposition of black-and-white photography, and sequences of dance in color, comments on the confrontation between these two domains of competency. The appearance of a photograph is always accompanied by an emphatic explosion and a freezing of the frame. Life stops; movement is arrested; an historical document for the records of posterity is born through the death of the moving image. Without the documentary authority of a black-and-white photograph, dance is, instead, a representation of bodies set in motion by sexual desire or by a sense of attachment to a national community. With its connotations of truthfulness, photography is the medium most easily associated with a traditional view of history. Black-and-white still photographs, however, exhibit a death-like quality which is antithetical to the ambition of cinema and dance. Both art forms seek to represent life-in-motion, a history of hidden layers in the making, with or without documents.

With this juxtaposition between photography and dance, document and movement, Scola furnishes a text within whose context I situate Foucault's remark on the rhythm of history. Foucault's new, "unmoving histories" can be situated within the history of Italian cinema itself, traditionally split between documentary realism and allegorical spectacle. A possible subtitle for *Le Bal* (and for this book) would be: Nouvelle Histoire, Italian Style.

Indeed, the French-Italian connection I have traced through Scola's film is stylistic as well as historiographical. In this way, the composite style of *Le Bal* sheds light on the role of Italian neorealism in the shift from the "Tradition of Quality" to the nouvelle vague, as well as on the impact of les enfants terribles of French cinema on the Italian cinema of today. This interweaving of competing cinematic traditions produces a fabric made up of the different positions taken on by a canonical mode—whether it be that of Fascist cinema, of Hollywood, or of the "Tradition of Quality"—against which the national cinemas of France and Italy have been set in an oscillation of love and hate, of rejection and recovery.

# Bibliography

Abba, Giuseppe Cesare. *The Diary of One of Garibaldi's Thousand*. 1880. Reprint. London: Oxford University Press, 1962.

Abruzzese, Alberto. *L'immagine filmica*. Rome: Bulzoni, 1974.

Agosti, Aldo, ed. *Togliatti e la fondazione dello stato Democratico*. Milan: Franco Angeli, 1986.

Alpers, Svetlana. *The Art of Describing: Dutch Art in the Seventeenth Century*. Chicago: University of Chicago Press, 1983.

Althusser, Louis. *Lenin and Philosophy and Other Essays*. New York: Monthly Review Press, 1971.

Amari, Vincenzo Maria. "Vico, Leopardi, Nietzsche: A Comparative Study of the Problem of Nihilism." Ph.D. diss., Columbia University, 1979.

Andreotti, Giulio. *De Gasperi e il suo tempo*. Verona: Mondadori, 1956.

Andrew, J. Dudley. *André Bazin*. New York: Oxford University Press, 1978.

*Gli anni trenta: Arte e cultura in Italia*. Milan: Mazzotta, 1982.

Aprà, Adriano, and Patrizia Pistagnesi, eds. *Comedy Italian Style 1950–80*. Turin: Edizioni Radiotelevisione Italiana, 1986.

———. *The Fabulous Thirties: Italian Cinema 1929–1944*. Milan: Electa International, 1979.

Argentieri, Mino. *Il film biografico*. Rome: Bulzoni, 1984.

Aristarco, Guido. *Sotto il segno dello scorpione—Il cinema dei Fratelli Taviani*. Messina-Florence: Casa Editrice G. D'Anna, 1977.

———. "*La Strada*." *Cinema Nuovo* 3, no. 46 (November 1954): 312.

Aristarco, Guido, ed. *Antologia di Cinema Nuovo 1952–1958*. Florence: Guaraldi, 1975.

———. *Il mito dell'attore*. Bari: Edizioni Dedalo, 1983.

Armes, Roy. *French Cinema*. New York: Oxford University Press, 1985.

———. *Patterns of Realism*. South Brunswick, N.J.: A. S. Barnes, 1971.

Aschieri, Pietro. "Scenografia e costumi di *Scipione l'Africano*." *Bianco e Nero* 1, nos. 7–8 (July 1937): 19–22.

Aspesi, Natalia. *Il lusso e l'autarchia: Storia dell'eleganza italiana 1930–44*. Milan: Rizzoli, 1982.

*Aspetti della realtà contemporanea italiana*. Bologna: Calderni, 1971.

*Atti del convegno di studi sulla resistenza nel cinema italiano del dopoguerra*. Venice: Biennale di Venezia, 1970.

Ayfre, Amédée. "Néo-réalisme et phénoménologie." *Cahiers du Cinéma* 3, no. 17 (November 1952): 6–18.

Baldelli, Pio. *Luchino Visconti*. Milan: Mazzotta, 1973.

Barbaro, Umberto-Luigi Chiarini. *L'arte dell'attore*. Rome: Bianco e Nero Editore, 1949.

Barkan, Leonard. *Nature's Work of Art: The Human Body as Image of the World*. New Haven, Conn.: Yale University Press, 1975.

Barraclough, Geoffrey. "The Sovereign State." *The Spectator*, (August 1, 1958): 171.

Barthes, Roland. *Mythologies*. Paris: Éditions du Seuil, 1957.

Battaglia, Roberto. "La storiografia della resistenza, dalla memorialistica al saggio storico." *Il Movimento di Liberazione in Italia* 9, no. 57 (1959): 80–131.

Baxandall, Michael. *Painting and Experience in Fifteenth-Century Italy*. London: Oxford University Press, 1976.

Bazin, André. *What Is Cinema?*. 2 vols. Translated by Hugh Gray. Berkeley: University of California Press, 1967–71.

Benamou, Michel, and Charles Caramello, eds. *Performance in Postmodern Culture*. Madison, Wis.: Coda Press, 1977.

Bencivenni, Alessandro. *Visconti*. Florence: La Nuova Italia, 1982.

Benjamin, Walter. *Illuminations: Essays and Reflections*. Edited and introduced by Hannah Arendt. New York: Schocken Books, 1969.

Bennett, Tony. *Formalism and Marxism*. London: Methuen, 1979.

Bernardi, Sergio. "La serie infinita delle immagini." *Filmcritica* 37, no. 363 (March–April 1986): 131–45.

Bernardini, Aldo. *Cinema muto italiano*. 3 vols. Bari: Laterza, 1980–81.

Bernardini, Aldo, and Jean A. Gili, eds. *Le cinéma italien: De la prise de Rome (1905) à Rome ville ouverte (1945)*. Paris: Centre Georges Pompidou, 1986.

"Bernardo Bertolucci Seminar." *American Film Institute Dialogue on Film* 3, no. 5 (April 1974): 14–28.

Berry, Thomas, C.P. *The Historical Theory of Giambattista Vico*. Washington, D.C.: The Catholic University of America Press, 1949.

Bestetti, Carlo. *Italian Movie Stars*. Rome: Edizioni d' Arte, 1952.

Beylie, Claude. "De l'acteur américain." *Etudes Cinématographiques* 14–15 (Spring 1962): 72–77.

Blasetti, Alessandro. "A proposito di *1860*." *La Rivista del Cinematografo* 7 (July 1966): 419–20.

———. *Scritti sul cinema*. Venice: Marsilio, 1982.

Bloom, Harold. *The Anxiety of Influence: A Theory of Poetry*. New York: Oxford University Press, 1973.

Bolzoni, Francesco. "Il paesaggio nel cinema e nella narrativa italiana del novecento." *Bianco e Nero* 17, no. 2 (February 1956): 14–63.

Bolzoni, Francesco, ed. *Il progetto imperiale: Cinema e cultura nell'Italia del 1936*. Venice: Edizioni de la Biennale, 1976.

Bondanella, Peter. *Italian Cinema: From Neorealism to the Present*. New York: Frederick Ungar Publishing Co., 1983.

————. "Neorealist Aesthetics and the Fantastic: *The Machine to Kill Bad People* and *Miracle in Milan*." *Film Criticism* 3, no. 9 (Winter 1979): 24–29.

Bondanella, Peter, and Julia Conway Bondanella. *Dictionary of Italian Literature*. Westport, Conn.: Greenwood Press, 1979.

Bordwell, David. "The Art Cinema as a Mode of Film Practice," *Film Criticism* 4, no. 1, 56–64.

Borges, Jorge Luis. *Ficciones*. New York: Grove Press, 1962.

Borradori, Giovanna. *Recoding Metaphysics: The New Italian Philosophy*. Chicago: Northwestern University Press, 1988.

Bossaglia, Rossana. "L'iconografia del novecento italiano nel contesto europeo." *The Journal of Decorative and Propaganda Arts 1875–1945* 3 (Winter 1987): 53–65.

Braudel, Fernand. *On History*. Translated by Sarah Matthews. Chicago: University of Chicago Press, 1980.

Bresson, Robert. *Notes on Cinematography*. Translated by J. Griffin. New York: Urizen Books, 1977.

Britton, Andrew. "Bertolucci: Thinking about Father." *Movie* 23 (Winter 1976–77): 9–22.

————. "The Ideology of *Screen*: Althusser, Lacan, Barthes," *Movie* 26 (Winter 1978–79): 2–28.

Brooks, Peter. *The Melodramatic Imagination: Balzac, Henry James, Melodrama, and the Mode of Excess*. New York: Columbia University Press, 1985.

Broude, Norma Freedman. "The Macchiaioli: Academicism and Modernism in Nineteenth-Century Italian Painting." Ph.D. diss., Columbia University, 1967.

Brown, Norman O. *Closing Time*. New York: Vintage Books, 1974.

Bryson, Norman. *Word and Image: French Painting of the Ancien Régime*. Cambridge: Cambridge University Press, 1981.

Brunetta, Gian Piero. "La migrazione dei generi dalla biblioteca alla filmoteca dell'italiano." *Italian Quarterly* 21, no. 81 (1980): 83–90.

————. *Storia del cinema italiano 1895–1945*. Rome: Editori Riuniti, 1979.

————. *Storia del cinema italiano dal 1945 agli anni ottanta*. Rome: Editori Riuniti, 1982.

Brunette, Peter. *Roberto Rossellini*. New York: Oxford University Press, 1987.

————. "Unity and Difference in *Paisan*." *Studies in the Literary Imagination* 16, no. 1 (Spring 1983): 91–111.

Bruno, Giuliana. "Towards a Theorization of Film History." *Iris* 2, no. 2 (1984): 41–55.

Bruno, Giuliana, and Maria Nadotti, eds. *Off Screen: Women and Film in Italy*. Introduced by Laura Mulvey. London: Routledge, 1988.

Buchsbaum, Jonathan. "Vote for the Front Populaire! Vote Communiste! *La Vie est à nous.*" *Quarterly Review of Film Studies* 10, no. 3 (Summer 1985): 183–212.

Burgoyne, Robert. "The Imaginary and the Neo-Real." *Enclitic* 3, no. 1 (Spring 1979): 16–34.

———. "The Somatization of History in Bertolucci's *1900.*" *Film Quarterly* 40, no. 1 (1986): 7–14.

Burke, Peter. *Vico.* New York: Oxford University Press, 1985.

Burke, Peter, ed. *A New Kind of History: From the Writings of Febvre.* Translated by K. Folca. New York: Harper and Row, 1973.

Calendoli, Giovanni. *Materiali per una storia del cinema italiano.* Parma: Maccari, 1967.

Calvino, Italo. *The Path to the Nest of Spiders.* Translated by Archibald Colquhoun. Preface by the author, translated by William Weaver. New York: The Ecco Press, 1987. *Il Sentiero dei Nidi di Ragno* (1947). Turin: Einaudi, 1956.

———. "Viaggio in camion." *Cinema Nuovo* 25 (April 1955): 292–95.

Camerini, Claudio. "La formazione artistica degli attori del cinema muto italiano." *Bianco e Nero* 44, no. 1 (January–March 1983): 7–43.

Camerino, Vincenzo, and Antonio Tarsi. *Dialettica dell'utopia. Il cinema di Paolo e Vittorio Taviani.* Manduria: Piero Lacaita Editore, 1978.

Cameron, Ian, ed. *The Films of Robert Bresson.* New York: Praeger, 1970.

Cammarota, M. Domenico. *Il Cinema Peplum.* Rome: Fanucci, 1987.

Cannella, Mario, "Ideology and Aesthetic Hypotheses in the Criticism of Neo-Realism." *Screen* 14, no. 4 (Winter 73/74): 3–60. Originally printed in *Giovane Critica* 11 (1966).

Cantelli, Gianfranco. *Mente, corpo, linguaggio: Saggio sull'interpretazione vichiana del mito.* Florence: Sansoni, 1986.

Canziani, Alfonso. *Gli anni del neorealismo.* Florence: La Nuova Italia, 1977.

Carocci, Giampiero. *Giolitti e l'età giolittiana.* Turin: Einaudi, 1961.

Carrà, Massimo. "Consapevolezza e nostalgie di Campigli." In *Omaggio a Massimo Campigli.* Cortina D'Ampezzo: Edizioni della Galleria d'Arte Falsetti-Prato, 1973.

Casetti, Francesco. *Bernardo Bertolucci.* Florence: La Nuova Italia, 1978.

Castello, Giulio Cesare. "Realismo, romanticismo e senso dello spettacolo nei film italiani sul risorgimento a partire dal 1930." *Bianco e Nero* 24, nos. 1–2 (January–February 1963): 94–100.

*Catalogo Bolaffi del cinema italiano 1945–1965.* Turin: Bolaffi, 1967.

Cavallaro, G. B., ed. *Senso di Luchino Visconti.* Bologna: Cappelli, 1955.

Cavani, Liliana. *Il Portiere di notte.* Turin: Einaudi, 1974.

Cavani, Liliana, Franco Arcalli, and Italo Moscati. *Al di là del bene e del male.* Turin: Einaudi, 1977.

Cecchi, Emilio. "Blasetti." *Tutto* 21, no. 13 (March 25, 1939): 16.

———. *Pittura italiana dell'ottocento*. Milan: Hoepli Editore, 1938.

———. *"Senso* e il colore nel film." *L'Illustrazione Italiana* (Christmas 1954): 16–21.

Cecchi, Emilio intro. *The "Macchiaioli": The First "Europeans" in Tuscany*. Critical notes by Mario Borgiotti. Florence: Leo S. Olschki, 1963.

Celati, Gianni. *Finzioni occidentali: Fabulazione, comicità e scrittura*. Turin: Einaudi, 1965.

Chabod, Federico. "Croce storico." *Rivista Storica Italiana* 64 (1952): 516–19.

*Cinema, storia, resistenza 1944–1985*. Istituto Storico della resistenza in Valle d'Aosta. Milan: Franco Angeli, 1987.

*Cinema e storia*. Vol. 3, *Rassegna cinematografica "Lido degli Estensi," 1959*. Ferrara: Amministrazione Provinciale di Ferrara, 1959.

*La cinepresa e la storia, fascismo, antifascismo, guerra e resistenza nel cinema italiano*. Milan: Bruno Mondadori, 1985.

Cluny, Claude-Michel. "Le Péplum." In *Cinéastes 2*. Paris, 1971.

Collet, Jean. "L'acteur à son insu dans les films de la nouvelle vague." *Etudes cinématographiques* 14–15 (Spring 1962): 38–47.

Comolli, Jean-Louis. "Historical Fiction: A Body Too Much." *Screen* 19, no. 2 (Summer 1978): 41–53.

Coradeschi, Sergio. "Lo stile novecento italiano: Grafica di massa e design esclusivo." *The Journal of Decorative and Propaganda Arts 1875–1945* 3 (Winter 1987): 67–82.

Corliss, Richard. Review of *Night of the Shooting Stars*. *Time* (February 21, 1983): 80.

Coward, Rosalind, and John Ellis. *Language and Materialism*. London: Routledge & Kegan Paul, 1977.

Cresti, Carlo. *Architettura e fascismo*. Florence: Vallecchi, 1986.

Crivellato, Valentino. *Tiepolo*. New York: W. W. Norton & Co. Inc., 1962.

Croce, Benedetto. *History as the Story of Liberty*. Translated by Sylvia Sprigge. New York: Meridian Books, 1955. *La storia come pensiero e come azione*. Bari: Laterza, 1954.

———. *History: Its Theory and Method*. Translated by Douglas Ainslee. New York: Harcourt and Brace, 1923. *Teoria e storia della storiografia*. Bari: Laterza, 1917.

———. *History of Europe in the Nineteenth Century*. Translated by Henry Furst. New York: Harbinger Books, 1963. *Storia d'Europa nel secolo decimonono*. Bari: Laterza, 1932.

———. *History of Italy from 1871 to 1915*. Translated by Cecilia M. Ady. Oxford: Clarendon Press, 1929. *Storia d' Italia dal 1871 al 1915* (1928). Bari: Laterza, 1967.

———. *The Philosophy of Giambattista Vico*. Translated by R. G. Collingwood. New York: Russell and Russell, 1913. *La filosofia di Giambattista Vico*. Bari: Laterza, 1911.

D'Amico, Masolino. *La commedia all'italiana: Il cinema comico in Italia dal 1945 al 1975*. Milan: Mondadori, 1985.

D'Annunzio, Gabriele. *Le novelle della Pescara*. Milan: Fratelli Treves, 1925.

*Da Togliatti alla nuova sinistra*. Il Manifesto, Quaderno no. 5. Rome: Alfani, 1979.

De Felice, Renzo. *Interpretations of Fascism*. Translated by Brenda Huff Everett. Cambridge, Mass.: Harvard University Press, 1977. *Interpretazioni del fascismo*. Bari: Laterza, 1969.

————. *Mussolini, Il rivoluzionario (1883–1920)*. Turin: Einaudi, 1965.

De Felice, Renzo, and Luigi Goglia. *Storia fotografica del fascismo*. Rome: Laterza, 1982.

De Giusti, Luciano. *I film di Luchino Visconti*. Rome: Gremese Editore, 1985.

De Grazia, Victoria. *The Culture of Consent: Mass Organization of Leisure in Fascist Italy*. Cambridge: Cambridge University Press, 1981.

De Lauretis, Teresa. *Alice Doesn't: Feminism, Semiotics, Cinema*. Bloomington: Indiana University Press, 1984.

————. "Semiotics, Theory and Social Practice: A Critical History of Italian Semiotics." *Cine-tracts* 2, no. 1 (1978): 1–14.

De Michelis, Cesare. "La resistenza nel cinema degli anni facili." *Cinema 60* 3, nos. 23–26 (May–August 1962): 87–91.

De Poli, Marco. "Paolo e Vittorio Taviani." *Belfagor* 30, no. 1 (January 31, 1975): 71–82.

————. *Paolo and Vittorio Taviani*. Milano: Moizzi Editore, 1977.

De Santis, Pier Marco. "Scola e Scarpelli dal disegno al film." *Bianco e Nero* 47, no. 1 (January–March 1986): 49–67.

Del Fra, Lino. "Il film storico e il neorealismo." *Rivista del Cinema Italiano* 3, nos. 5–6 (May–June 1954): 67–73.

Doane, Mary Ann. "The Abstraction of a Lady: *La Signora di Tutti*." *Cinema Journal* 28, no. 1 (Fall 1988): 65–84.

————. "The Dialogical Text: Filmic Irony and the Spectator." Ph.D. diss., University of Iowa, 1979.

————. "Film and the Masquerade—Theorizing the Female Spectator." *Screen* 23, nos. 3–4 (September–October 1982): 74–88.

Dorfles, Gillo. *Kitsch: The World of Bad Taste*. New York: Universe Books, 1969.

Dombroski, Robert. "Timpanaro's Materialism: An Introduction." *The Journal of the History of Ideas* 44, no. 2 (April–June 1983): 311–26.

Dosse, François. "History in Pieces: From the Militant to the Triumphant Annales." *Telos* 67 (Spring 1986): 163–76.

Dumas, Alexandre, ed. *The Memoirs of Garibaldi*. Contributions by George Sand and Victor Hugo. London: Ernest Benn Ltd., 1931.

Dumoulin, Michel. "Bibliographie annuelle d'histoire italienne contemporaine (1980–81)." *Risorgimento* 2–3 (1981): 287–99.

Durbè, Dario. *I Macchiaioli*. Florence: Centro Di, 1976.

———. *Pittura garibaldina da Fattori a Guttuso*. Galleria Nazionale d'Arte Moderna. Rome: De Luca Editore, 1982.

Durgnat, Raymond. "Homage to Hercules." *Motion* 6 (1963): 48–50.

Eco, Umberto. *The Role of the Reader*. Bloomington: Indiana University Press, 1979.

Eisenstein, Sergei. *The Film Sense*. New York: Harcourt Brace and Co., 1942.

Ellero, Roberto. "Le fortune presunte del cinema italiano in Francia." *Bianco e Nero* 47, no. 1 (January–March 1986): 60–65.

Elley, Derek. *The Epic Film: Myth and History*. London: Routledge & Kegan Paul, 1984.

Elsaesser, Thomas. "Myth as the Phantasmagoria of History: H.-J. Syberberg, Cinema and Representation." *New German Critique* 24–25 (Fall–Winter 1981–82): 108–54.

Falaschi, Giovanni. *La resistenza armata nella narrativa italiana*. Turin: Einaudi, 1976.

Faldini, Franca, and Goffredo Fofi, eds. *L'avventurosa storia del cinema italiano raccontata dai suoi protagonisti 1935–1959*. Milan: Feltrinelli, 1979.

———. *Il cinema italiano d'oggi, 1970–1984: Raccontato dai suoi protagonisti*. Milan: Mondadori, 1984.

Farassino, Alberto, and Tatti Sanguineti, eds., *Gli uomini forti*. Milan: Mazzotta, 1983.

Ferrero, Adelio, ed. *Visconti: Il cinema*. Modena: Ufficio del Cinema del Comune di Modena, 1977.

Ferro, Marc. *Analyses de film, analyses de société*. Paris: Hachette, 1975.

———. *Cinéma et histoire: Le cinéma agent et source de l'histoire*. Paris: Denoël, 1977.

———. *The Use and Abuse of History or How the Past Is Taught*. London: Routledge and Kegan Paul, 1984.

———. *Film et histoire*. Paris: Éditions de l'École des Hautes Études en Sciences Sociales, 1984.

*Il film storico e la sua influenza negli altri paesi*. Rome: Edizioni di Bianco e Nero, 1963.

*Film Studies Annual: Theory-French-German-Italian*. Lafayette, Ind.: Purdue University Press, 1976.

Fink, Guido. "*Neorealismo* Revisited." *Twentieth-Century Studies* 5–6 (September 1971): 72–82.

Fletcher, Angus. *Allegory: The Theory of a Symbolic Mode*. Ithaca, N.Y.: Cornell University Press, 1964.

Forgacs, David, and Geoffrey Nowell-Smith, eds. *Antonio Gramsci: Selections from Cultural Writings*. Translated by William Boelhower. Cambridge, Mass.: Harvard University Press, 1985.

Foucault, Michel. *The Archaeology of Knowledge and the Discourse on Language*. Translated by A. M. Sheridan Smith. New York: Pantheon Books, 1972.

Friedlander, Saul. *Reflections on Nazism: An Essay on Kitsch and Death*. New York: Harper & Row, 1982.

Furno, Mariella, and Renzo Renzi, eds. *Il neorealismo nel fascismo: Giuseppe De Santis e la critica cinematografica 1941–43*. Quaderni della Cineteca, no. 5. Cineteca e Commissione Cinema del Comune di Bologna. Bologna: Edizioni della Tipografia Compositori, 1984.

Fusco, Maria Pia. "Ecco la famiglia secondo Scola." *La Repubblica*, January 21, 1987, 20.

Galasso, Giuseppe. *Il mezzogiorno nella storia d'Italia*. Florence: Le Monnier, 1977.

Gallagher, Tag. "NR = MC²: Rossellini, Neo-Realism, and Croce." *Film History, An International Journal* 2, no. 1 (1988): 87–97.

Gentile, Giovanni. *Studi vichiani*. 2d ed. Florence: Felice Le Monnier, 1927.

Ghirardini, Lionello. *Il cinema e la guerra*. Parma: Maccari, 1965.

Gili, Jean A. *Arrivano i mostri: I volti della commedia italiana*. Bologna: Cappelli, 1980.

―――. "Avignon 1974: Raffaello Matarazzo." *Écran* 30 (November 1974): 16.

―――. "Fascisme et résistance dans le cinéma italien." *Etudes Cinématographiques* 82–83 (1970).

"Giovanni Gentile." *Enciclopedia Filosofica*. Vol. 3. Florence: Sansoni, 1968.

Gobetti, Paolo. *I film del 1945 dall'occupazione alla liberazione: Recensione di 188 film*. Turin: Archivio Nazionale Cinematografico della Resistenza, 1985.

―――. *Risorgimento senza eroi e altri scritti storici* (1926). Introduction by Franco Venturi. Turin: Einaudi, 1976.

Gori, Gianfranco, ed. *Passato ridotto*. Florence: La Casa di Usher, 1982.

Gramsci, Antonio. *Letteratura e vita nazionale*. Rome: Editori Riuniti, 1971.

―――. *La questione meridionale*. Edited by Franco De Felice and Valentino Parlato. Rome: Editori Riuniti, 1966.

―――. *Il risorgimento*. Turin: Einaudi, 1966.

Grayson, Cecil. Review of Ernst H. Kantorowicz's *The King's Two Bodies:*

*A Study in Political Medieval Theology. Romance Philology* 15, no. 2 (November 1961): 179–84.

Grazzini, Giovanni. *Federico Fellini: Intervista sul cinema.* Bari: Laterza, 1983.

Green, Martin, and John Swan. *The Triumph of Pierrot.* New York: Macmillan Publishing Company, 1986.

Greene, Naomi. "Fascism in Recent Italian Films." *Film Criticism* 6, no. 1 (1981): 31–42.

Grosoli, Fabrizio. "Cinema/Storia: Memoria del passato e lettura del contemporaneo." *Cinema e Cinema* 5, nos. 16/17 (July–December 1978): 117–28.

Hanson, Anne Coffin. "Manet's Subject Matter and a Source of Popular Imagery." *Museum Studies* 3 (1968): 63–80.

Hay, James. *Popular Film Culture in Fascist Italy.* Bloomington: Indiana University Press, 1987.

Hess, John. "La Politique des Auteurs." *Jump Cut* 1–2 (May–June 1974): 19–22.

Hillier, Jim, ed. *Cahiers du Cinéma: The 1950s, Neo-Realism, Hollywood, New Wave.* Cambridge, Mass.: Harvard University Press, 1985.

*History and Film: Methodology, Research, Education.* Copenhagen: Eventus, 1981.

Hoare, Quintin, and Geoffrey Nowell-Smith, eds. *Antonio Gramsci: Selections from the Prison Notebooks.* New York: International Publishers, 1971.

Horton, Andrew, and Joan Magretta, eds. *Modern European Filmmakers and the Art of Adaptation.* New York: Ungar, 1981.

Iggers, George G. *New Directions in European Historiography.* Middletown, Conn.: Wesleyan University Press, 1975.

*Italia moderna: Immagini di un'identità nazionale.* 2 vols. Milan: Electa, 1983.

Jacobitti, Edmund E. "From Vico's Common Sense to Gramsci's Hegemony." In *Vico and Marx: Affinities and Contrasts,* edited by Giorgio Tagliacozzo. Atlantic Highlands, N.J: Humanities Press, 1983.

Jodi, Rodolfo Macchioni. *Il mito garibaldino nella letteratura italiana.* Caltanisetta-Rome: Edizioni Salvatore Sciascia, 1973.

Jolly, Penny Howell. "On the Meaning of the Virgin Mary Reading Attributed to Antonello da Messina." *The Journal of the Waters Art Gallery* 40 (1982): 25–35.

Kantorowicz, Ernst H. *The King's Two Bodies: A Study in Political Medieval Theology.* Princeton, N.J.: Princeton University Press, 1981.

Kaplan, E. Ann, ed. *Postmodernism and Its Discontents.* London: Verso, 1988.

Kline, T. Jefferson. *Bertolucci's Dream Loom: A Psychoanalytic Study of Cinema*. Amherst: The University of Massacchusetts Press, 1987.

———. "Orpheus Transcending: Bertolucci's *Last Tango in Paris*." *International Review of Psychoanalysis* 3 (1976): 85–95.

Kolker, Robert Philip. *The Altering Eye*. New York: Oxford University Press, 1983.

———. *Bernardo Bertolucci*. New York: Oxford University Press, 1985.

Kracauer, Sigfried. *Theory of Film: The Redemption of Physical Reality*. New York: Oxford University Press, 1960.

Kubler, George. *The Shape of Time: Remarks on the History of Things*. New Haven, Conn.: Yale University Press, 1962.

Landy, Marcia. *Fascism in Film: The Italian Commercial Cinema 1931–43*. Princeton, N.J.: Princeton University Press, 1986.

Laqueur, Walter, and George L. Mosse, eds. *The New History: Trends in Historiographical Research and Writing since World War II*. New York: Harper and Torch Books, 1967.

Laura, Ernesto G. *Alida Valli*. Rome: Gremese Editore, 1979.

Lawton, Ben. "Italian Neorealism: A Mirror Construction of Reality," *Film Criticism* 3, no. 2 (Winter 1979): 8–23.

Li Pera, Lucia. *Il fascismo dalla polemica alla storiografia: Un saggio introduttivo con i confronti antologici da Antonio Gramsci*. Florence: G. D'Anna, 1975.

Liehm, Mira. *Passion and Defiance: Film in Italy from 1942 to the Present*. Berkeley: University of California Press, 1984.

Lizzani, Carlo. *Il cinema italiano dalle origini agli anni ottanta*. Rome: Editori Riuniti, 1982.

Lotman, Jurij. *Semiotics of Cinema*. Michigan Slavic Contributions no. 5. Translated from Russian and introduction by Mark E. Suino. Ann Arbor: University of Michigan, 1981.

Lucente, Gregory. *Beautiful Fables: Self-Consciousness in Italian Narrative from Manzoni to Calvino*. Baltimore, Md.: The Johns Hopkins University Press, 1986.

Lukács, Georg. *The Historical Novel*. Translated by Hannah and Stanley Mitchell. Atlantic Highlands, N.J.: Humanities Press, 1974.

———. *Writer and Critic and Other Essays*. Edited and translated by Arthur D. Kahn. New York: Grosset & Dunlap, 1971.

Mack Smith, Denis. *Italy: A Modern History*. Ann Arbor: University of Michigan Press, 1959.

McLennan, Gregor. *Marxism and the Methodologies of History*. London: NLB, 1981.

McNair, William A. *In Search of the Four Musketeers*. Sydney: Alpha Books, 1972.

McRobbie, Angela, and Mia Nova, eds. *Gender and Generation*. London: Macmillan, 1984.

Magretta, William, and Joan Magretta. "Lina Wertmuller and the Tradition of Italian Carnivalesque Comedy." *Genre* 12 (Spring 1979): 25–43.

Major-Poetzl, Pamela. *Michel Foucault's Archaeology of Western Culture: Toward a New Science of History*. Chapel Hill: University of North Carolina Press, 1983.

Manacorda, Giuliano, ed. *Antonio Gramsci: Marxismo e letteratura*. Rome: Editori Riuniti, 1975.

Mancini, Elaine. *Luchino Visconti: A Guide to References and Resources*. Boston, Mass.: G. K. Hall, 1986.

———. *Struggles of the Italian Film Industry during Fascism 1930–35*. Ann Arbor, Mich.: UMI Research Press, 1985.

Mancini, Michele, and Giuseppe Perella, eds. *Pier Paolo Pasolini: Corpi e luoghi*. Rome: Theorema Edizioni, 1981.

Mango, Achille. *Cultura e storia nella formazione della commedia dell'arte*. Bari: Adriatica Editrice, 1972.

Marcus, Millicent. *Italian Film in the Light of Neorealism*. Princeton, N.J.: Princeton University Press, 1986.

Margadonna, Ettore M. "Cinema." *L'Illustrazione Italiana* 61, no. 15 (April 15, 1934): 560–61.

Matteucci, Nicola. *Dal populismo al compromesso storico*. Rome: Edizioni della Voce, 1976.

Matthaei, Rupprecht, ed. *Goethe's Color Theory*. New York: Van Nostrand Reinhold Company, 1971.

Maturi, Walter. *Interpretazioni del risorgimento*. Turin: Einaudi, 1962.

Meccoli, Domenico. *Il risorgimento italiano nel cinema e nel teatro*. Rome: Editalia, 1961.

Melchiorre, Virgilio, and Anna Maria Cascetta, eds. *Il corpo in scena: La rappresentazione del corpo nella filosofia e nelle arti*. Milan: Vita e Pensiero, 1983.

Mellen, Joan. "A Conversation with Bernardo Bertolucci." *Cineaste* 5, no. 4 (1973): 21–24.

Metternich (Prince). "Letter, 19 November 1849." In *The Oxford Dictionary of Quotations*, 338. 2d ed. London: Oxford University Press 1966.

Mida, Massimo, and Fausto Montesanti. "*1860*." *Cinema* 6, no. 129 (November 10, 1941): 287.

Mida, Massimo, and Giovanni Vento. *Cinema e resistenza*. Florence: Luciano Landi Editore, 1959.

"Mille facce per un duce." *La Repubblica*, July 10–11, 1983, n.p.

Mitchell, W. J. T., ed. *On Narrative*. Chicago: University of Chicago Press, 1981.

Molinari, Cesare. *Storia universale del teatro*. Milan: Mondadori, 1983.

Montesanti, Fausto. "La parabola della diva." *Bianco e Nero* 13, nos. 7–8 (July–August 1952): 55–72.

Monti, Raffaele. *Les Macchiaioli et le cinéma: L'image du XIX siècle et la peinture des Macchiaioli dans le cinéma italien.* Paris: Éditions Vilo, 1979.

Monticone, Alberto. *Il fascismo al microfono: Radio e politica in Italia (1924–1945).* Rome: Studium, 1978.

Mora, Teo. "Il melodramma di Matarazzo." *Filmcritica* 312 (February 1981): 71–76.

Morante, Elsa. *History: A Novel.* Translated by William Weaver. New York: Knopf, 1977. *La Storia.* Turin: Einaudi, 1974.

Moravia, Alberto. *The Conformist.* Translated by Angus Davidson. New York: Playboy Paperbacks, 1982. *Il Conformista.* 2d ed. Milan: Bompiani, 1951.

———. *The Time of Indifference.* Translated by Angus Davidson. New York: Farrar, Straus and Young, 1953. *Gli Indifferenti.* 4th ed. Milan: Edizioni Alpes, 1930.

Mosse, George L. *Nationalism and Sexuality: Respectability and Abnormal Sexuality in Modern Europe.* New York: Howard Fertig, 1985.

Mulvey, Laura. "Visual Pleasure and Narrative Cinema." *Screen* 16, no. 3 (Autumn 1975): 6–18.

Mura, Antonio. *Film, storia, storiografia.* Rome: Edizioni della Quercia, 1963.

Narducci, Emanuele. "Sebastiano Timpanaro." *Belfagor* 40, no. 3 (May 31, 1985): 283–314.

Nichols, Bill, ed. *Movies and Methods: An Anthology.* Berkeley: University of California Press, 1976.

Nietzsche, Friedrich. *The Use and Abuse of History.* Translated by Adrian Collins and introduction by Julius Kraft. New York: The Library of Liberal Arts Press of New York, 1957. *Vom Nutzen und Nachteil der Historie für das Leben.* Basel: Verlag Birkhäuser, n.d.

Nowell-Smith, Geoffrey. *Luchino Visconti.* Garden City, N.Y.: Doubleday, 1968.

Orto, Nuccio. *La notte dei desideri: Il cinema dei Fratelli Taviani.* Palermo: Sellerio Editore, 1987.

Overbey, David, ed. *Springtime in Italy: A Reader on Neo-Realism,* Hamden, Conn.: Archon Books, 1979.

Palumbo, Mario. *La Sicilia nel cinema.* Palermo: Ed. Sicilia Domani, 1963.

Pandolfi, Vito. *Il cinema nella storia.* Florence: Sansoni, 1957.

Pasolini, Pier Paolo. "The Catholic Irrationalism of Fellini." *Film Criticism* 9, no. 1 (Fall 1984): 63–73.

Pavone, Claudio. "Le idee della resistenza: Antifascismo e fascismo di fronte alla tradizione del risorgimento," *Passato e Presente* 7 (1959): 850–918.

Perlini, Tito. "Left-Wing Culture in Italy since the Last War." *Twentieth-Century Studies* 5–6 (September 1971): 6–17.

Pinel, Vincent. "Le paradoxe du non-comédien." *Études Cinématographiques* 14–15 (Spring 1962): 78–84.

Pintus, Pietro. *Storia e film.* Rome: Bulzoni, 1980.

Piscicelli, Salvatore, ed. *San Michele aveva un gallo: Allonsanfan di Paolo e Vittorio Taviani.* Introduction by Guido Aristarco. Bologna: Cappelli, 1974.

Pistagnesi, Patrizia. "Risi, Comencini e altri: La dialettica delle maschere." *Cinema e Cinema* 3, nos. 7–8 (April–September 1976): 108–14.

Pizzetti, Ildebrando. "Significato della musica in *Scipione l'Africano*," *Bianco e Nero* 1, nos. 7–8 (July 1937): 1–18.

Podestà, Attilio. "Roma: Mostra di dipinti restaurati di Antonello da Messina." *Emporium* 97 (January 1943): 33–36.

Polan, Dana B. "Brecht and the Politics of Self-Reflexive Cinema." *Jump Cut* 17 (1978): 29–32.

Quazza, Guido. *Resistenza e storia d'Italia: Problemi e ipotesi di ricerca.* Torino: Giappichelli, 1976.

Quinsac, Annie-Paul. *Ottocento Painting.* Columbia, S.C.: Columbia Museum of Art, 1972.

Ragghianti, Carlo Ludovico. *Cinema arte figurativa.* Turin: Einaudi, 1952.

Richards, Nancy Jane. "Maria Schell." *The International Dictionary of Films and Filmmakers: Actors and Actresses* 3:558–59. Chicago: St. James Press, 1986.

Rivera, Fausta Drago. *De Vulgari Eloquentia: La questione della lingua da Dante a domani.* Milan: Centro Nazionale di Studi Manzoniani, 1980.

Riverso, Emanuele, ed. and intro. *Leggere Vico: Scritti di Giorgio Tagliacozzo ed altri.* Milan: Spirali, 1982.

Robins, Anthony W. "The Paintings of Antonello da Messina." *The Connoisseur* 188, no. 757 (March 1975): 186–93.

Romano, Carlo. *Lo spettacolo e i suoi prodigi.* Rome: Arcana Editrice, 1975.

Romeo, Rosario. *Il risorgimento in Sicilia.* Bari: Laterza, 1950.

———. "La storiografia italiana sul risorgimento e l'Italia unitaria (1815–1915) nel secondo dopoguerra." Vol. 3 of *Il Giudizio Storico sul Risorgimento*, 105–41. Catania: Bonanno Editore, 1967.

———. "Gli studi italiani di storia contemporanea (1815–1915) nel secondo dopoguerra." *I Quaderni di Rassegna Sovietica* 1 (1965): 109–31.

Rondi, Brunello. *Il neorealismo italiano.* Parma: Guanda, 1956.

Rondolino, Gianni. "L'antifascismo nel cinema italiano recente." *Il Nuovo Spettatore Cinematografico* 5, no. 4 (August 1963): 4–26.

Rondolino, Gianni, *Luchino Visconti*. Turin: Utet, 1981.

Rosen, Phil. "History, Textuality, Nation: Kracauer, Burch, and Some Problems in the Study of National Cinemas." *Iris* 2, no. 2 (1984): 69–84.

Rossellini, Roberto. *Il mio metodo: Scritti e interviste*. Edited by Adriano Aprà. Venice: Marsilio, 1987.

Salvatorelli, Luigi. *Nazionalfascismo* (1923). Introduced by Giorgio Amendola. Turin: Einaudi, 1977.

Sasso, Gennaro. *La "Storia d'Italia" di Benedetto Croce: Cinquant'anni dopo*. Naples: Bibliopolis, 1979.

Sassoon, Donald. *Togliatti e la via italiana al socialismo: Il PCI dal 1944 al 1964*. Turin: Einaudi, 1980.

Saviane, Sergio. "Una Donna e Una Motocicletta." *L'Espresso*, February 12, 1961, 11.

Sedgwick, Eve Kosofsky. *Between Men: English Literature and Male Homosocial Desire*. New York: Columbia University Press, 1985.

Severino, Galante. *La fine di un compromesso storico: PCI e DC nella crisi del 1947*. Milan: Angeli, 1980.

Siclier, Jacques. "L'Age du Péplum." *Cahiers du Cinéma* 22, no. 131 (May 1962): 26–38.

*Significato attuale del film sulla resistenza europea*. Genoa: Comune di Genova, 1964.

Silva, Umberto. *Ideologia ed arte del fascismo*. Milan: Mazzotta, 1973.

Silverman, Kaja. "Dis-Embodying the Female Voice." In *Re-Vision: Essays in Feminist Film Criticism*, edited by Mary Ann Doane, Patricia Mellencamp, and Linda Williams, 131–49. Frederick, Md.: University Publications of America and the American Film Institute, 1984.

Silverman, Michael. "Italian Film and American Capital, 1947–1951." In *Cinema Histories/Cinema Practices*, edited by Patricia Mellencamp and Philip Rosen, 35–46. Frederick, Md.: University Publications of America and the American Film Institute, 1984.

Snyder, Joel. "Benjamin on Reproducibility and Aura: A Reading of 'The Work of Art in the Age of Its Technical Reproducibility.' " *The Philosophical Forum* 15, nos. 1–2 (Fall–Winter 1983–84): 130–45.

Sontag, Susan. *Under the Sign of Saturn*. New York: Farrar, Straus and Giroux, 1980.

Solmi, Sergio. "Il film della resistenza." *Filmcritica* 9, nos. 47–48 (April–May 1955): 131–32.

Sorlin, Pierre. "Cinema and Unconscious: A New Field for Historical Research." *Working Papers and Pre-Publications* 112 (March 1982).

———. "Fascisme en images, fascisme imaginaire." *Risorgimento* nos. 2–3 (1981): 225–45.

———. *The Film in History: Restaging the Past*. Oxford: Basil Blackwell, 1980.

————. *Sociologia del cinema.* Milan: Garzanti, 1979.

Spadolini, Giovanni. *Tre maestri: Croce, Einaudi, De Gasperi.* Rome: Unione Italiana per il Progresso della Cultura, n.d.

"Special Dossier on Ettore Scola." *Revue du Cinéma* 391 (February 1984): 49–60.

Spinazzola, Vittorio. *Cinema e pubblico: Lo spettacolo filmico in Italia, 1945–65.* Milan: Bompiani, 1974.

————. *Film 1962.* Milan: Feltrinelli, 1962.

————. *Film 1963.* Milan: Feltrinelli, 1963.

Spini, Giorgio. *Disegno storico della civiltà.* Vol. 3. Rome: Edizioni Cremonese, 1984.

Spriano, Paolo. *Problemi di storia del partito comunista italiano.* Rome: Istituto Gramsci, Editori Riuniti, 1971–73.

————. *Sulla rivoluzione italiana.* Turin: Einaudi, 1978.

Stoianovich, Traian. *French Historical Method.* Ithaca, N.Y.: Cornell University Press, 1976.

*La storia: Fonti orali nella scuola.* Venice: Marsilio, 1982.

Tannenbaum, Edward. *The Fascist Experience: Italian Society and Culture 1922–45.* New York: Basic Books, 1972.

Timpanaro, Sebastiano. *Antileopardiani e neomoderati nella sinistra italiana.* Pisa: ETS Editrice, 1982.

————. "The Pessimistic Materialism of Giacomo Leopardi." *New Left Review* 116 (1979): 1–12.

Tinazzi, Giorgio. *Michelangelo Antonioni.* Florence: La Nuova Italia, 1985.

Troyer, Nancy Jane. "The Macchiaioli: Effects of Modern Color Theory, Photography, and Japanese Prints on a Group of Italian Painters, 1855–1900." Ph.D. diss., Northwestern University, 1978.

Valiani, Leo. *L'Italia di De Gasperi (1945–1954).* Florence: Le Monnier 1982.

Vasoli, Cesare. "Italian Philosophy after Croce," *Twentieth-Century Studies* 5–6 (September 1971): 31–59.

Verdone, Mario. "Il film atletico e acrobatico." *Centrofilm* 3, no. 17 (1961): 3–36.

Verga, Giovanni. *Mastro Don Gesualdo: A Novel.* Translated and introduced by Giovanni Cecchetti. Berkeley: University of California Press, 1979. *Mastro Don Gesualdo.* Milan: Fondazione Arnaldo e Alberto Mondadori, 1979.

Vico, Giambattista. *The New Science* (1725). Translation of the 3d ed. (1744) by Thomas Goddard Bergin and Max Harold Fisch. Ithaca, N.Y.: Cornell University Press, 1968.

Villari, Rosario. *Storia contemporanea per le scuole medie superiori.* Bari: Laterza, 1982.

Vitali, Lamberto. *Il risorgimento nella fotografia.* Turin: Einaudi, 1979.

Vittorini, Elio. *Conversation in Sicily*. Translated by Wilfred Davis. London: Drummond, 1984. *Conversazione in Sicilia*. Manchester: Manchester University Press, 1978.

Vogel, Amos. "Bernardo Bertolucci: An Interview." *Film Comment* 8, no. 3 (Fall 1971): 25–29.

Warshow, Robert. *The Immediate Experience*. New York: Atheneum, 1979.

Weaver, William. *The Golden Century of Italian Opera from Rossini to Puccini*. London: Thames and Hudson, 1980.

White, Hayden. *Metahistory: The Historical Imagination in Nineteenth-Century Europe*. Baltimore, Md.: The Johns Hopkins University Press, 1987.

———. *Tropics of Discourse: Essays in Cultural Criticism*. Baltimore, Md.: The Johns Hopkins University Press, 1986.

White, Miriam. "An Extra-Body of Reference: History in Cinematic Narrative." Ph.D. diss., University of Iowa, 1981.

Wicks, Ulrich. "Borges, Bertolucci and Metafiction," In *Narrative Strategies*, edited by Syndy M. Conger and Janice R. Welsch, with an introductory essay by Dudley Andrew, 19–36. Macomb: Western Illinois University, 1980.

Wilkinson, James D. *The Intellectual Resistance in Europe*. Cambridge, Mass.: Harvard University Press, 1983.

Wilson, Edmund. *To the Finland Station: A Study in the Writing and Acting of History*. London: Macmillan, 1972.

Wolff, Richard J. "Catholicism, Fascism and Italian Education from the Riforma Gentile to the Carta della Scuola 1922–39." *History of Education Quarterly* 20, no. 1 (Spring 1980): 3–26.

Woolf, Stuart J. "Risorgimento e fascismo: Il senso della continuità nella storiografia italiana." *Belfagor* 20, no. 1 (January 31, 1965): 71–91.

Zagarrio, Vito. "Il Fascismo e la politica delle arti." *Studi Storici* 17, no. 2 (1976): 235–56.

Zavattini, Cesare. *Toni Ligabue*. Milan: All'Insegna del Pesce d'Oro, 1974.

———. *Ligabue*. Parma: Franco Maria Ricci, 1967.

# Index